The Total Workplace

Facilities Management and the Elastic Organization

The Total Workplace

Facilities Management and the Elastic Organization

Franklin Becker

Professor
Facility Planning and Management Program
New York State College of Human Ecology
Cornell University

VNR VAN NOSTRAND REINHOLD
_____ New York

Copyright © 1990 by Van Nostrand Reinhold

Library of Congress Catalog Number: 90–11929
ISBN 0-442-23811-8

Printed in the United States of America

Van Nostrand Reinhold
115 Fifth Avenue
New York, New York 10003

Van Nostrand Reinhold International Company Limited
11 New Fetter Lane
London EC4P 4EE, England

Van Nostrand Reinhold
102 Dodds Street
South Melbourne 3205, Victoria Australia

Nelson Canada
1120 Birchmount Road
Scarborough, Ontario M1K 5G4, Canada

16   15   14   13   12   11   10   9   8   7   6   5   4   3   2   1

Library of Congress Cataloging-in-Publication Data

Becker, Franklin D
    The total workplace: facilities management and the elastic
organization/Franklin Becker.
        p.   cm.
    ISBN 0-442-23811-8
    1. Facility management.   I. Title.
TS177.B43   1990
658.2—dc20   90-11929
                                                            CIP

To Robert O'Neal and Pat Mitchell, who helped inspire this book, and to Harriet, Zoe, and Miles for making it possible.

Contents

Preface

This book is about quality. What an elusive concept! Think of Venice. Dilapidated, stucco-peeling, sagging rust-colored walls punctuated with faded turquoise shutters. Awful? Hardly! It's all charm. Bathed in light and color, the stench of the sewer retreats to the back alleys of awareness. Although I did not know it then, *The Total Workplace* was born in the midst of a ten-day tour of Italy in September 1988. In Italy, surrounded by beautiful ruins, I realized that my work over the last twenty years had a common thread. It was a passion for quality—in planning and design processes, in buildings, and in how these are managed over time.

Venice charms, surprises, unfolds from narrow, twisting alleys delicately connected to piazzas that open without warning, like sun bursting from behind the clouds, to delight the unsuspecting eye. The quality of Venice is its thousands of paths beaten into shape by hundreds of years of human labor to create a texture and patina whose genius is time. But can we wait that long for our "everyday" environments to befriend us, and do we have any confidence that time will improve them?

For me, Venice's inspiration was its lessons about context. It is impossible to think about studying "housing conditions" in Venice without a corresponding study of "piazza conditions." The same is true of London, where, at the moment, I sit writing. Can anyone make sense of London without reference to its parks and gardens? From iron-corseted square to gentrified heath its gardens are—quite literally—a breath of fresh air. Only in the underground, the dreary, windy, dust-filled but efficient "tube," can one remain impervious to the random patch of green guarded by dignified Victorian houses, with carved cornice like lace on a prim lady's collar.

Quality is embedded in context, yet we ignore it without a second thought when we think of places like offices, twentieth-century information factories. We worry about the ergonomic chair, the adjustable work surface, wire management, glare-free lighting. Excellent. But what are the "piazza conditions?" Where is the patina, light that sparkles rather than flickers, furniture that you want to touch, smells that make the mouth water not the nose wrinkle, sounds that soothe or stimulate instead of "white noise" that "tunes" the friction of air whistling down metal ducts to create a uniform noise that merely dulls our senses?

Great soaring atria, filled with bent and polished steel are not a "town square" or "city center" any more than is a promenade the strip development known as "autorow" that (dis)graces most American cities. Where in our corporate atria is the Piazza San Marco? Where is the counterpart to the lacework of tiny tables decorating the sidewalk like frosting on a wedding cake; the smell of fresh-roasted coffee; the texture of stone that is cool, solid, and reassuring to touch? Where the variety, the hum of voices, the spontaneous dance, the skateboard or soccerball? What have we instead? The fortified reception desk, hushed voices, the "bing-bong" of the electronic elevator. This is more museum than piazza, but what marvels are we to contemplate? Is it the detritus of our work, sodden foam cups and half-eaten doughnuts left like stray weeds in a field of paper?

Too much time is spent in the office by too many people to let such questions languish and finally wither, discarded as unanswerable or, even worse, unquestionable. Organizations spend millions of dollars annually on their physical facilities, and much more on the employees using them. Such vast sums are allocated to the physical surroundings of the office to create "quality environments," presumably to help the organization achieve its objectives. But do they? More precisely, how well do they do it? Can they do it better?

The answer must be yes, for all our sakes. This book is about and for those responsible for creating quality workplaces, for architects and interior designers and, even more so, for the new professionals who have emerged over the last ten years: facility managers. Then there is a third group, usually overlooked when talking about the quality of the built environment, which is senior management, the corporate planners, financial officers, and division managers who often initiate and typically approve facility-related decisions.

This book is, then, about management and organizational effectiveness, and the shape it takes in what I call the *elastic organization*. Elasticity is an attitude as much as a set of techniques, structures, policies and procedures. The elastic organization has the capacity to balance and to harness what often seem on the surface to be the competing, if not conflicting, needs of the individual, the group, and the organization as a whole.

What sets the elastic organization apart from other types of organizations is its commitment to succeeding in a competitive world by using all of its resources to their fullest potential. Prospering in such an organization means making tough decisions, not mindless or short-sighted ones. It means using imagination to create facilities that enhance individual and organizational effectiveness and that at the same time give pleasure and promote human dignity. Great challenges these are but worth pursuing, even more so as organizations struggle to control costs and "add value" in the face of ferocious competition and soaring costs.

The ideas presented in *The Total Workplace* are based on my own research, teaching, and consulting over the past twenty years in organizations in the United States, Britain, Europe, and, most recently, Asia. A friend of mine, a facility manager at a giant American corporation, often chides me that his views on facility management are practical, rooted in what facility managers actually do, whereas mine, he likes to say, are about what facility management could be. He means, of course, that mine are academic, in the sense of being impractical and unconnected to (his?) reality. In fact, the ideas, tools, and techniques discussed in this book are rooted in practice, the practice of elastic organizations' trying to invent new ways of providing high-quality workplaces while containing costs and maintaining flexibility and adaptability. My intent, in any case, is not to generate blueprints but to stimulate thinking, which seems to have a longer shelf life.

This book is organized into five parts, all of which have a strong planning and organizational focus. The reason for this is simple: Other books address technical issues of facility management such as project and construction management, architectural design to accommodate information technology, database development, and financial forecasting. What they lack are detailed discussions of how to think about the social and organizational context of some of these more specialized aspects of facility planning and management and, even more importantly, how decisions about everything from planning processes to space planning and performance evaluation can affect an organization's ability to meet its business objectives.

Part 1, "The Changing Role of Facility Management," puts facility management into a historic context and suggests some of the ways in which it is evolving toward a more active, even innovative, service function in large organizations today. Part 2, "Planning the FM Process," explores some of the processes for creating quality facilities, from strategic planning to managing the briefing and environmental change processes. Part 3, "Designing and Managing Workspace," focuses on new approaches to space planning and management being implemented around the world, particularly in the United States, Europe, and Japan. Part 4, "Assessing Performance," looks at new techniques for appraising buildings and for measuring and defining the effectiveness of the FM function. The Conclusion looks at the management of control in the continued evolution of facility management.

All of the chapters describe ways of thinking about how to plan, design, and manage office buildings that are rooted in practical experience. I do not claim to discuss exhaustively the concepts, tools, and techniques presented, nor is my intent to provide a step-by-step "how to" manual. I have been selective, concentrating on what I consider to be innovative approaches to planning, designing, and managing complex office environments. I am sure that many more innovations exist than I am aware of. But, if I can capture some of the flavor of a new field working hard to become more professional and more effective, then I will have succeeded.

Acknowledgment

Many people contributed to this book in ways small and large. Over the past ten years Bill Sims and I have worked together very closely on many different projects, of which the most visible and important was establishing Cornell's Facility Planning and Management Program. His contribution to my thinking and work in facility management has been invaluable. Fritz Steele has played a similarly important role, especially in relation to my thinking about the facility management process. My thanks go also to Bob O'Neal and Pat Mitchell, who in their own ways actually got me started on this book; to Thomas Allen for developing my insights into how architecture and communication affect each other and the R & D process; to Wayne Pierce, Wayne Veneklasen, Dwayne Bucklin, and many others at Steelcase for the opportunity to put theory into practice in the Corporate Development Project; to Frank Duffy and DEGW for giving me the opportunity to work in London on sabbatical leave and to learn from their considerable and often pioneering efforts in the field of space planning and building appraisal; to PROJECT Office Furniture in England for supporting my facility management research during my sabbatic year in England; to John DeLucy, Karl Gruen, and many other outstanding facility management professionals for their strong support in my research efforts; and to Gerald Davis for including me in the ORBIT-2 and other ground-breaking projects. My special thanks go to Bethany Davis who helped in innumerable ways in the preparation and reading of the manuscript; to John Allen and Elizabeth Daley of *Premises Management and Facility Planning* magazine for publishing my monthly articles on FM over the past two years; to Anne Falluuchi and *Facilities Design and Management* magazine for their ongoing support; and to *Illume* magazine in Japan, which commissioned a major article on the Steelcase CDC. Many of the articles I have written over the past two years for these magazines were the starting points for the chapters in *The Total Workplace*. In that regard special thanks goes to Fritz Steele, Tom Allen, and the Steelcase and WBDC CDC project team, all of whom contributed substantially to the development of the ideas and illustrations concerning the CDC, as well as to my thinking generally. And finally, I want to thank the many students with whom I have had the good fortune to work over the past ten years. Their own research forms some of the pioneering work in the facility management field and has helped launch this new field with a strong research tradition. This book reflects the ideas and experience of all these people and many others. Over the years they have become friends as well as colleagues, and for that, in particular, I am truly grateful.

PART 1

The Changing Role of Facility Management

The Hidden Resource

The English call them *bogs* and *loos*. We call them *toilets*. Whatever the terms, until recently facilities management was associated with—to the extent it was consciously considered at all—cleaning, maintenance, and other routine building-related functions. You can imagine the real estate advertisement: "Charming three bedroom house with eat-in kitchen and two-and-a-half facilities." In the mind of top management, especially, facilities management resided in the basement, not the boardroom. This is odd, really, when one considers that facilities account for a huge proportion of most large organizations' total assets. They are a hidden resource.

A study by *Corporate Design and Realty* (Yee 1986) of Fortune 1000 companies showed that their corporate real estate executives managed a median of 131 facilities representing five million square feet of space. Yet a 1983 study by Harvard Real Estate, Inc. (Zeckhauser and Silverman 1983), a subsidiary of Harvard University, found that only 40 percent of American companies consistently evaluated the performance of their real estate. Many organizations consider facilities a necessary evil: like a washer and dryer, you appreciate them but would rather spend money and energy on something else.

Top management's interest in a new high-image headquarters project, which probably had its beginnings in the pyramids, is nothing new. But until quite recently few organizations have paid much attention to how the planning, design, and management of their buildings and the associated systems, equipment, and furniture affected the organization's ability to meet its business objectives. Historically, even less attention has been paid to actively and creatively managing these resources after they are occupied.

Business success was viewed, not without reason, to reside in finely wrought management structures or the personal dynamism and vision of corporate leaders. Information technology (IT) and competition, which stimulated wrenching organizational change, have placed enormous new demands on organizations' physical facilities, pushing awareness of facilities into management consciousness slowly but inexorably.

Convincing top management that the way in which a building is planned, designed, and managed affects the organization's ability to achieve its business objectives has not been easy. It has often felt a bit like trying to chop down an oak tree with a butter knife: hard going. But things are changing. The principal reason is that for organizations to benefit from their enormous investment in facilities they have had to begin managing them actively and creatively, with commitment and a broad vision. They have had to link facility planning and management to the kinds of social and organizational trends widely publicized by a number of American writers.

Many senior managers avidly read books like Peters's and Waterman's (1982) *In Search of Excellence* or John Naisbett's (1982) *Megatrends*. Yet, ironically, they rarely link trends like higher levels of employee involvement in decision making, more group-based work, and a more diverse and demanding work force to the nature of their physical facilities or the policies and processes for planning and managing them. It is as though Columbus planned his voyage to the Indies without worrying about the design of the *Santa Maria*.

Under the pressure of economic and social changes, piecemeal approaches to organizational change are a common survival technique. Specialized task forces are assigned to study one or another aspect of the total picture. In one corner the human resources people dig into demographic statistics and the consequences for labor force patterns. In another corner the computer experts absorb every new hardware and software development and look to see how these might be employed to the organization's advantage. In a third corner architects and engineers investigate the latest developments in automated building systems. And in the fourth corner sits the facility management team, often waiting to be invited to a party that nobody has planned. The consequences of treating organizational and technical trends in isolation are, in hindsight, predictable: huge numbers of new computers purchased but used far below their potential or, in some cases, never even turned on because there was no place to put them, or inadequate staff training, insufficient budgets for data entry, or failure to determine in advance exactly how and for what they would be used; or new buildings costing millions of dollars whose design makes it expensive and difficult to install new information technology and unpleasant for staff to use and undermine desired communication patterns.

As the demand for highly qualified professional staff increases—and often exceeds their supply—such findings become critical organizational concerns in the race to hire and retain the best staff. Table 1-1 describes some of the facility implications of a number of organizational trends, while other trends of importance fall within the categories of organizational, group, and individual levels which are described below. These form the crucible from which modern facility management has evolved.

Table 1–1. Facility Impact of Social and Organizational Trends

Trends	Pressures	Implications
Social Organizational	*Simultaneous Increase in:*	*Process/Product*
Participation Health/Well-being Multiple Choice Networking High Touch Decentralization Information Age Work Groups World Economy	Control Coordination Cooperation	Space Planning Policy/Standards Building Design Building systems Furniture Information Technology
Work force		
Better Educated More Women/Working Mothers Multiple Wage Earners/Part time Handicapped Older		

Source: Davis et al. 1985.

FACILITY IMPLICATIONS OF SOCIAL AND ORGANIZATIONAL TRENDS

Organizational Level

More specifically adapted spaces

More easily subdivisible/expandable buildings

More support spaces to attract/retain staff (e.g., cafeteria, day care, library, exercise)

Changing level and pattern of cabling

Connecting electronic equipment

Protecting hardware operations

Meeting the demand for electrical power

Providing security to the outside

Providing security to the inside

Providing facilities that convey a positive image to outsiders and to employees

Group Level

Systems designed from ground up to support group work

More social space that maximizes interaction

Development of computer simulations/games that foster cooperation, communication skills, and build group cohesiveness

Furniture (and layout) that easily accommodate differences in group size and work style/churn

More physical cues to reinforce group identify

Redistribution rather than reduction of total space

New furniture/space standards that less tied to job level and more to task and individual needs

Individual Level

More access to daylight

More individual control over air, temperature, lighting, furniture, and privacy

Smaller individual spaces at top; larger at bottom

More shared space

More movement among loosely-coupled settings that differ in function (e.g., social vs. concentrative) and location (e.g., home, central office, neighborhood work center as well as multiple locations within a central office).

More attention to the human factors of workstation design (e.g., furniture, lighting, sound, air quality) and layout.

FACILITY MANAGEMENT

A Definition

From mud and stone to concrete, steel, and glass, facilities planning and management have had a very long, if unwritten, history, and the function of planning, designing, and managing buildings has existed as long as have buildings. What is new is not the function but its deliberate, conscious, and planned practice.

Facility management, a term that I use to encompass the activities in planning, designing and managing complex facilities such as offices, hospitals, and schools, differs from architecture and interior design, at least as they have been practiced historically, in the following way: Facility management refers to buildings in use, to the planning, design, and management of occupied buildings and their associated building systems, equipment, and furniture to enable and (one hopes) to enhance the organization's ability to meet its business or programmatic objectives. Facility management thus refers to organizational effectiveness.

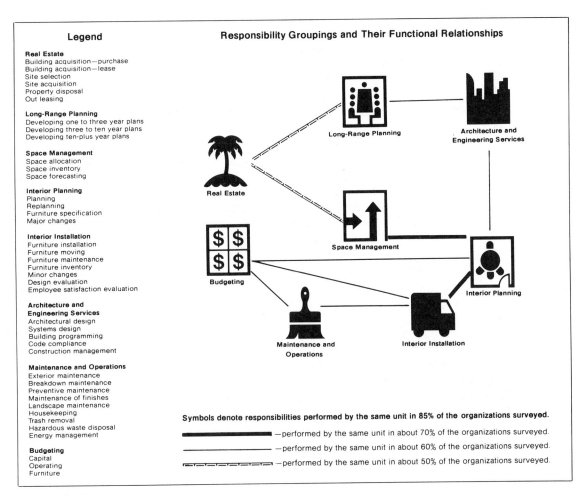

Legend

Real Estate
Building acquisition—purchase
Building acquisition—lease
Site selection
Site acquisition
Property disposal
Out leasing

Long-Range Planning
Developing one to three year plans
Developing three to ten year plans
Developing ten-plus year plans

Space Management
Space allocation
Space inventory
Space forecasting

Interior Planning
Planning
Replanning
Furniture specification
Major changes

Interior Installation
Furniture installation
Furniture moving
Furniture maintenance
Furniture inventory
Minor changes
Design evaluation
Employee satisfaction evaluation

**Architecture and
Engineering Services**
Architectural design
Systems design
Building programming
Code compliance
Construction management

Maintenance and Operations
Exterior maintenance
Breakdown maintenance
Preventive maintenance
Maintenance of finishes
Landscape maintenance
Housekeeping
Trash removal
Hazardous waste disposal
Energy management

Budgeting
Capital
Operating
Furniture

Responsibility Groupings and Their Functional Relationships

Long-Range Planning

Architecture and
Engineering Services

Real Estate

Budgeting

Space Management

Interior Planning

Maintenance and
Operations

Interior Installation

Symbols denote responsibilities performed by the same unit in 85% of the organizations surveyed.
—performed by the same unit in about 70% of the organizations surveyed.
—performed by the same unit in about 60% of the organizations surveyed.
—performed by the same unit in about 50% of the organizations surveyed.

Figure 1-1. The facility management function embraces many disciplines and types of expertise. (Source: International Facility Management Association 1984)

As Figure 1-1 shows, facility management includes space and furniture allocation, building acquisition and leasing, building operations and maintenance, architecture, engineering, and interior design. It concerns policy and procedure, human behavior and management style, as much as it does steel and glass, preventive maintenance, and automated building systems. It is fundamentally a management function, as the following definition (Becker 1987, p. 82) suggests: "Facility management is responsible for coordinating all efforts related to planning, designing, and managing buildings and their systems, equipment and furniture to enhance the organization's ability to compete successfully in a rapidly changing world."

This definition contains three ideas. First, facility management is a function, or a series of linked activities; therefore its primary role is to coordinate all efforts pertaining to the planning, design, and management of an organization's physical resources. It is not a reactive function that takes over once planning processes have been completed and building decisions have been made. Facility managers thus must be familiar with a wide range of building disciplines, but they do not have to be expert in all of them. That is, broad-based specialization is required.

Second, facility management is responsible for coordinating planning processes and managing the building's continuous development and changing use patterns, as well as for maintaining the building. Facility management begins before architecture and design and never disappears. When the building is occupied and the architect's role diminishes, the facility manager's comes into sharper focus. The building as a concept becomes the building as a living organism, and like other living things, it needs to be nurtured, understood, and its full potential developed.

Third, facility management is not in the business of such things as wire management, space planning, furniture selection, building maintenance, or lease negotiation per se. Rather, the goal is organizational effectiveness: helping the organization allocate its physical resources in a way that allows it to flourish in competitive and dynamic markets. As such, strategic policy and procedure governing planning processes and resource allocation are (or should be) central themes in facilities management. The challenge is to integrate operational decisions into a broader strategic framework.

History

Although facility management has existed as long as building, its recorded history is a nanosecond in time. In the United States, 1980 seemed to me the critical demarcation point, the time at which several creeks quickly formed into a fast-flowing stream that then began to grow into a river, with tributaries flowing around the globe, from the United States and Britain to Japan, Australia, New Zealand, the Netherlands, and other parts of Europe.

Five factors coalesced to propel facility management from the basement to the boardroom, from a hidden function entrusted to the sleepy, the slow, and the steady to the increasingly bright-eyed and dynamic facility managers who can be found in public and private sector organizations today (see Figure 1-2).

Information Technology

The first factor concerns computers, which in the beginning were huge, heavy affairs whose enormous size and weight, as well as concern about information security, dictated that they be located in basements. Mysterious, secreted away in windowless rooms, and run by esoteric wizards working with the incomprehensible foreign languages of arcane programs, computers were viewed as frightening, dehumanizing machines, the harbingers of a robot-driven brave new world. But now they sit on almost every desk, and most people who have used them cannot imagine having survived without them (see Figures 1-3, 1-4, 1-5, and 1-6).

The first step out of the basement led to "dumb" terminals located at individual workstations. These in turn linked individual workers to huge mainframe computers ideal for processing enormous amounts of routine data or, in the case of financial

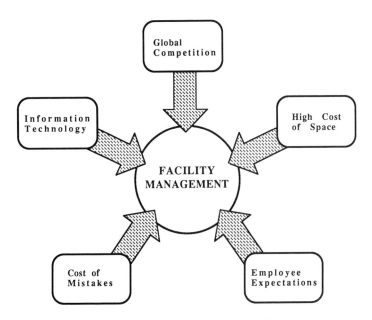

Figure 1-2. Five factors stimulating the growth of facility management.

institutions, running complex econometric models used for financial forecasting. All the remaining steps have led to personal computers. Indeed, even in that bastion of conservatism, English law firms, computers are now becoming commonplace. According to a report of professional firms in the city of London (DEGW 1988), about one in four solicitors were using personal computers, a figure that was expected to rise rapidly. In financial institutions, one-to-one or higher ratios of computers to staff are typical.

Computers at the workstation have not eliminated computers in the basement, but they have been matched by continued developments in automated building management systems (BMS) for security, fire control, lighting, temperature, ventilation, and elevator service. Interest in linking what have until recently been isolated but large databases for human resources, maintenance, inventory, purchasing, and real estate to an integrated network is creating a new impetus for using mainframe computers.

The proliferation of information technology, in the form of both office automation and automated building management systems has placed enormous new demands on buildings. Technical characteristics such as floor-to-floor heights; the capacity and zoning capability of heating, ventilation, and air conditioning (HVAC); the size, accessibility, and location of cable risers; and the need for an uninterrupted power supply (UPS) have literally changed the way in which buildings are designed.

Information technology also impinged on the visible office. Furniture designed to carry cables linking computers to one another and to the secondary power supply, and special lighting that increases staff comfort and reduces fatigue by controlling reflected light on VDU (visual display unit) screens have helped shape interior design into a far more technical discipline.

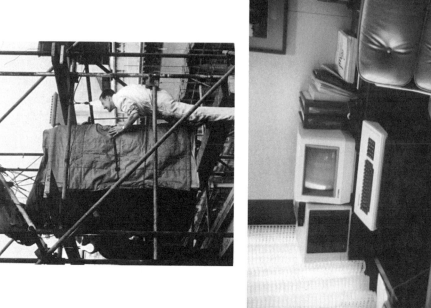

1-4

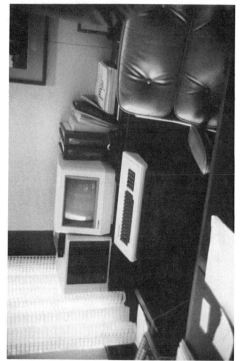

1-6

1-3

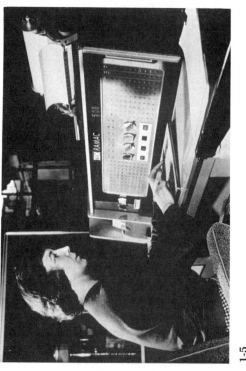

1-5

Figures 1-3 to 1-6. The change in the size and number of computers has driven the transformation of the office over the past eight years. (Photos 1-3, 1-4, and 1-5: Source: Archivist, Lloyd's Bank PLC, London)

Planning, designing, and managing buildings in traditional ways have become a form of corporate gambling, a high-risk venture in organizations that otherwise pride themselves on being careful and cautious. The cost of acquiring the new information technologies (IT) is bad enough, but to acquire them and then not be able to install them where one wants to, or to do so only at high cost and higher levels of disruption to work—often alienating (if not making ill and uncomfortable) a well-paid staff—epitomizes poor value for money. To achieve organizational quality, the interface between IT, the building, and its occupants must be managed efficiently. Facility management—shakily, erratically, with little information and less experience—began to evolve as the coordinating function.

Global Competition

The second factor was recognized by John Naisbett (1982) in his best-selling book *Megatrends*. He was one of the first to capture the enormous enlargement of the marketplace, often unbeknownst to those trading in it, from the local, regional, and national scene to a complex web of international competition. Financial services companies and computer, automobile, television, and appliance manufacturers all began to realize that to survive they needed not only to improve their products and services, but also to become more efficient, "lean and mean," using to maximum advantage their increasingly expensive professional staff, equipment, and buildings to meet the competition at home and abroad.

Thus the first wave of concern for improved buildings, furniture, and building systems to accommodate new information technologies that many naively believed would be the plug stopping the flow of profits down the drain of international competition quickly evolved into a more direct set of management concerns. Policies and procedures for the efficient and effective use of space, equipment, and furniture to support rapidly changing, often unpredictable business practices became paramount. Although acquiring technology turned out to be easy, using it effectively was enormously difficult.

High Cost of Space

Figure 1-7 demonstrates a third factor in the upsurgence of facilities management. That is, with a few exceptions the cost of space goes in one direction: up. Older buildings that are at best marginally able or, in some cases, not able to support new information technologies become cash drains for firms paying rates (in London) of around $60 to $90 per square foot. These kinds of economic pressures stretch conventional wisdoms to the breaking point. Questions of how important it is for different groups to occupy such space and which groups might be moved to less expensive "back office" locations with more modern and efficient buildings better able to accommodate organizational change and new information technology become unavoidable. Property strategies (to sell or lease, to renovate, or to build new) once viewed as securely within the domain of the real estate department can no longer be made in isolation from organizational strategies, from the cost of operating buildings, or from decisions about information technology or their effect on attracting and retaining top-quality staff. These are, in fact, business decisions. A comprehensive, integrated facility management framework by definition thus spans departmental and disciplinary boundaries.

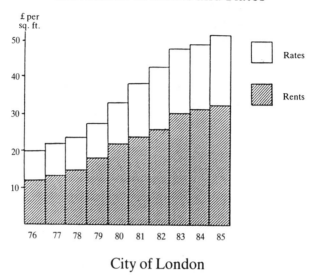

Movement of Rents and Rates

City of London

Figure 1-7.   Excalating space costs require innovative thinking about how facilities should be planned and managed. (Source: Becker 1988a)

Rising Employee Expectations

The facility manager's lament: "Wouldn't it be great if there weren't any employees!" (Many university professors would prefer college without students; architects like commissions without clients.) The world would undoubtedly be much simpler if we did not have to contend with other people's expectations, desires, needs, preferences; that is, their idiosyncracies. But although it would be much easier, it also would be exceedingly boring, if not pointless.

The fast-rising expectations of employees is the fourth reason behind the advancement of facilities management. People expect more than safe environments; they want comfortable, pleasant—amiable—working conditions. They want the chance to work productively, to form meaningful relationships, and to make a contribution and be recognized for it. They want to be treated with dignity, to be recognized as individuals. For many, these may be the preconditions for accepting a job or for staying in it and working productively. They want the information and equipment resources needed to do their job well, and they want to be able to structure their work with some discretion. These are not new issues, but despite the efforts over the past thirty years of human resource and organizational development experts to increase worker participation and create more humane work environments, little had changed until quite recently. Yet the time and location of work—for the last eighty years controlled without significant challenge by management—will, in the future, be much more often a part of negotiated working conditions.

Providing employees with acceptable environmental conditions, especially in sectors in which the demand for highly qualified staff exceeds their supply, becomes central to organizational effectiveness. And as the baby boom generation goes bust and the pool of qualified workers shrinks, meeting these expectations will become a matter of survival. It is the staff who represents 92 percent of organizational costs over the life of a building, and it is the staff who ultimately determine the success or failure of any enterprise. Again, understanding employees' environmental expectations and meeting them while coping with the kinds of demands we noted now require considerably greater effort and imagination than in the past.

The Cost of Mistakes

A fifth factor underlining the greater recognition enjoyed by facilities management is money, for $40 to $60 per square foot in leasing costs, one hundred million dollar buildings, $10,000 workstations, and millions of dollars in office automation and automated building management systems make mistakes expensive. Spending time, effort, and money on initial analysis and planning thus becomes good value for money. As many companies have discovered, getting it right the first time is less costly than buying "cheap" and then having either to suffer the consequences or to spend even more money to rectify the initial mistakes.

In combination, it is these five factors that have combined to pull facility management out from the dark and into the open, from the basement into the boardroom.

FACILITY MANAGEMENT AND ORGANIZATIONAL QUALITY

It has been the concern for organizational survival, however, not design quality that has driven the evolution of facility management from a low-level, routine function—more serendipitous than planned—to one that was highly centralized and controlled, to the current state of affairs in which the facility management division is likely to view employees as "customers" and itself as a vital service group. This is the kind of organization I call, in the next chapter, the *elastic organization.*

The goal of elastic organization is to develop control mechanisms that are taut but not brittle; that can bend, shrink, expand, or be reconfigured; and that can take new and unpredictable shapes without snapping, having to be jury-rigged, scrapped, or simply suffered.

Like any ecological system, it does not really matter where one breaks into the system: Tracing interdependencies links parts of systems initially considered independent. In the case of facilities, the pressures for a more elastic organization were stimulated by the repercussions of costly errors, for example, expensive computers used far below their potential capacity or new (and expensive) buildings more alienating than old ones. Like Robert Burns's famous line: "The best laid schemes of mice and men gang aft agley and leave nought but grief and pain for promised joy," too many facility managers have championed modern buildings in which good intentions and bad planning end up undermining the organization's ability to locate or configure work groups in ways that made good business sense. Only the richest organizations can afford space standards that may require enormous time and effort to develop but then may be too complicated and cumbersome to be continually updated or to be of any practical use.

Quality and the Elastic Organization

Organizations exist—at the very least—to perpetuate themselves, but most want to prosper, to expand, to increase their profitability, to serve more people at a higher level, to invent more and better products, and to contribute to the fund of knowledge. "Quality" means excellence. To me, it means more than profits or just running in the black, necessary as these are for survival. Rather, quality has a time perspective, being able to prosper over time in the face of changing conditions, whether they be the emergence of new markets and the withering away of old ones, shifting staff and customer expectations, or obsolete technologies giving way to modern ones.

Excellence is a relative measure. For example, few of us would choose the "excellent" medical treatment of two hundred years ago over the "excellent" treatment available today. Thus excellence is, for most things, a moving, not a stationary target. Static approaches, useful in their own time, are unlikely to remain so as the world around them changes.

In an organizational context, quality refers to creating those conditions under which motivation, commitment, shared ideas, energy, creativity, dignity, interdependence, control, and cooperation can flourish. With a little sunshine these seeds can sprout the policies and procedures, the structures and designs, the new ideas that enable organizations to survive if not prosper.

If we define organizational quality in this way, then facility management contributes to it directly and indirectly in a number of ways, such as:

- Asking questions about organizational and demographic trends and how they will affect facility planning and design
- Providing information about the design and layout of buildings that will promote effective communication within and across work groups, departments, divisions, and regions
- Developing policies and procedures for the allocation and use of space, furniture, and equipment that will enable staff to work effectively, comfortably, safely, and efficiently
- Creating approaches to building design and space planning that enable the organization to organize (and reorganize) work teams, departments, and divisions quickly in response to changing market conditions
- Designing and implementing planning and design processes that promote a sense of cooperation and interdependence among diverse disciplines, departments, and areas
- Establishing cost control procedures that use financial resources in a way that will maximize their benefit
- Using processes and procedures for selecting sites and buildings that can easily accommodate new technologies and also meet the needs of staff and management

Reducing the enormous fixed costs of these facilities is the aim of many facility management programs. A less visible but equally important goal should be to use the organization's physical resources closer to their maximum potential; that is, to ensure that whatever is planned, designed, and used actually supports the ways in which employees work most effectively. Sharing control and systematically involving a cross section of employees in facility decisions can transform the design process from a rather sterile, often pro forma data collection exercise into a dynamic, energizing form of organizational development that promotes positive employee attitudes while generating better designs and facilities.

Facility management that supports organizational quality in this way is an invaluable hidden resource. "Hidden" because we are self-centered: People, not buildings, make things happen. But the same car runs differently depending on the octane level of the gasoline powering it. Water can flow uphill, but not without energy-intensive pumps. Humans are unbelievably adaptable, but why should we spend millions of dollars to build, furnish, and then use facilities that test the limits of human adaptability? Facilities are the structure around which working practices are built, and the policies and procedures for making facility-related decisions are the glue that binds facility management to the broadest issues of organizational excellence.

Skeptics Speak

What evidence is there that facility management really does affect an organization's profitability? Without this evidence, why should any company make a big effort to improve its facilities operation?

At the moment, there are few published data from formal research that assess the organizational consequences of FM policies and procedures. But organizations make major decisions all the time without such data and merely on the basis of fashion. Think of the rush toward decentralization today (see Chapter 6). Organizations will always have to act without all the necessary information. But the absence of formalized research does not mean that there is no "evidence" that good facility management makes a difference. Indeed, there is a wealth of powerful anecdotal evidence that suggests just the opposite.

Companies like TRW, Union Carbide, and John Hancock have saved millions of dollars over the past several years by implementing energy savings programs that use computers to monitor and control energy use. By using innovative space-planning concepts, firms like IBM and Hewlett-Packard in England, Digital Equipment Corporation in Finland, and the Shimizu Institute of Technology in Tokyo have been able to use space over 30 percent more efficiently.

Firms like Steelcase Corporation with its Corporate Development Center and Corning Glass with its Decker Engineering Building have produced buildings and space-planning concepts that they believe have significantly improved informal communication among their professional and technical staff. Professor Thomas Allen's research at the Massachusetts Institute of Technology (one instance of a long-term research program) has repeatedly shown that such informal communication is associated with higher-quality products and a faster product development cycle. Companies like Herman Miller that use computerized space and furniture inventory report both cost savings from not purchasing unnecessary furniture and increased responsiveness, because reconfigurations and renovations can draw on available furniture inventories made accessible through computer inventory processes.

Thus, facility planning and management are affecting direct costs as well as the indirect costs of communication processes, response time, and a faster product development cycle. All of these contribute significantly to the organization's ability to meet its basic objectives.

It seems to me that another sense of FM as a "hidden resource" is that the facilities, if well planned and designed, should be invisible: People should not even know that they are there. Why promote a function that ought to remain hidden?

In a sense the facility is a big tool. Good tools get the job done quickly, efficiently, and safely. They also bring pleasure to those using them: the heft and balance of a hammer, the feel of the handle, its texture and temperature, its simple sinuous shape. The building should not irritate its users, drain their energy, increase medical risk. But why shouldn't it—as fine architecture always does—bring a smile to their lips, a bounce to their walk, a sense of joy? Good architecture does not have to cost more than bad does, but it does require an act of will and a commitment to excellence that mediocre facilities lack.

CHAPTER 2

The Elastic Facilities Organization

An organization involves hundreds of its rank-and-file employees in a model programming process to develop new space and furniture standards. Another devotes a corner of its building to the construction of a full-scale mock-up of several new workstations and then invites intact work groups to use them. Their reactions are monitored by the facility manager by means of informal interviews and brief questionnaires. The final selection of furniture is based on the employees' feedback. Using a survey form that elicits employees' reactions to their physical environment, a third organization initiates a regular post-occupancy evaluation (POE) of the work environment. Its goal is to create a database against which the success of building renovation and interventions can be determined. A fourth organization develops a more systematic, quantitative, and comprehensive building appraisal process to assess the suitability of its building stock for different operating units.

These organizations are IBM, Shell Oil, Lloyd's Bank, Union Carbide Corporation, Steelcase, and the World Health Organization. Each is exploring new ways of planning, designing, and managing its physical facilities. Some require new organizational structures and new briefing processes, and others involve new information technologies, new procedures for collecting and analyzing data, computer-aided energy management, space and furniture inventory systems, and FM training programs. The nature of the innovation differs from organization to organization, but the stimulus behind the pressure for innovation is frequently the same. Rising employee expectations, increasing national and international competition, escalating space and land costs, and rapidly fluctuating markets make innovation necessary to the organization's survival.

Neither these kinds of innovation nor the pressures stimulating them affect all organizations at the same time or with the same intensity. Yet few organizations will remain immune to them. The evolution of the facility management organization can be viewed as a trajectory of change, with individual organizations located all along the change path, some more advanced than others.

A MODEL OF THE FM ORGANIZATION

Organizations are different and they change over time; two simple ideas that have guided my thinking about facility management. They underscore the importance of understanding the "fit" or match between organization policy and practice and the organization's stage of evolutionary development, its organizational culture, and its business and operating environment. What works well when a company is small is not likely to work as well when it is large and, what works in a stable operating environment is unlikely to work well in a turbulent one.

I see the facilities organization as falling into roughly three types: The *loose-fit,* the *tight-fit,* and the *elastic* organization (see Table 2-1). In practice, elements of each can be found in all three types, but the framework helps focus attention on organizations as dynamic organisms whose policies and practices should evolve with the organization over time. FM's role evolves from merely helping the organization survive to eventually acting to enhance its potential to prosper in a volatile, unpredictable business climate.

Loose Fit: From Indifference to Complacency

The loose-fit facility organization is characteristic of organizations at two different stages of development: very small start-up companies and medium to large mature companies operating in a stable business climate. Hallmarks of the loose-fit organization in either stage of development are little formal control over facilities and, in small firms, decisions negotiated directly between users (in small firms rarely is there someone who is formally assigned to making facilities-related decisions). Instead, decisions tend to be *ad hoc* and informal. Chairs, desks, and computers are unlikely to match and layout is decided by the people directly involved. Concern for corporate image is minimal. Little information is collected or used to guide decision making. Written space or furniture standards do not exist.

Indifference to facilities, especially in regard to their image and appearance, is characteristic of organizations that are busy launching themselves. The neophyte organization's embryonic structure—small, highly personal, and interactive—makes the concern for facilities beyond a place to sit, a telephone, and computer—let alone formalized rules and procedures for allocating space and furniture—unthinkable and unnecessary. If you cannot afford the boat, no need to worry about how to sail it. Nor do you need to hire an expert to maintain it. Garages, basements, a corner of the den, part of a warehouse, or a few rooms in a converted house often define the "facilities." All energies are directed toward developing and marketing the business's products and services.

Table 2-1. Model of the Changing Facilities Organization

	Types of Organization	
Loose Fit	Tight Fit	Elastic Fit
Ad hoc	Central Standard	Central Guideline
Minimum Information	Maximum Information	Selected Information
Minimum Control	Maximum Control	Selected Control
Service	Cost	Cost & Service
Reactive	Reactive	Proactive
Tactical	Tactical	Strategic
Unplanned Diversity	Planned Uniformity	Planned Diversity
Negotiated Decisions	Dictated Decisions	Consensus Decisions

Source: Becker 1988a.

Complacency rather than indifference applies to larger, mature organizations firmly established in a stable operating environment. The facilities function is a distinctly back stage, basement operation. Business as usual, mind-numbing but reassuringly routine, is the order of the day. The organization is like a train running smoothly on a level plain, tracks stretched out endlessly until they disappear over the distant horizon. Other than making sure that everyone has a place to sit and that senior management is satisfied with their own work areas, little self-consciousness exists anywhere in the organization in regard to the role or importance of facilities to overall organizational success. Role differentiation and specialization among facilities staff are minimal (though highly differentiated elsewhere in the organization). Inefficiency can be endemic, but the firm's profits help mask it and render stringent controls unnecessary. The focus is on keeping things "ticking over."

Facilities people in this type of organization tend to be competent lower-level administrative staff or older professionals at the twilight of their career. Taking care of cleaning and basic maintenance and making sure that broken door locks are fixed and that everyone has a desk to sit at occupy a good deal of their time. Little more is required. The proverbial "Old Joe" keeps things running, carrying all the information around in his head about who has a spare chair, where a desk can be found, and who to call when the toilet backs up. When he needs some resources, he calls on the president, his old friend, and asks for what he needs. Tradition guides decisions more than information does. Sailing in becalmed waters does not take much skill or imagination. Risk taking and courage are history, not living theater.

Tight Fit: Survival Is the Goal

Much more typical of large organizations operating in a turbulent business environment, the tight-fit organization is the most stressful and frustrating. Running it is like sailing in uncharted waters in rough seas. Surviving the storm is the goal: Phones ringing are a constant threat, incessant, clamoring for attention, with callers rarely satisfied. Toughness, stamina, steel nerves, and a sense of humor carry the day. Finding order in seeming chaos is the sheltered harbor.

The hallmark of the tight-fit organization is the formalization of the facility management function. Deliberate, planned management control settles like a layer of dust everywhere, typified by a bureaucratization of the facility management functions. Someone is now assigned responsibility for managing the facilities, which account for a much larger proportion of the firm's total assets. In marked contrast with the negotiated, *ad hoc* decentralized decision-making style of the loose-fit organization and the consequently highly diverse nature of the facilities, decision making in the tight-fit organization is highly centralized. Formal space and furniture standards, space and equipment inventories, and formal request procedures for products and services such as new furniture or furniture rearrangements typify this stage. Such an organization is reactive, tactical, often unbending, upright, vigilant, and harangued.

Facility management becomes more self-conscious and deliberate. It has to. A great deal of information is likely to be collected, especially to justify major capital expenditures, but relatively little information is closely analyzed to identify patterns that emerge over time or locations. Systematic databases and benchmarking are uncommon. Operational decisions are often confused with strategic policy, and the distinction between the two is likely to be unclear.

In the face of frequent and unpredictable change, constantly putting new and often extreme pressures on the facility, the facility function attracts complaints like flies to sticky paper. In a turbulent environment, the major concern is simply getting things under control and reducing chaos. Key issues for the facility manager are such things as wire management, power capacity, running costs, and more efficient space utilization.

This makes sense. The explosion of demands on the facility from new information technologies and a dynamic organization constantly shifting in size and structure, at the same time that space costs spiral upward, can create a sense of panic and chaos. Control is needed as a necessary first step toward managing the facility.

Unfortunately, the controls exercised usually evolve outside any explicit philosophy concerning the facilities management function. Attention focuses on management directives to control costs and "get things under control." Users (employees) are often viewed by the facility manager, whose own needs for control and order tend to be quite high, as disobedient children: unruly, messy, whiny, demanding, unable to exercise good judgment, occasionally rude to their surrogate parent (the facility manager), and even sneaky (when making "midnight" requisitions of furniture, for example).

Stringent controls help make the facilities managers job easier and increase efficiency, but they often run the risk of alienating staff and can impede organizational effectiveness if they become static gatekeeping devices. As a transition stage, the tight-fit organization can buy breathing room to allow preparation for moving on to the next stage.

Elastic Fit: From Efficiency to Effectiveness

The elastic facility organization builds on, and integrates, both of the earlier stages. One of its hallmarks is that what typically seem like contradictory or conflicting policies and procedures in the tight-fit organization—like promoting the corporate image while allowing individuals to help design their own workstations, or containing energy costs while providing individual control over temperature and humidity—are reconciled in the elastic organization. Decision making is more a matter of "both/and" than "either/or" thinking.

Thus the elastic organization recognizes the need for some central control, but it also accepts the value of decentralized decision making and some forms of diversity. Control is taut but dynamic; hence the concept of elasticity. The elastic organization encourages diversity within well-defined frameworks, and it provides clear guidelines within which decentralized groups can quickly make decisions to respond to changing conditions. Broad-based and well-structured employee participation is seen as a means of enriching the information base that drives decisions, increasing the employees' commitment to the decisions that are made, and helping attract staff whose expectations include being consulted about decisions that will affect their work life.

Facility management is stronger and (no longer a contradiction) both more management and more employee oriented. Strategic policy and operations and the people expected to carry them out are clearly distinguished. Central facility management becomes more of an expert resource than a gatekeeper. More (and sometimes less) information is collected and regularly analyzed and used to guide both strategic and operational decisions. Benchmarking and databases are common.

For the first time there is a strong emphasis on facilities quality, defined not only in terms of administrative ease, corporate image, and cost containment (hallmarks of the tight-fit organization) but also in terms of user satisfaction and the effect of the facilities on internal communication and the ability to attract and retain high-quality staff. Innovation and risk taking, fundamental to business success at the time of organizational launch, are now equally critical to the success of established firms operating in a turbulent business environment.

Managers and staff at almost every level are likely to be given the authority to make well-defined categories of decisions within frameworks developed by a centralized facility management function. Relatively rigid centrally-developed space standards, for example, evolve into more flexible space guidelines. Technically advanced building management systems allow employees to set their own heating and cooling levels within predetermined limits and, at the same time, monitor actual energy use so that facility management can recoup its occupancy costs. Rather than setting a single standard for every piece of computer equipment (virtually impossible in many large companies, particularly when they cross national boundaries), the headquarters facility group is more likely to install software that allows communication among different kinds of hardware than to beat its head against the wall trying to police uncooperative user groups throughout its organization.

The elastic facilities organization is proactive and strategic. The facilities group concentrates on process and product. It integrates the tactical focus of the survival stage but begins to view operational decisions within a broader strategic arena. The goal is to contain costs while adding value, and so, using the ways in which facilities are planned, designed, and managed to help the organization attract and keep the highest-quality staff is vital. Yet because the cost constraints make it impossible to give everyone large offices and expensive furniture, the need to add value while containing costs thus demands innovation and the ability to stretch the mind in the search for new solutions. It is this willingness to innovate, to involve many diverse groups in the planning process, and to analyze information that defines the elastic organization.

ESTABLISHING AN FM PHILOSOPHY

Elastic organizations have a clear facilities philosophy, for facility innovation cannot occur without it. "Keep costs down" has entirely different implications than does "Contain costs and add value." Is the facilities organization the "central gatekeeper" or the "staff resource"? Are staff viewed as children, needing to be disciplined, or as the firm's most valuable resource? How these questions are answered and the kind of reward systems set in place to reinforce them will guide the nature of the solutions that the organization will seek. Whether developed from the top down or from the bottom up, the facilities philosophy must be communicated to and understood by all the staff. It also helps if they accept it. Why is this so important?

A good philosophy provides a framework for action and guides decision making. If it works well, it can actually increase individual autonomy (because people know what is expected of them and what to expect from others) without sacrificing overall organizational control. Ultimately, the value of any philosophy is tested by its daily application. In a major computer company, for instance, quality slogans abound, mounted on foamcore and hung on the wall or propped on a desk. Yet when I asked a young staff person in this firm how facility management quality was assessed, she looked confused, not knowing what to say. I am sure the company, especially top management, believes in quality, but the philosophy has failed if the staff cannot easily and quickly point to events, actions, and procedures that illustrate how value statements are transformed into action.

In another computer company the facility philosophy was captured in a few words: "Keep it simple and efficient." Any staff person could point to simple straightforward space guidelines or photographs of facilities worldwide to show how those values were put into practice. Detailed specifications were unnecessary, because over time the staff had built up a strong mental image of what "simple and efficient" meant and had incorporated the philosophy into their daily decisions almost without thinking.

CHARACTERISTICS OF AN ELASTIC FACILITY ORGANIZATION

To create an elastic organization in which facilities management is designed to cope with an unpredictable business environment, a better-educated and more professional (and demanding) work force, and constantly evolving information technologies, the following issues must be considered.

Systems Thinking and Organizational Ecology

The factors affecting facility decisions and the technical, financial, human, and organizational ramifications of these decisions have become enormously complex. They demand not only more information, but also an understanding of the relationships among areas, disciplines, and departments once considered unrelated, if not irrelevant, to one another.

Organizational ecology is the study of how the planning, design, and management of offices' physical settings (everything from site, building form, interior design, and space planning to the furniture, equipment, and building systems) affects and is affected by organizational patterns and practices (culture, values, decision and organizational structures, and staffing). It links what are likely to appear to top management as trivial, or technically narrow, facility issues to fundamental management concerns. HVAC (heating, ventilation, and air conditioning) illustrates this point.

In itself, looking a bit like a Rube Goldberg contraption with its brightly painted blue, green, red, and yellow ducts, chillers, blowers, and filters twisted into wonderful forms, HVAC may attract senior management's attention, but it is more likely to be for its sculptural appeal than because its role in supporting basic organizational objectives is understood. Yet HVAC in a modern, high-tech office can (and often does) dictate how the organization runs.

HVAC incapable of fine-grained zoning can, for example, make it difficult to place heat-generating computers where they would make most sense from an organizational perspective because there is no way to direct extra cooling at the subarea of a floor where, ideally, they should be placed. So the computer goes where the rigid air conditioning system dictates, or it is located in its desired location and everyone working near it either sweats or shivers. In one of the Big Eight accounting firms, for example, a new office layout could not give partners the privacy they desired in their offices. Why not? The HVAC zone control did not match the office layout. The only way to cool and heat the partners' offices was to leave off the doors.

The ability to reorganize departments quickly in response to changing market conditions and business plans is also essential to many organizations. Does the HVAC have the flexibility to accommodate the reorganization of departments that may have boundaries different from the existing ones? Can a personnel department, with its needs for privacy in fully enclosed interviewing rooms, be located where a data-processing group was sitting the week before—and still have appropriate heating and cooling?

Professional and highly qualified staff are critical to the success of many organizations, and they also are in short supply. Given comparable pay and similar job challenges, the quality of the physical environment can be what differentiates two otherwise comparable organizations. Does the HVAC system meet employees' expectations for a comfortable and healthy work environment?

These are management issues, but they are caught in the facilities web. Thus, decisions even about something as seemingly technical as HVAC systems require information about the number and adaptation of new information technologies, organizational changes, spatial and temporal characteristics of work patterns, air pollution and human factors, user needs and preferences, and work-styles and organizational culture.

To achieve organizational quality with this degree of interdependence, the answer is both more data and a wider sharing of information across department and discipline barricades at early stages in the decision process. Integrated organizational structures in which previously isolated facility functions (e.g., design and construction, building operations and maintenance, catering and security) report to a single high-ranking facility management executive is one approach. Informal working parties and task teams are another approach. More frequent review meetings are still another. Electronic mail and design that maximizes informal contacts can also ease communication. The key is top management's actively supporting and rewarding cooperation across departmental and discipline boundaries.

Accountability

The cost of mistakes is high. When change is infrequent, more effort is devoted to justifying it than to evaluating it. Frequent change pushes assessment to the fore. Yes, management wants to know why they should purchase new furniture, renovate a floor, or develop a CAD capability. But because decisions in these areas will come often, not just once in a decade or less, management will also want to know whether the benefits claimed in the original proposal to renovate a building or purchase a new technology have been realized. Have operating costs been cut? Staff morale increased? The time and disruption in responding to a departmental reorganization reduced?

Demanding evidence about projected outcomes after a decision, when there is concrete experience with the effects of that decision, often makes more sense than asking for justification before making the decision. The reason is simple: There will never be published research findings, or even the informally shared experiences of colleagues in other organizations, that demonstrate the costs and benefits of every decision. In the absence of available evidence, or experience in one's own organization (which most top managers value more), asking for "hard data" often is simply a means of stalling a decision or imposing one's personal views.

Linking the Facility and the Corporate Plan

Historically, the access of facility planning and management (with the possible exception of corporate real estate) to corporate decision makers and to their strategic organizational, marketing, and financial plans was limited or nonexistent. Like a Buster Keaton film in which everyone races madly around and around, colliding, narrowly escaping crashing boulders and careening cars, all action and no direction, the results of keeping facility management at arm's length from corporate planning might be funny if they were not so debilitating. Typical is an organization in which field operations staff spends six months looking for a new site. About the time they finally find the site they learn that a corporate business decision was made six months earlier to relocate the organization entirely out of the region. Thus enormous effort has been wasted.

In another company it is purely accidental that a facilities manager is at a meeting in which it is decided to expand immediately into a new region. The business managers are shocked to learn that it will take about eighteen months to provide the manufacturing facility they need, by which time the new operation has been predicted to be profitable!

In large organizations with regional branches and sites, strategic planning is sometimes linked to facilities planning by having facilities managers report directly to the business manager at the site, rather than to a headquarters facility management group. This ensures that facilities decisions will be made in the context of local business decisions, but it may prevent the facility manager from gaining corporatewide expertise and thus producing an overall facilities program for the organization.

More informal procedures, revolving around periodic meetings and informal discussions based on managers' understanding that any facility or business decisions should be assessed according to their wider effects is another alternative. Such procedures are often much easier to establish than an organizational restructuring, and there is no conclusive evidence that the more difficult and time-consuming structural approach to enhancing communications and cooperation necessarily works better than do informal approaches.

Employee Involvement

Employees' expectations are rising, and on the whole employees are becoming better educated. A recent Steelcase/Harris (1987) survey of American office workers supported earlier research that has consistently shown that American workers are permitted much less participation in decisions about their work, and workplace, than they want.

My own and others' research has shown that increased employee involvement is associated with greater satisfaction with work environment and a stronger commitment to decisions made about it (Becker 1988b, 1988c; Brill, Margulis, and Konar 1984; DIO 1983; Froggatt 1985; Wandersman 1979). Involving rank-and-file employees in workplace decisions can also save an organization thousands of dollars by reducing the likelihood that money will be allocated to physical designs that workers consider unacceptable. Subsequent modification of the original design can cost hundreds of thousands of dollars, thereby compounding the cost of the original mistakes.

The recent Lloyd's of London MORI poll (Becker 1988b), showing that 75 percent of the people working at Lloyd's found the new building less satisfactory than its predecessor, is a powerful example of the consequences of not involving occupants in decisions about their work environment. My own research on the Lloyd's building showed that many of the aspects of the building that the staff do not like (concrete block, exposed ducting, and rubber floors in support areas; black ceilings and light fixtures; frosted glass that prevents views outside; the layout of the different insurance groups on the floors) were made with minimal or ineffective occupant input and review. The irony is that this occurred even though formal structures for involving staff had been created. But the real cost is yet to come. Eighteen months after its initial occupancy, Lloyd's was considering hiring new architects to make relatively major changes to one of the most expensive buildings ever built.

There are many ways of involving employees in planning and design decisions (see Chapter 8, "Managing the Briefing Process"). Some companies use surveys; others use structured focus groups to react to schematic design proposals. Special committees and working parties are common and full-scale furniture mock-ups are no longer rare. In some cases employees respond only to design proposals. In others, they may actually help design their own workstations by selecting their furniture or laying out their own work areas. No single approach is best. But the key is to involve employees in decisions they care about and to demonstrate to them that their ideas actually contributed to the final decision.

More Expertise

No single person is competent in all facets of facility planning and management, which now include mechanical engineering, architecture, interior design and space planning, human factors, organizational behavior and psychology, personnel, finance, telecommunications, CAD, construction and project management, acoustics, and lighting. Even within a given field, specialization may be required. Clean rooms require different engineering expertise for design and maintenance than do computer rooms; the design of a trading floor bears little resemblance to the design of an executive suite or reception area.

A much wider variety of expertise is needed. One of two approaches can be used. The first is to hire more outside consultants, typically for a specific project (see Chapter 4, "Staffing the FM Organization"). Developing selection criteria and knowing how and when to use consultants are important issues. In some cases the use of outside consultants may be radical, such as reducing the in-house staff to a few managers, with virtually the entire facility function contracted out to specialty firms. Many firms now do this for security, catering, and cleaning, and in the future they may also do this for furniture inventory, internal reorganization, and monitoring of programs and activities. Knowing exactly what needs to be done and having a procedure to gauge the effectiveness of the outside consultants are essential (the issue of accountability).

An alternative approach is broadening in-house expertise, often by hiring new people. Another approach is in-service training for existing staff, such as through nondegree residential training programs, like those run by MIT's Sloan School of Management for executives granted leave by their companies. Cornell University's Facility Planning and Management Program is currently exploring this type of high-level training program for facility planning and management.

Benchmarking

Organizations are complex, multifaceted organisms in which growth and development among their parts is generally uneven. Thus, it is not unusual to find a facility management group that appears to have developed either more slowly or rapidly than its surrounding parts have. It seems out of kilter, skewed, rough edged. Yet as a management function, the ways in which facilities are planned, designed, and managed should be compatible (but not necessarily identical) with basic organizational values, goals, and objectives. To make sure that facility management fits its own organization and its operating environment, some form of organizational benchmarking is useful.

THE VALUE OF ORGANIZATIONAL BENCHMARKING

Organizational benchmarking allows managers to see how close or far they are from some wider corporate pattern, within their own as well as among comparable other organizations. They can then decide whether this is about right for their organization or whether they should consider changing in some areas. Organizational benchmarking also serves as an organizationwide or industrywide indicator of organizational performance, analogous to data regarding operational performance. For example, when one organization's operating costs are much lower than those of comparable organizations (or different units among the same organization), performance is generally considered good, whereas a space efficiency ratio below the norm suggests poorer-than-average performance. Knowing where an organization stands in relation to others can help justify facility expenditures, policies, and procedures to senior management who rarely have any "benchmark" against which to judge the facility group's proposals or performance. Without such a benchmark, management is likely to invoke personal experience that may be wholly inappropriate to the actual situation.

Organizational benchmarking can serve similar purposes, as it provides a yardstick against which an organizational unit, such as the facility group, can measure its fit with other groups within and outside the organization. By thinking in terms of organizational rather than operational benchmarking, one can begin to ask whether the organizational structure of the FM function, its decision-making policies and procedures, its service philosophy, or its management style reflects broader, and perhaps more rapidly changing, corporatewide values and practices, as well as those in comparable leading-edge organizations.

Benchmarking and Underachievement

One should remember, of course, that if the industrywide or internal organizational standard is low, simply matching a typical profile is not necessarily an indication of high-quality performance or of what might be achieved, even with the same resources. Jan Carlzon (1987), president of Scandinavian Airlines (SAS) tells a story that illustrates the potential of benchmarking for encouraging underachievement.

SAS, despite strenuous efforts, was unable to match the profitability of a leading English tour group operator. When Carlzon finally asked the British company how it managed to be so profitable, he was astonished to learn that he had misunderstood the basis for its profitability calculations. In fact, SAS had considerably exceeded the English firm's profitability. He thus realized that if he had understood the standard in the first place, he never would have tried to improve on it (as SAS had already met the highest industry standard). Yet if he had not had any benchmark, he would have had no basis for even considering whether his own company's performance was acceptable.

Ultimately, each organization has to decide whether it wants to be average or to excel. Standards, like sport records, are made to be broken. But not every organization has the will, the resources, or the skills to be a leader.

What Kind of Facility Organization Are You?

In terms of the facility organizational model described earlier, every facility group needs to address three issues: (1) What is its own organizational profile? Which of the three organizational types does it most closely resemble? (2) How similar is this profile to its own firm's organizational model? (3) How does this profile compare with competitor FM organizations? Once the facility group knows where it stands, it can begin to calculate the value to the organization of its way of doing things. It can also discuss with top management, if necessary, any conflicts between how management thinks about the organization as a whole, and the kinds of directives it gives to the facilities group. And it can use information from competitors or other organizations for rethinking internally and talking with senior management about where the FM organization not only is but also should be going.

To find out whether your own facility group is closer to a "loose," or "tight," or "elastic" organization, try asking yourself some of the following questions:

- What exactly are your strategic policies, and are they distinct from specific long-range plans (e.g., space forecasting, headcount projections) and from your day-to-day operational decisions?
- What information do you collect? How much of its has been analyzed formally?
- What decisions have been influenced by the information you collected and analyzed? How much information do you collect but never use?
- What kind of control do you have over facilities? Do you try to control every decision made by any group, or do you concentrate on developing guidelines that allow different operating units, groups, and individuals to exercise some choice?
- Who are your customers? Do you think primarily in terms of cutting costs, or are you always trying to balance cost containment with better service?
- How are facility decisions made, and by whom? Are you told what to do, or do you work with others to reach a consensus based on a review of information in light of organizational goals?
- What staff are involved? What decisions, if any, are made by rank-and-file staff? Is their input and feedback sought formally, regularly, or not at all?
- Is the diversity in office layout or in the components found in offices seen as improving performance or indicating that facility management has insufficient control?

By comparing your answers to these kinds of questions with the categories in the organizational model, you can begin to get a rough picture of what kind of facilities organization you are. Then you can address the question of how you fit into the organization as a whole and compare with competitor or other organizations. Answering this question requires looking at and talking with people from other departments and divisions in your own and other organizations, reviewing published annual reports and (at least within your own organization) corporate planning documents and organizationwide handbooks and manuals. IFMA (International Facility Management Association) and BOMA (Building Owners and Managers Association) research reports provide data on a cross section of industries and organizations of varying sizes. All provide clues to how top managers and other facility managers think about the issues described earlier in this chapter.

Using this information, you can begin to chart and compare the facility group's organizational profile with what you believe to be top management's view of the organization as a whole and with what you understand to be profiles from other organizations. Where does the profile overlap? Where does the FM group seem out front, behind, or well matched? Perfect matches will never occur; the point is to know where and, more importantly, why discrepancies occur, that is, to discover why things are the way they are and to see how they might change. Simply talking with senior management in human resources, in corporate planning, and finance about these organizational profiles can be useful in establishing FM's view of itself as a management function and as an integral part of the total organization.

Is What You Do Beneficial?

Once the facilities group knows where it stands, it might begin by asking a few simple questions:

- Is there evidence to suggest that the way the group allocates space or furniture, assesses the suitability of buildings, decides to own or lease buildings, or manages a construction project is better than some other way of doing the same things to meet FM as well as corporate goals and objectives?
- Is there information to show that doing something in a different way would be less effective than how you do it now?

Try to identify deeply rooted working assumptions that may, in fact, be unsubstantiated by fact and counterproductive. American office planning, for example, is guided by the belief in the organizational imperative of close physical adjacencies among members of the same department, even when a department has fifty, a hundred, or even more people in it. The spatial consequences are huge, expensive, uninterrupted floor areas, and tremendous cost and time devoted to moving employees every time a department is organizationally restructured. Yet in a recent tour of Dutch and Swedish offices I found an equally strong belief in designing work areas to accommodate only about ten to twenty workers. Areas larger than this were considered alienating and unconducive to effective communication.

Given the cost and planning implications of such space-planning premises, collecting information in order to test basic working assumptions seems justified. This might be done by using surveys or analyzing existing organizational records (e.g., absenteeism, turnover, medical complaints, employees' grievances, requests for physical changes, costs of moving people or building certain kinds of buildings). Focus groups and interviews with representative employees as well as specially selected informants are also useful.

The objective of organizational benchmarking should not be to lower one's aspirations, to limit one's imagination, or to feel comfortable being "average." Some companies undoubtedly will use organizational benchmarking to reinforce the status quo. But for other companies the value of organizational benchmarking is that it not only defines the boundaries of mediocrity, tradition, and complacency but also suggests barriers to be broken and new standards to be set.

Operational Benchmarking

More common than organizational benchmarking is operational benchmarking. Procedures for monitoring factors such as cost (construction, maintenance, repair, furniture, equipment), response time, and employees' reactions are becoming more routinized. These data serve as a useful performance indicator. Does our firm (or site or region) use space more efficiently or have lower operating costs than a competitor (or another site or region) does? They also can be used to explain and justify costs, programs, or plans that might otherwise seem "out of line" to senior managers asked to approve something for which they have no experience or yardstick.

The basis of benchmarking is trend analysis rather than scrutiny of a single event. Building engineers at Lloyd's of London, for example, have linked a request for repairs procedure to a computer program, which allows facility managers to track the time between the lodging of a complaint and its resolution, the cost to solve the problem, and the location of the problem in the building. With this system, they can instantaneously trace maintenance patterns over time and use these data for management decisions. Are some products more troublesome than others? How much is this costing us (useful in price or service contract negotiations)? Is a more expensive product less expensive to maintain (thereby justifying its higher initial costs)? Is there a reason to assign more staff to a particular site because of its special maintenance problems?

In addition to tracking such things as operating costs (e.g., energy, cleaning, maintenance), operational benchmarking can include square footage per person, space efficiency ratios (e.g., usable to rentable or to gross), amount of "churn" or office reconfigurations by department, cost of moving a typical workstation or so many linear feet of panel or drywall, or the average rating of employees' satisfaction with their workplace. The idea is not to generate a list that is long enough to wrap around the earth three times, but to highlight those few important pieces of information that management cares about (ask, do not assume) and that one can directly relate to widely shared strategic goals, and that would significantly affect one's operating budget, staff levels and patterns, and capital expenditures.

Thus an annual post-occupancy evaluation (POE) in which staff attitudes toward their workplace are systematically measured is a good database because it directly relates to attracting and retaining high-quality staff, which is likely to be a strategic objective. IBM, for example, conducts an annual employee survey that incorporates questions about the workplace, generating a database on the quality of the workplace from the employee's perspective. These data can be linked, if desired, to other data on, for instance, absenteeism, turnover, and annual sales volume. IBM sets a minimum acceptable average score, and managers of buildings that do not reach this level must show specific plans for rectifying the situation.

National Westminster Bank has detailed procedures for monitoring at every stage of a construction project the relation between the projected and the actual expenditure. The value of the procedure itself also can be determined in relation to cost overruns before and after initiating the procedure. Operational benchmarking is a way of containing costs and adding value. Cost data, when linked to customer satisfaction surveys, are

---

To: All Department Heads   Subject: Occupancy Charge

From: Manager, Management Services   Date: 1st February 1988

Attached are copies of floor plans for .... showing areas occupied by
Cost Centre based on post restack plans from 1st February 1988. Occupancy
charge will be based on these areas.

Common areas have been kept to a minimum so as to increase the space
occupied and reduce occupancy charge. All common areas are shared equally
by departments based on space occupied.

If a Cost Centre vacates an area they will remain liable for its occupancy
charge until another user agrees to take the space.

It is anticipated that the overall space plan will be reconfigured each quarter to
take account of changes in occupancy, so the next plan will be produced on
May 1st 1988.

The occupancy charge for 1987/88 is £58.1 per square foot and this covers:
1. All premises costs (rents, rates, service charge), cleaning, guards, and
    maintenance contracts
2. All photocopier costs
3. All costs associated with the Staff Restaurant
4. Furniture and Archive storage costs at Verney Road
5. All messenger and post costs
6. All vending costs

Costs associated with the Executive Dining Rooms and Printing are being
charged out on an as used basis.

Figure 2-1. An example of an easily understood communication between facility manager's
and business managers. (Source: Becker 1988a)

a means of appraising buildings and facility management, in the form of a cost–performance ratio (see Chapter 14, "Assessing FM Performance").

Communicating with Management

Developing databases and tracking trends can influence an enormous range of decisions,
including the allocation of space; the progress of a project; the performance of vendors
and contractors, staff, equipment, and systems; and the purchase of services and
supplies. But data resting in their electronic home or buried in piles of computer printouts
on the facility manager's desk are of no use. For data to be useful they must be
transformed into information, that is, selected, analyzed, and communicated to those
who can benefit from seeing them.

Figures 2–1 and 2–2 are examples of how one facility manager regularly used information from his database to communicate to top managers and to the managers of the
user groups occupying his building. His purpose in both cases was to answer the question
that many managers have a hard time understanding: "Where are you spending all that
money?" He wanted to give managers a realistic picture of how the facilities group
budget was spent and also to show managers who must pay for the space they occupy
exactly how their facilities charges are derived.

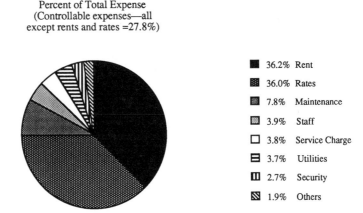

Building Operating Expense Plan
Percent of Total Expense
(Controllable expenses—all
except rents and rates =27.8%)

■ 36.2% Rent

▨ 36.0% Rates

▨ 7.8% Maintenance

▨ 3.9% Staff

☐ 3.8% Service Charge

☰ 3.7% Utilities

⊞ 2.7% Security

▧ 1.9% Others

Figure 2-2.   Simple charts are the most effective for communicating with top management.
(Source: Becker 1988a)

The effectiveness of these figures lie in their simplicity. They convey, in a single page or a single chart, just enough information to answer the question in easily understood terms. This facility manger did not try to impress management with the fact that the facility group has mountains of data or is comfortable with business graphics; the information about the occupancy charge alone was very helpful in taming the managers' expansionist visions. The pie chart helped the CEO understand that his demand that facilities reduce their budget by £7 million was nonsense. If all controllable expenses were eliminated, the most that could be saved would be £1.3 million. This chart prompted realistic questions and focused on what might be sensibly pared down.

INNOVATION AS POLICY

Control is essential, for without it facility management could never achieve top management's support. But control does not have to be an "either/or" zero-sum game proposition; it can be a "both/and" situation in which imagination backed by technological and facility innovation allows facility management to contain costs while adding value to the organization's most valuable resource: its employees.

The challenge of managing the facility management organization is to address issues of cost and profitability within the broader context of quality and organizational effectiveness. It requires using technology to support both the organization's and individual and group needs. It requires an organization with enough elasticity to accommodate unplanned, unpredictable changes in labor force patterns, in organizational size and structure, in technology, in the nature of markets, and in economic conditions.

Pressures for systems thinking, accountability, benchmarking, employees' involvement, more expertise, and closer links between corporate and facility planning exist for all organizations. In responding to them, organizations face three challenges:

1. To recognize such pressures as part of a pattern rather than regarding them as individual events, each seemingly demanding an entirely separate response. This seems self-evident, but often the only experience is of crisis.
2. To explore alternative practices, procedures, and technologies rather than fixing on one or two familiar ones. What works for a competitor or another well-known company may not be appropriate for your organization.
3. To initiate policy, design, and procedure changes on a small scale, if possible, and then to monitor the results. In this way, a series of small changes can be made, each one incorporating the lessons learned from the previous experience.

Organizations that can—and will—try new ways of planning, designing, and managing their buildings, equipment, and furniture in response to these pressure points will be able to compete successfully.

FM As an Organizational Change Agent

In many organizations FM is still regarded by the rest of the organization as a relatively low level, largely reactive service function, certainly not at the cutting edge of organizational policy and practice. But why not? There is no reason that FM, just as well as any other unit within the organization, cannot serve as an organizational model. In many ways, given the need for facility management to understand every part of the organization, the FM group is ideally placed to understand the overall picture of the company and how the different pieces fit together.

What is required is a clear idea of what FM is now and what it can and may have to become in the near future. Organizational benchmarking can help the FM organization see that at least it does not fall behind the evolution in management styles and practices occurring in the rest of the organization. And it can go further. Facility management can—given its need for understanding finance and capital planning, human resource planning and organizational structure, forecasting, budget control, public relations, and marketing—develop policies and practices whose basic principles are relevant to and can be applied to many other parts of the organization. Reconciling centralized and decentralized decision making, devising cost–effective means of involving staff in workplace decisions, balancing the corporate image with individual and group needs for identity, improving service while containing or reducing costs—all everyday FM concerns—are pertinent to the whole organization.

Skeptics Speak

You make it sound as though FM were a top management function. This doesn't make sense to me. FM is a support function that should respond to basic business objectives set by senior management.

I think it is important to distinguish between being supportive and being reactive. In order to support business objectives, FM must know what these are very early in their development. Ideally, FM should participate in their basic development, for a few simple reasons. First, facility functions such as leasing and fitting out space and selecting and ordering furniture generally have long lead times. In the case of leasing or buying buildings, six-month to one-year lead times are not unusual. If major renovation or building is involved, lead times can easily stretch from one to three years or more. Under these conditions it is obviously important that FM know early what support they are expected to provide. Their assessment of the feasibility of getting appropriate facilities on line within a given time period may, in some cases, make an otherwise strong business case impractical.

Second, FM is like the marketing function in the sense that in order to do your job you have to know a great deal about all aspects of the company: what work is being done, the equipment needed to carry it out, the ways in which people need and want to work, management philosophy, and financial structures and procedures. This knowledge is critical to strategic planning.

It is for both this reason and the length of the facilities planning development cycle that I believe FM can and should be integrated at the highest levels of corporate decision making.

Systems thinking is a good concept, but wouldn't it take a lot more time to make a decision if everything is reviewed by three or four different departments, representing different expertise?

It might, but it doesn't have to. The first point is knowing when to involve different types of expertise, and the second is making it clear exactly what kind of advice you want. Periodic review meetings are an obvious technique for reviewing project progress, but there are others. Electronic mail or bulletin boards can be used to solicit responses from geographically distributed staff. Focus groups and selected interviews with informants also are useful. The fundamental issue is total project time. A little more time initially may save enormous time and the cost of rectifying (e.g., through building change orders, cancellation and replacement of purchase orders, new layouts) superficially efficient decisions made without precise information about user and organizational requirements and without adequately considering how decisions about furniture, cabling, HVAC, or building form will affect space planning, organizational change, security, and the like.

I like the idea of accountability. Using numbers to justify one's decisions makes sense. But we do it already. What's new about what you are proposing?

I hope very little! The real issue is not collecting data; it is analyzing them. Far too many organizations collect enormous amounts of data and then haven't a clue about how to use them in their decisions. The challenge is to collect as little information as possible but to know exactly how it can be used.

Financial accountability is also not new. When we invest money, we carefully measure its return. Possibly because facilities are often seen as a cost, with no clear sense of their positive contribution to the organization, little effort has been made until recently to determine the return on facility investment in regard to its support of basic business objectives. Much energy, including number crunching, has been spent on justifying decisions. Given the frequency today with which money is invested in facilities, the emphasis must shift from initial justification to ongoing performance assessment. I will talk about this in more detail in Chapter 10).

When you talk about stages of FM development, you make it sound like being in calm seas is a bad idea. I'd sure as hell like to be there! My problem is that our company runs in cycles—now for centralization, now for decentralization. How does this relate to your evolutionary model?

The answer lies in the concept of elasticity. In a business climate in which the only thing predictable is that things will change—including organizational philosophy regarding centralization and decentralization—good facilities management must be capable of accommodating organizational oscillation. Establishing elastic policies, procedures, and buildings that can stretch and be reformed to fit an array of possible (but unpredictable) organizational requirements without breaking is the hallmark of being effective. Policies and procedures that are dynamic are likely to represent broad guidelines rather than detailed specifications, frameworks rather than detailed action plans, and strategic rather than tactical control. The tight-fit stage is a kind of bridging phase, temporarily allowing the complacent organization to reorganize itself to be competent in the long term in dealing with change and unpredictability.

CHAPTER 3

Defining FM Quality

The phrase "value for money" resounds in the corridors of facility management departments on both sides of the Atlantic. What does it mean? The implication is that the quality of facility management services should be enhanced while (at the least) containing costs and (ideally) reducing them. In theory, "value for money" weds facility management policy and procedure, as well as bricks and mortar, to organizational quality—a kind of ménage à trois. Streamlined procedures, detailed cost controls, more standardized reporting of data, space and furniture guidelines, more systematic building appraisal procedures—all are intended to contain costs while improving organizational quality. Calculating the cost side of the equation is comparatively simple and straightforward, but determining what constitutes value or quality is much more difficult. Yet without doing so, there is no question, only blunt-edged cost cutting, possibly to the point of damaging the organization's ability to meet its objectives. It is easy, for example, to reduce energy costs. Just turn down the heat or lower the air conditioning. Cheaper furniture and less adaptable buildings reduce first costs. But at what price to the organization?

Quality is an elusive concept. Its relativity makes it slippery, worth stalking but difficult to capture with any certainty. Yet in thinking about facility management "quality," certain themes can be identified. Perhaps the most important, and a major theme of the elastic organization, is the concept of "fit."

THE CONCEPT OF "FIT"

Who lives in apartments, houses, condominiums? Who lives in suburbia, the city center, a leisure community, or a planned development? In North America the answer is "It depends." Both stage of the life cycle and life-style determine where we live (or wish we lived). Stage of the life cycle refers to relatively distinct phases in our lives, stages we typically pass through as we grow older. From children living in our parents' home we become young, unmarried adults, part of a married couple without children, a married couple with children, an older couple without children ("empty nesters"), and eventually older persons living alone. In nomadic America, where housing choice and availability make residential mobility relatively easy, families shed their housing skins with the passing of life's seasons and within each "season" select housing options that reflect their life-style. Following what Constance Perin (1974) calls the "correct chronology," we move from family house to apartment to house to apartment, often with several moves within each category intended to help us move "up" in the quality and size of accommodation.

Life-style refers to the relative value that people assign to certain ways of living, such as choices about how to spend income, what activities to follow, what clothes to wear, and what language to use. Life-style is family-style organizational culture. Two families at the same stage in the life cycle and with the same income may choose to live very differently: One is family-centered, focused inward, home based and child directed. The other is leisure-centered; focused on entertainment, travel, and theater; city-based; and self-directed. To know something about appropriate housing for each family, we need to know something about both their life cycle and and their life-style. The same principle applies to organizations.

Policies, procedures, organizational structures, management styles, corporate strategies—and the sites, buildings, equipment, and furniture that give physical form to social structure—appropriate to one organization may not be for another, for the same organization at different points in time, or for different parts of the same organization. Corporate headquarters buildings rarely look like data-processing centers. The level of fit, finish, and furniture, power capacity, building adaptability, security, heating, and ventilation acceptable for a company ten years ago is rarely acceptable today. The issue is not money per se. Instead, life-style and life cycle pertain to how one allocates available resources, not raw spending levels. They refer to values, self-concept, image, functional needs, priorities, growth, and evolution.

Organizational quality is the result of a good fit or match between an organization's requirements and the characteristics of a building. Corporate headquarters of large, mature firms are showplaces, physical advertising. Prestige sites, impressive facades, landscaped grounds, palatial lobbies, wood-paneled dining rooms, the aroma of leather, the sheen of silk and mahogany, and large enclosed offices and conference rooms are physical manifestations of headquarters work-style and organizational culture. The facilities speak to the organization about its identity as much as they do to customers and clients. Headquarters buildings are the parlor, the front room.

The same organization's data-processing center, occupied by systems analysts and technicians, is likely to be located five, fifty, or a hundred miles away, in a back office.

Clean, modern, and simple, metal, drywall, plastic, and polyester (not wood, leather, and wool) are the materials of the day. Not always unpleasant, the back office is the den, the lounge, the country kitchen, worn but sometimes more comfortable than the parlor, vital but hidden from the visitor.

Quality is a moving target, and so the goal is to shoot neither too high nor too low. In facility terms, this means buildings and fit-out that neither overperform nor underperform. Overperformance wastes resources on building capacity, image, or flexibility that the organization does not need in order to succeed and prosper. Underperformance makes it difficult, expensive, or time-consuming for the organization to communicate, process information, reorganize, that is, to structure itself in the way it believes will allow it to prosper. Thus, one worries about both a small, start-up firm that spends its meager resources on expensive offices (unless these are a direct form of marketing), and a large mature one that prefers a cheaper, poorly serviced, inadequately powered building fitted out in the typewriter era but living in the computer age.

Where quality rests at any moment is determined by the size and age of the firm, the nature and behavior of its competitors, the composition and availability of its staff, and, of course, its work-style or organizational culture. Facility management exists to ensure that the facilities—including policies and procedures for governing not only what is built but also how space, equipment, and furniture are allocated and used—support organizational quality by creating a good fit with organizational requirements.

In the elastic organization, good facility management prevents overperformance, spending scarce resources where they have little payback to the organization, while at the same time minimizing the likelihood of underperformance. Getting facilities right demands an understanding of the organization, including its current and projected business and staffing plans, its culture, its overall operating environment, and evolving information and building technologies.

ORBIT-2: MATCHING FM AND THE ORGANIZATION

ORBIT-2 (Davis et al. 1985) is a study that was sponsored by eighteen major American and Canadian organizations representing both the public and private sectors. First, it sought to identify characteristics of high-quality buildings and high-quality facility management. Second, it wanted to develop a method of systematic building appraisal, a simple, practical tool that could help organizations determine the suitability of different buildings and facility management strategies for their organization over time (see Chapter 13, "Assessing Building Performance," for details of the ORBIT 2.1 Rating Process developed by the author and William Sims). The starting point was to link organizational characteristics to building and facility management characteristics.

The premise of the ORBIT-2 project was that "one size does not fit all." That is, each organization requires information technology, buildings, and facility management strategies that fit its particular social and organizational contexts. One outcome of this project was the development of a model of different types of organizations (see Figure 3-1).

We differentiated organizations along two dimensions: *nature of change* (high versus low) and *nature of work* (routine versus nonroutine). In combination these two dimen-

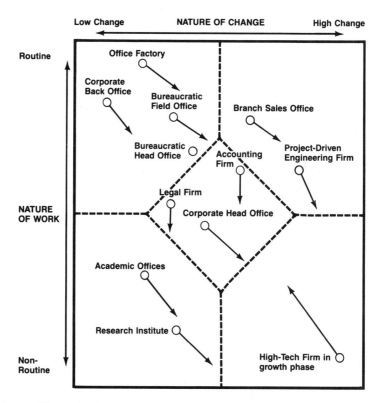

Figure 3-1.   All organizations are different, but they can be classified into groups with common facility requirements. (Source: Davis et al., 1985)

sions can describe organizations or, more usefully, their constituent departments or divisions, at a level useful to thinking about facility decisions. Nature of change, for example, refers to the likelihood of internal reorganizations, the frequency of relocating workplaces or information technology within the office, and changes in overall staff size.

Each of these aspects of organizational change has obvious implications for design. For instance, to accommodate changes in overall staff numbers, a building shell should be configured to permit easy expansion or subletting. To relocate the staff, interior fitting out should lend itself to the rearranging, rewiring, and rezoning of HVAC. Thus, high-change organizations are likely to use quite differently their environmental resources than are low-change ones.

The second dimension of the organizational model, nature of work, was defined as the extent to which the predominant work patterns within an organization or its subunits are either routine and predictable (e.g., processing claims, filing, filling sales orders) or were more varied and unpredictable (e.g., financial analysis, systems programming, market research, organizational development).

These aspects, too, have facility implications. Organizations characterized by highly routinized work, for example, are much more likely to rely on central mainframe computers and an omniscient MIS (management of information systems) department than is a research institute or high-tech firm in which computing intelligence is likely to be widely dispersed and based on powerful engineering workstations and personal computers.

These two dimensions together form a field of change in which the movement that all organizations experience can be traced (Figure 3-1). The corporate back office that today is highly routinized may over time, for example, move toward being less routine in accordance with new job designs and changing attitudes toward computing. The high-technology firm will probably follow an opposite trajectory; that is, as the firm matures, changes will slow and routine operations will increase.

Although we are speaking of whole organizations, in fact as firms grow they tend to break into differentiated parts, each playing a specialized role and often occupying a different facility or a different part of the same building. Thus the movement toward less change and more routine operations in a high-tech firm may apply only to the administrative part of the firm (accounting, purchasing), while the R & D component continues in the early, more freewheeling tradition. The difference between the Xerox Corporation's Palo Alto, California, research park and its corporate headquarters in Stamford, Connecticut (where in the late 1970s bean bag chairs could be found in the former and Knoll seating in the latter) reflects just this kind of split.

FACILITY MANAGEMENT PROFILES

The ORBIT-2 study argued that, because organizations are different and their needs change over time, the fit between strategies for planning and managing facilities and the type of organization is just as important as the fit between the type of organization and its physical facilities. The challenge we faced in the ORBIT-2 study was identifying FM strategies that were appropriate to different types of organizations.

The ORBIT-2 Facility Management Model

We selected two facility management dimensions, the degree of staff involvement and the amount of coordination among facility management functions (see Figure 3-2). Amount of coordination was selected because as organizations grow and the environment in which they operate becomes more unpredictable, facility decisions increasingly re-quire expertise from areas as diverse as engineering, real estate, human factors, design and space planning, environmental psychology, and finance. The extent to which such expertise is used in planning and design decisions was viewed as significantly distin-guishing facility management strategies.

Degree of staff involvement was selected because the work force as a whole is becoming better educated and more professional. People's expectations about the nature of their work and the conditions under which they perform it are rising. Because staff are the greatest cost (and resource) to any organization, involving them (as the Japanese have made apparent) makes sense both for the better solutions that are likely to emerge and for the greater commitment to the decisions that are made. The question no longer is whether to involve staff, but how to involve them (see Chapters 5 through 9).

These two characteristics—degree of staff involvement and amount of coordination—

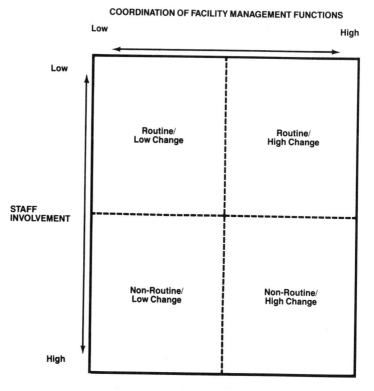

Figure 3-2. A model of different types of organizations (see Figure 3-1) can be compared with a model of different facility management strategies to suggest those strategies most suitable for different types of organizations. (Source: Davis et al., 1985)

by no means exhaust the universe of factors that could be used to characterize FM strategies. They do, however, capture themes that, depending on how they are used, are likely to make facility management more or less effective for different kinds of organizations.

Each quadrant of the matrix formed by the two dimensions (Figure 3-2) describes a pattern of policies and procedures, whose components include

- Organizational structure
- Decision authority
- Briefing processes
- Staff involvement
- Postoccupancy evaluation
- Space and furniture policy
- Expertise

Within each of these categories, we described a number of different options or approaches. For example, in an *integrated* organizational structure, the design and construction (typically including real estate) and building operations report to the same senior manager. In a *disaggregated* structure, they report to different senior managers. Some organizations do their postoccupancy evaluation *systematically and regularly,* whereas others do it *informally and periodically.*

The particular combination of policies and procedures defines an overall FM strategy for planning, designing, and managing buildings, space, equipment, and furniture. The ORBIT-2 FM Rating Process identified a number of prototypical FM profiles (strategies reflecting a combination of policies and procedures) and then rated their suitability for different types of organizations (using the ORBIT-2 organizational model).

The Low-Change/Routine Organization

As Figure 3-2 shows, low-change/routine organizations are likely to have a combination of low-coordination/low staff involvement facility management policies and procedures. Found in relatively mature organizations operating in a stable business climate (a rarity these days), this loose-fit FM management is likely to include:

- Little (but still some) coordination among related FM functions such as real estate, telecommunications, design and space planning, and building operations
- Minimal integration among specialists from MIS, human factors, environmental psychology, and human resource planning in facilities decisions, as either an in-house staff team or external consultants
- Written space and furniture standards that are often outdated and little used
- Minimal involvement of a cross section of staff in facility decisions. If the rank-and-file staff does participate, it usually is as a part of a general attitude survey conducted by the human resource department
- Department heads directly involved usually only for staffing projections and general space requirements
- Lip service paid to minimizing facility costs, but little actual rationalization of facilities based on systematic analysis and innovative policies and procedures
- Top management willing to accept complaints and dissatisfaction of middle- and lower-lever staff if the former considers facilities adequate for tasks

The Low-Change/Nonroutine Organization

Figure 3-2 shows that the low-change/nonroutine organization is typified by a low-coordination/high staff involvement FM profile, which is typical of organizations like universities and research institutes, a kind of hybrid of the loose- and tight-fit organization.

These kinds of organizations are staffed by several highly trained, opinionated, relatively powerful and autonomous professionals, are independent, confident, protective of their own turf. They demand to be heard, especially in regard to their own work and work environment. Although their work is creative and nonroutine, the overall institution changes slowly in comparison with start-up companies or others operating in an unpredictable business climate.

Such organizations put little emphasis on image, internally or externally; most stress functional work environments. The intrinsically rewarding nature of the work itself often diverts employees' attention from the physical context in which it is performed. Staff are indifferent to the style or image of the physical environment (yet are intensely interested in the equipment and layout in their own labs or workspace). They often wish to remain uninvolved in general office planning or design but react vigorously to plans proposed by others. It is, on the whole, an inefficient FM strategy, with the following features:

- Distinct but related FM functions are somewhat coordinated.
- Specialists from areas such as MIS, human factors, and human resources in the form of in-house staff reviews or as external consultants are involved in decisions about facilities.
- Allocation of space and furniture is based on tradition and implicit but widely accepted and known precedents. There will be some anomalies between rank and office size, but over time people of higher rank and status will gravitate toward bigger and better-located offices.
- Staff are likely to participate in facility decisions through focus groups or a building committee. Small numbers of staff meet with representatives of facilities management to respond to proposed design solutions and to articulate their environmental requirements.
- Involvement is likely to be broad, covering not only specific task functions but also issues such as control, privacy, communication, and work-style.
- Minimizing costs is a management concern, but equally important is generating user acceptance, particularly among the top echelons of professionals, who may have no direct management responsibility and are often in scarce supply.

The High-Change/Routine Organization

The facility management profile for a high-change/routine organization is high-coordination/low staff involvement. It is an efficient operation that works in organizations with many highly motivated staff dedicated to their work (e.g., brokers, sales staff) and operating in a competitive business environment. In the face of unrelenting competitive pressures, survival is the key and central control is tight.

Characteristics of this FM strategy, which has many of the features of the tight-fit organization, are

- A strong centralized FM structure.
- Strong coordination among specialized FM-related functions (telecommunication, MIS, design, and construction).
- Detailed space and furniture standards intended to maximize space utilization and to control corporate image.
- A narrow focus of concern in facility planning, emphasizing specific functional task requirements, ergonomics, and work flow.

- Little staff involvement outside department heads and other supervisory staff.
- Highest priority placed on facilities that accept technological and organizational change.

The High-Change/Nonroutine Organization

High coordination/high staff involvement facility management strategies, like those that typify the elastic organization, can be found in the high-change/nonroutine organization. They are the most advanced of the FM stages, having reached this point by a combination of growth in size and unpredictability in the operating environments. Under other conditions, the effort and sophistication of this profile, though desirable, is not essential to an organization's success. Frequent and unpredictable change makes coordination imperative, unlike the situation in organizations such as universities with similar kinds of staff but a much less volatile operating environment.

This FM strategy has the following features:

- Coordinated FM functions, both in structure and the use of multidisciplinary task forces and project teams
- Space and furniture guidelines, not detailed standards, intended to provide a consistent framework for space planning while accommodating idiosyncratic and unpredictable situations
- Planning focused on employee satisfaction (to attract and keep a qualified work force whose demand exceeds their supply) and on flexibility and efficiency

These ORBIT-2 FM profiles are rough and crude but interesting. By identifying policies and procedures likely to be appropriate to different organizations (or different parts of the same organization or the same organization over time), ORBIT-2 made a first step toward defining facility management quality in management terms, that is, in regard to policies and procedures that improve organizational quality by creating a good fit between physical resources and organizational requirements.

FM QUALITY: THE ELASTIC ORGANIZATION AND COMPLEMENTARY OPPOSITES

One interesting aspect of the elastic organization is that policies and procedures that are likely to be seen as contradictory or incompatible in earlier stages, such as planning efficiency stemming from centralized control coexisting with high levels of staff involvement, are viewed by the elastic organization as part of an integrated management strategy. The Japanese do this by combining very strict and formal hierarchies with widespread staff involvement in quality circles and multiple layers of staff review. The Japanese hierarchies are, in fact, so secure that no senior manager can be threatened by good ideas from subordinates! Everyone wins, and credit is shared throughout the group.

The principle of complementary opposites requires clearly distinguishing strategic and tactical decisions. The role of top management in the elastic organization is to create decision frameworks that enable lower levels of management and staff to make their own decisions within predetermined boundaries. A facility example is the thirty furniture "packages" developed by the architect and facility manager, with top management approval, at the Union Carbide Corporation's corporate headquarters in Danbury, Connecticut. These packages represent a central framework within which every employee (over three thousand) was able to select whichever package they prefer, based on his or her own professional identify and personal work-style. Any choice was acceptable.

To apply the principle of complementary opposites successfully—which requires the ability to balance and integrate competing needs for control among the individual, the group, and the organization—the following conditions must be met.

Serving the Customer

Over time the greatest expense (and the greatest resource) for an organization is its staff. An elastic organization requires a culture that truly values its employees, viewing them as "customers" whose needs, values, preferences, and habits must be understood and met to be successful. Staff are beginning to expect comfortable, safe, and pleasant work surroundings. In the elastic organization, therefore, providing quality requires understanding the attributes that diverse users associate with quality, plus a commitment to building this diversity into facility designs and policies.

Distinguishing Requirements from Solutions

If quality refers to concepts such as fit and serving the customer, its starting point is being able to understand what is required to achieve a particular objective. Yet too often the search for quality starts with solutions: access floors, systems furniture, greenfield site, cost control procedure, CAD system. Are these the right solutions or the current fashion? Analysis requires transforming data into information, with the goal of collecting not as many data as possible but as few as needed to make an informed decision.

A Systems Perspective

Political gerrymandering is a way in which American politicians define their own voting districts so that they will contain as many of their supporters, and as few of their opponents, as possible. System gerrymandering occurs when one selects from the whole range of potential outcomes of an organizational intervention only those that indicate that a valuable organizational objective has been achieved. For example, if costs are the prime issue, reducing the "headcount" by hiring more contract staff is a form of system gerrymandering (because it ignores what may be the same, or possibly higher, costs of the contracted labor force, by locating it in a different accounting category). Comparing total costs, including the cost of the contract staff, with greater staffing flexibility or better service is a more honest analysis and avoids system gerrymandering.

Quality should be embedded in systems thinking by gauging how decisions in one area will affect decisions and outcomes in others. Facility managers ordered by their management to reduce costs should first determine the systemswide implications of such reductions. They should then present these to their management before spending time achieving an outcome that may be counterproductive to broader organizational objectives.

These three themes—customer service, organizational requirements before facility solutions, and a systems perspective—should be reflected in the policies and procedures of facility management strategies: briefing processes that solicit information from diverse users, POEs that systematically obtain feedback about how implemented projects and programs really work, and organizational structures and project teams that cut across departmental and disciplinary boundaries.

QUALITY AS PROCESS NOT PRODUCT

For the FM organization committed to improving its quality, the first step is to discover what policies and procedures are actually in place. What seemed (to some people) like clear policies will inevitably turn out to be more a personal interpretation of a vague directive or a departmental norm. Explicit, written directives (i.e., policies) need to be separated from common practice or informal (even if widely shared) expectations.

As a second step, policies and procedures should be evaluated in light of strategic objectives, existing (and shifting) organizational values and practices, existing (and evolving) work patterns and labor force patterns, availability and suitability of new information technologies, and organizational change (often in response to shifting market and economic conditions). Are policies and procedures equally appropriate (the question of fit) to all parts of the organization? How well do they use different kinds of expertise (the question of systems)? To what extent do they involve users (the question of serving the users)? Are there procedures for accurately and precisely identifying requirements (the question of separating requirements and solutions)?

Such analyses will not magically produce quality facility management, but they are likely to stimulate critical thinking that may.

Skeptics Speak

You argue that every organization is different yet propose only four types of organization, using the ORBIT-2 model. What good is such a model in helping an organization establish facility management programs and practices?

You are right. By itself the ORBIT-2 model does not provide answers to specific problems. But then, it wasn't designed to. Consistent with the idea of the elastic organization, the ORBIT-2 FM model is intended as a framework for analyzing one's own situation, not a detailed blueprint for action (the ORBIT 2.1 Building Rating Process, described in Chapter 13, is designed as a decision tool). It does suggest useful questions to ask about FM policies and procedures and which of these combinations is most likely to work for a particular type of organization.

Your analysis indicates that for some types of organizations, such as a low-change/routine work organization, low coordination among different FM related functions, minimal staff involvement, and so on, are acceptable. Is this true?

Partially. It means that some companies, depending on the business environment in which they operate, will be able to compete effectively by using policies and procedures that for another kind of company would be disastrous. Integrating FM-related services, for example, is always desirable, but the consequences of not doing this when the rate of change is very high are likely to be much more severe than when they are lower. For example, the disruption of telephone and computer lines for a financial services group, for even a few minutes, can result in millions of dollars lost in sales. Thus, making sure the computer and telecom people are working closely with the furniture installers as part of an office relocation or reconfiguration is not merely desirable; it is essential. But the same would not be true for a records retention group in an insurance firm.

In the same way I would argue that some form of broad-based employee involvement offers benefits in terms of higher morale, a better design, and more commitment to and satisfaction with the design. However, with professionals whose influence can be very strong, such involvement, again, becomes not a matter of desirability but critical to the success of the project.

In effect, the issue relates to over- and underperformance. The goal is using scarce organizational resources to the maximum advantage, which means knowing where to spend time and money. The ORBIT-2 FM model suggests the kinds of policies and practices that, at least, will not impede the achievement of organizational objectives.

Staffing the FM Organization

A man, about fifty years old, balding or maybe with a crew cut, wearing a short-sleeved shirt with a plastic pen protector in the pocket and baggy pants, who is gruff, down to earth, loyal to the company, more a detail man than someone with the big picture, comfortable taking orders (and giving them), short on imagination but long on tenacity; in sum, he is a caricature of the type of facility manager that is becoming an increasingly rare species.

The introduction of vast amounts of new information technology, combined with dynamic organizations that restructure departments and divisions with the abandon of a ten-year-old-child playing with a Lego set, has flooded the corporate basement (where facility management was often housed symbolically, if not literally) with new complexities, new challenges, and new expectations. In the process, facility management has floated upwards, if not to occupy the boardroom, then to at least move in that direction. Meeting these challenges with staff who more or less fell into the facilities area or were dumped there by management skeptical of their architectural, engineering, or management skills no longer worked very well. And so facility management as a more professional function began to evolve.

THE PROFESSIONALIZATION OF FM

In a recently completed research study (Becker 1988a) entitled "The Changing Facilities Organization," which involved ten major multinational firms from the banking and computer industries, every firm cited raising the professionalism of its FM function as one of its main facility management objectives. They used one or a combination of three approaches.

Train Existing Staff

The first approach was to increase the competence of the existing staff, especially the younger, non-college-educated workers who had been identified by higher management as having high potential and strong motivation but relatively little formal training in any particular field. This approach was also directed at older middle-level managers whose new job responsibilities exceeded their experience and competence, even when they had been trained in a specific field like engineering, architecture, or real estate and property management. In either case, the intent was to broaden the staff's understanding of their responsibilities and stimulate new thinking, as well as to help them acquire specific job-related skills.

Both internal and external staff development seminars were used as the teaching vehicle, especially for training existing workers. Regardless of the ease or difficulty of hiring and firing staff, several organizations preferred ongoing staff development because of the constant need to update all employees' skills and knowledge.

Hire New Staff

Not all existing staff have the desire and capacity to grow in their jobs. It is difficult (but not necessarily impossible) for an electrician skilled in the shop to acquire, through occasional seminars and workshops, a sufficiently deep understanding of electronics or computers to maintain them at the required level.

The second stage of professionalism, then, is the hiring of new staff. Armed with degrees in facilities planning and management from programs at colleges and universities in the United States, England, the Netherlands, and Canada, such staff raise the skill and knowledge of facility management. Specially trained staff are more expensive and more demanding. They want intellectual challenge and freedom to enhance and use their training. They want to contribute to the organization and to progress up its management ladder. Thus, they bring new resources while, at the same time, challenging an existing organizational culture that has historically looked at a position in facilities as more or less a dead end.

Attracting and keeping such highly qualified staff is not easy. By the end of my study in Britain I found that almost every facility manager I had worked with had left his or her company either to take a higher-level job in another company or to move into consulting. These facility managers were a talented, ambitious, and energetic lot, and they seemed to outgrow their company's ability to tolerate and nourish the innovative facility management approaches they were moving toward.

There is another problem. The sophisticated skills required to plan, design, and maintain complex facilities can be provided only by well-paid professionals, whose skills may not be needed on a full-time basis. But when they are needed, in response to a building systems failure, for example, they are needed immediately. And to cover during holidays, illness, and other absences, more than one person with the same skills is needed. Because many organizations find supporting such staff financially unacceptable, the wide-ranging contracting of staff has emerged as a third way of enhancing FM professionalism.

Contract Staff

Until recently, many organizations in Britain and the United States maintained their own catering, security, cleaning, and maintenance staffs. In-house staff were considered to be more loyal and also more effective. Because they were familiar with the nuances of the building systems and understood how the organization worked, they could more quickly solve any problems. A desire to lower costs by cutting down on staff, increasing the existing staff's flexibility, and, at the same time, improving their performance has inspired many organizations to consider hiring contract staff for everything from cleaning and security to engineering, space planning, and architectural services.

Some organizations have addressed the fear that contract staff could not be controlled and that performance would suffer by drawing up more stringent contract procedures, which follow one of two models.

In the Ivy League model, few people qualify for admission, but once admitted relatively few flunk out. In facility management this takes the form of extremely detailed contract procedures intended to ensure that the contractors are fully qualified to provide the services for which they are bidding and that they bid on exactly the same basis, that is, that they will provide exactly the same services. If these criteria are met, then the lowest bid will automatically be accepted. John de Lucy, an English facility manager who has adapted this approach to contracting at the Chase Manhattan Bank, the Canadian Imperial Bank of Commerce, and at the accounting firm Ernst & Young believes that detailed screening of contractors provides the following benefits: (1) It demonstrates to outside auditors that contracts have been fairly and competitively awarded; (2) it ensures that all contractors are tendering bids on exactly the same basis; (3) it ensures that all contractors bidding are qualified and can, in fact, offer the service at the required level; (4) it demonstrates to senior management that the costs are the lowest possible for a given level of service; and (5) it spells out exactly what the contractor has to do to succeed.

This procedure is time-consuming and can be daunting to the contractors at first, but there are benefits to them as well: Contract periods are longer (three years, reviewed yearly), and more services are bundled into single contracts (e.g., all cleaning falls under a single contract, rather than having separate contracts for offices and interior spaces, toilets, and the exterior). The result is that the client has to manage fewer separate contractors and issue and review fewer bids.

I call this the Ivy League model because it emphasizes detailed contract documents and screening procedures rather than over detailed and formalized written performance assessments intended to make sure that certain service levels have been achieved, after the contractor has been hired. The examples below show clearly defined performance criteria for contracted services.

In the so-called state university model, admission is relatively easy (compared with top private colleges and universities), but many students flunk out after the first year. In facility management this takes the form of detailed, formalized performance standards. The contractor's ability to meet these levels may be tracked on a monthly or even weekly basis. At IBM UK, for example, outside contractors participate in several days of training to make sure that they understand the performance standards and how their work will be measured against them and also to learn about IBM's service culture in general.

An interesting twist in the case of IBM UK is that the contractors' actual performance, as measured by the groups receiving the service, is made public in contractors' work areas by posting performance ratings on a weekly basis. Thus work quality, good or bad, is continually determined. This approach differs from the formal annual review, which often is based as much on informal impressions or complaints as on any kind of formal performance review by those receiving the service.

PERFORMANCE CRITERIA FOR CONTRACTED SERVICES

Definition of Cleaning Terms

- *Track Off Areas*
  That area of any carpet which collects foot soil tracked from outdoors or from hard surface areas indoors. For maintenance planning it must be considered that track off areas at building entrances average 60 sq ft, at internal doorways 6 sq ft, and for partially carpeted corridors 40 sq ft.
- *Funnel Areas*
  Where foot traffic is squeezed through a concentrated area, such as doorways, stairwells, lift lobbies, in front of vending areas, etc. funnel areas should be averaged at 6 sq ft on each side of a door jamb, or 12 ft in front of lifts or vending areas.

Cleaning Performance Specification

Vending Areas
- Visit each vending area twice daily
- Damp dust chilled water foundations and polish dry
- Replenish cup dispenser, damp wipe container and dry
- Empty all waste receptacles and dispose of rubbish
- Empty and damp wipe all ashtrays; contents collected in separate container

CONTRACTED LABOR AND COSTS

Little research has been done on the advantages and disadvantages of contract labor. Even though contracted labor is often justified to top management on the basis that fewer permanent employees will be needed, it is unlikely to be significantly cheaper, as the "notional profitability" analyses of one of the firms in "The Changing Facilities Organization" study suggested. This firm, a major international bank, developed a detailed procedure for measuring and then comparing the cost of its in-house professionals with the cost of hiring similarly qualified outside consultants.

Essentially, the bank instituted a job-tracking system in which each employee had to record the number of hours worked on particular jobs. To calculate the cost—and profitability—of each staff person these hours were then multiplied by the standard rates recommended by the Royal Institute of British Architects. If the the cost exceeded the individual's salary, this was considered "notional profit." If the person's salary exceeded the cost, this was considered a loss; that is, it would have been cheaper to hire an outside consultant. Included in the calculations were the cost of managing outside consultants and the fact that VAT (value-added tax) must be charged against outside contractors but not employees. In almost every case the internal employees were a bargain.

This kind of notional profitability analysis does not, of course, consider quality. Outside consultants, possibly more motivated to stay current in their field and to be good simply to remain competitive, may provide better service. At issue, especially in an emerging multidisciplinary field like facility management, is what are the relevant competencies and personal qualities associated with an outstanding practitioner.

FM EDUCATION

Founded in 1980, the International Facility Management Association has devoted considerable effort to developing and supporting an educational agenda, both for professionals returning for continuing education and for persons who want to pursue a full-time degree course. Similar efforts are now well under way in England, Japan, and the Netherlands.

Cornell University's Facility Planning and Management Program, the first facility planning and management degree program anywhere, offers both a four-year undergraduate degree and a master's degree. Many of the ideas embodied in Cornell's approach to facility planning and management were included in IFMA's (1989) "Facility Management Model Curriculum Bachelor Degree Program."

Model FM Curriculum

The IFMA core curriculum encompasses seven content areas:

- Facility planning and design
- Facility operations and maintenance
- Human and environmental factors
- Organizational management
- Financial theory and practice

- Real estate planning and development practices
- Research and analytical methods

All of these content areas are to be developed in the context of two process areas, integrative and problem-solving skills and communication skills. Table 4-1 lists the kinds of competencies IFMA believes are associated with each of the areas.

First, facility management is a function not, an individual. Expertise in all seven content areas is needed at different times by most large organizations, but the same individual is unlikely to be an expert in all of them. The IFMA model curriculum distinguishes, in fact, among different exposure levels for competencies within each content area, while recognizing that people should have a working knowledge of the purposes, values, appropriate applications, benefits, and drawbacks of most of them.

Second, not all of these functions will be performed by in-house employees. Many will be contracted out, particularly in specialized areas such as project and construction management, interior and architectural services, and building systems maintenance.

Third, many of these competencies are developed in a single class, or sometimes in a single project, in an academic setting. IFMA also recognizes that these competencies are developed outside the classroom, through various kinds of work experiences. The professional internship program at Cornell, for example, in which students work in the facilities management departments of major companies throughout the United States, Europe, and Japan is based on the belief that theory should be tested by practice (and vice versa).

The thread that ties together different approaches to FM education is what we call at Cornell *broad-based specialization,* that is, the need to supplement a broad understanding or working knowledge of many areas with specialized knowledge or expertise in one of them. This is quite different from the facility manager trained as an architect who is convinced that no one can be a good facility manager without architectural training (or engineering training if the person is an engineer, business training if the person has this background, and so on).

Although knowledge-based competencies are important, keep in mind that there are many other important skills, attributes, and qualities. Whether called *people skills* or *good communication skills,* they mean that to be effective and able to climb up a career ladder requires more than technical skills and knowledge.

FM TRAINING PROGRAMS

Few organization today provide specialized in-house facility management training programs (in contrast with more general management training programs, which are often provided internally). To develop FM skills and knowledge, staff are usually sent to outside seminars, conferences, and training programs. These teach basic skills and knowledge but do not focus on the particular problems of any single organization. There are two ways of providing training to solve specific problems and help people work more effectively in their own organization. One, as the Facility Planning and Management Program at Cornell has been doing with the facility group at a major bank in New York City, is to bring the education, in the form of seminars on particular FM topics (e.g.,

Table 4-1. IFMA Model Curriculum: Basic Competencies by Content Area

Facility Planning and Design	Facility Operations and Maintenance
• role of facilities in organization • architectural design concepts • cost estimating techniques • forming & managing design team • furniture, finishes & equipment • interior design concepts • post occupancy evaluation • site planning • space inventory • design & corporate standards • workstation configuration • building and interior construction • basic building types • building plans & documentation • Computer aided design • building programming • forecasting • space planning and management	• building systems and related technologies • building diagnostics • inventory management • communications management • energy management • facility operations and maintenance • procurement • principles of contracting • custodial management • security and life-safety management • wire management • workstation reconfiguration • annual budgeting • facility performance appraisal • construction management • move management • computer-aided facility management
Organizational Management	**Financial Theory and Practice**
• human resource issues • contracts and contract documents • contracted services/use of consultants • organizational theory • principles of management • conflict management • techniques of work integration • organizational models	• accounting • life-cycle costing • asset management • budget formulation and execution • capital budgeting • payback analysis • depreciation • financial analysis and business plans
Real Estate and Development	**Research and Analytic Methods**
• urban planning • property acquisition and disposal • site evaluation and selection • leasing and lease management • marketing and market analysis • Taxation and real estate finance	• research design • data collection and analysis • display of statistical information • statistical methods

Adapted from IFMA Educational Committee 1989.

the sick building, project management, space planning and design), to the firm. This allows the training to concentrate on the organization's particular problems. Questions from participants pertain to their own problems, and the seminar leaders can respond to them without worrying about alienating other participants from different firms with different problems. Yet even these kinds of seminars are more general than many staff people want and need.

The Targeted Workshop

The alternative is to run tailor-made training workshops for a specific problem, situation, or opportunity. These kinds of workshops, at least in my experience, are much more effective than are more generalized seminars, for several reasons.

First, the targeted workshop addresses the particular problem with which the participants are grappling at the moment. Getting help in resolving a specific problem is highly motivating for most staff. Even though project management may be important, it always differs from organization to organization, and generic seminars cannot, by definition, focus on the particular.

Second, the size of the targeted workshop tends to be small, between five and fifteen people, which is an ideal size for working intimately with a group. Hands-on exercises, role playing, informal interaction and banter, group presentations, and other effective interactive teaching techniques are feasible with small groups. Many public seminars, on the other hand, have from twenty-five to sixty or more people. For this size the only viable format is some form of lecture, which severely limits the participants' opportunities to apply new ideas and concepts to their own situation within the workshop structure.

Third, although the workshop organizers have created a structure and have a good sense of the general issues, the small size of the targeted workshop format enables a more open-ended approach. Rather than talking about role relationships or a service orientation in general, the workshop can discuss what service means in an organization that prides itself on meeting without delay every customer's request or what the roles are in two agencies, both of whom believe they have the right (and responsibility) to shape the form of the facility, or how the culture of a particular organization defines being a "good" employee or manager and how that might interfere with doing specific tasks that might violate these norms.

Fourth, running an effective targeted training program requires that its leaders be familiar with the organization itself: its structure, culture (norms, values, typical work patterns, management expectations, departmental rivalries, some of the players' personalities), operating environment, and labor force characteristics. This kind of information allows the workshop leaders to target their remarks and apply general concepts, methods, and knowledge far more directly.

Fifth, targeted workshops are more likely to be an ongoing rather than a one-shot experience. In targeted workshops, participants have the chance to let new concepts and ideas seep in for a bit, both during the workshop and for several days, weeks, or

Table 4-2. Facilities Manager Profile

Experience and Qualifications	Skill with People
• Minimum 'O' levels or equivalent • Management of multi-site complex, preferably hi-tech	• Able to influence; listen • Give and receive feedback • Negotiating skills
Mental Abilities	**Ability to Get Things Done**
• Good written and verbal communication • Able to understand and monitor budget process • Innovative; able to think on feet • Able to explain decisions; use information effectively	• Anticipates problems; forward planning • Manages time effectively • Delegates responsibility while remaining accountable
Attitudes and Values	**Motivations and Interests**
• Willing to learn; flexible • React positively to change; approachable • Can cope with pressure • Risk-taking	• Sets high standards; goal oriented • Self-motivated; determined to succeed and help others do so • Ambitious, seeks senior management role

Source: Becker 1988a

months afterward. They know that they will have the opportunity—as more questions arise and as some of the concepts become confused or forgotten—to get feedback from the group and its leaders that clarifies and elaborates workshop ideas and to get ideas about applying them to their own situation. The targeted workshop acknowledges that learning rarely occurs in isolation, and is much more likely to be effective when it is interactive and continuous.

FM CAREER PATHS

Regardless of which competencies (skills, knowledge, techniques) a specific job emphasizes, all organizations must attract and retain the best staff they can. Good people are concerned about their career. They want to know what is expected of them so they can perform at high levels, and they want to know how their careers might progress within the organization. Unfortunately, until recently few FM departments have been helpful in this regard, but this is changing. Table 4-2, for example, which was designed

Table 4-3. Property Management Awards

Awards Specific to Property Management
• Balanced Manager Award • Property Professional Excellence Award • Quality Shield • Quality College • Quality Improvement Project Completion

Balanced Manager Award	
Criteria	**Award**
• Achieve overall rating of 2 on basic job objectives	• £400
	• Piece of Glass (£25)
• Good balance between Task and People	• Engraved Cup for 6 months
• Constructive relationships with other property departments	• Guest together with partner at Annual Dinner

Source: Becker 1988a.

for a major computer manufacturer to help select and promote FM staff, highlights a number of personal qualities that this firm associates with a good facility manager: innovative, able to think on feet, willing to take risks, able to cope with pressure, able to negotiate well, and ambitious. These qualities are not a substitute for technical qualifications or relevant experience, but they underscore the fact that effectiveness is not merely technical. Some organizations have stretched the relation between job demands and job skills even further.

One organization identified the specific skills required to manage each of its sites and then measured the skills of the person occupying that position and compared the two profiles. The organization found that in some cases personal skills exceeded job demands, but that in others the job demands exceeded the personal skills. There was little uniformity in pay levels across sites in relation to the skills actually demanded by the characteristics of the site. With these analyses the organization could begin to link pay to actual job demands and could identify existing staff for relocation or additional training. It also had a much clearer picture of characteristics to look for when hiring new staff. For example, career paths were matched to specific FM job levels so that those entering the FM department would have a sense of how they might progress and, also, what was expected of them.

Staff who perform well want recognition. Annual salary increases are obviously part of this, but one firm in the study also offered a series of "property management" awards (see Table 4-3) that reward the facility staff publicly. These awards underscore the organization's commitment to excellent performance and to rewarding in tangible and public ways those who meet its exacting demands.

Hiring Consultants

The enormous scope and complexity of facilities planning and management mean that, even in the largest organizations, outside consultants will play an increasingly important role. Reducing the number of staff, a kind of organizational shell game in which costs are often simply moved from one financial pocket (fixed costs) to another (controllable expense) without the actual cost decreasing, is partially responsible. But more relevant is the need to use specialized expertise at particular times, for which neither permanent hiring nor long-term contracts make sense. Building a new headquarters or creating a new data-processing center, for example, requires a wide range of expertise for technical, organizational, and project management issues. Staff with this expertise are unlikely to exist in-house in areas such as fire and security, lighting design, ergonomics and human factors, mechanical and electrical engineering, organizational ecology and environmental psychology, and automated building systems design.

Hiring consultants is easy, but hiring the right consultants often seems to require divine intervention. I have seen several firms set up elaborate selection processes that include interviewing programs, site visits to previous jobs, and major presentations and yet not end up with consultants with whom they were really pleased. What good is an elaborate screening process if you do not know what questions to ask, how to interpret the information you are given, or what to look for in a site visit? Selecting the right consultant may be an art, but there can be some method to it, including:

- Having a clear vision before starting the selection process of the kinds of persons (not just the kind of expertise) for whom you are looking. Call other firms who have recently endured a similar project and ask them detailed questions about what kind of expertise they feel, with hindsight, would have been valuable. Ask them (others besides the project manager or senior business manager) to evaluate their own selection process.
- Valuing "chemistry" as well as technical expertise. Are the consultants the kinds of persons or team with whom you feel comfortable? Do you trust them to protect your and the firm's confidentiality? Do you feel reluctant (stupid or silly or ignorant) to ask questions or for an elaboration or explanation, and is the answer defensive, evasive, or patronizing? Do you cringe when the consultants call or walk through the door, or do you look forward to it?
- Looking at their work-style, that is, looking at how they work. How do they involve different user groups (interview the senior manager, use a survey, do informal walk-about interviews)? How do they evaluate their work on other jobs? Have them explain their methods. Do they blame the client, and have they learned and changed their own methods over time?
- Evaluating past clients' responses. Too often only the project manager is questioned. It also is useful to ask whether the project was systemically evaluated (not just a few highly selected "cheers" from key players). Talk to several different end users at different levels and ask them about the process as well as the final product.
- Ascertaining whether the consultants understand their role. Do they see themselves as advisers or gurus who will help management make informed decisions or as ad-

vocates for a particular position, style, or technology? In other words, are they good listeners, responsive, ready to apply their knowledge and experience to your problems (not to fit your problem to their worldview)? Try asking them to describe (and demonstrate) the kind of evidence, procedures, or presentations (written and oral) they have made to help decision makers make good, informed judgments. Are these likely to be persuasive in your own organization?

• Deciding whether they are leaders in terms of ideas and innovation or simply in terms of volume, size, and billable hours. In some cases you may want a consultant with relatively little experience but interesting ideas rather than a well-established person or group that can get the job done but is more or less running on automatic pilot with respect to innovation.

• On site visits, noticing what you do not see or are not told about. Who was not involved, what evidence was not presented, or what technology or methodology was not used? Ask why certain decisions were made and who made them. How often is the prospective consultant mentioned in these kinds of discussions, and in what way?

• Having your own staff experts interview the prospective consultants. From their viewpoint, are the consultants responsive, easy to work with, knowledgeable, and the like?

• Deciding who will actually be working on your job (not who made the presentation). Ask former clients how much they saw of the principal person or partner or senior consultant (and in what role) and how much of his or her staff.

• Determining whether the consultants understand the interdependence of expertise. Ask them to discuss how they see their work (recommendations, decisions) affecting other players in the process. Which players do they mention? Do they understand how something like HVAC, for example, affects people and will affect organizational change efforts? Does the interior designer understand the communication implications of different furniture layouts (based on what evidence, in addition to personal insights and beliefs)?

Asking these questions is no guarantee that the right consultant will be hired, but not asking them is pretty good assurance that you will have to rely heavily on divine intervention.

THE CHANGING CONSULTANCY ROLE

Facility management must come to grips with the problems presented by new technologies and changing social and organizational patterns, for example, terrorism; telecommunications; office automation; continuous internal organizational change; frequent shifts (up and down) in the organization's population size; changes in management style; escalating land, building, and maintenance costs; and rising expectations among a more educated and demanding work force. Organizations are demanding more of their buildings, and a prime role of facility management is to make sure that the organization's physical resources are an asset and not a liability. The goal is organizational effectiveness; that is, helping the organization allocate its physical resources in a way that will allow it to flourish in competitive and dynamic markets.

Implications for Consultants

What this means for consultants, quite simply, is that clients are becoming more sophisticated and more confident. They can better articulate their requirements to consultants, and they are prepared to scrutinize the extent to which design proposals meet them. For consultants, this can be a boon.

It recognizes, for example, that architects have often been asked to design in response to poorly formulated design requirements set out in inadequate briefs. These often impose rigid requirements on relatively precise issues (e.g., number of people to accommodate and total square footage required) while providing almost no information on how the organization actually works, its philosophies and values, its anticipated plans and goals, and its management style and typical work practices. Such latter factors, of course, are the ones that typically end up haunting the project after the building has been built. More sophisticated and articulate facility management should improve this state of affairs, with the result being buildings that better meet clients' needs beyond initial occupancy and that may help reduce design time and costs.

COLLABORATION

Over the next decade only those organizations committed to building a good staff, to providing ongoing training and education programs, to offering clear and challenging career paths, and to rewarding good performance will be able to attract and keep the kind of bright and imaginative FM staff they need to cope with complex and sophisticated facilities.

Yet the building process is simply too complicated today for any single discipline to master by itself, and failures are too expensive to leave the process to a well-intentioned but underskilled project team. They key to successful buildings is understanding how decisions in any one area affect decisions in others. Architects, being some of the longest-standing consultants, must understand, for example, the ways in which information technologies affect working patterns, maintenance requirements, and building servicing. To create an effective planning and design process they must understand organizational culture: how the organization makes decisions, the basis on which such decisions are made, how it views its employees and its business market, the role it assigns to the physical environment, and how this is connected to corporate planning processes. The concern must shift from a building product, essentially considered complete upon occupancy, to a dynamic view of buildings as part of a continuing organizational development process. At the same time the facility manager and the business unit manager must understand something about architectural and interior design processes and principles so that they can effectively communicate with these professionals.

No architect, nor any other single professional group, can do it all, but the building must, and so the internal facility management team, permanent contract staff, and peripatetic consultants must work together. This means building a team, a design challenge in its own right, which is discussed in Chapter 7, "Organizing the Project."

Skeptics Speak

The kind of degree educational requirements IFMA has proposed are wonderful on paper, but they would be impossible to fulfill in an actual program in short of a lifetime. Doesn't it make more sense to suggest that someone specialize in one of the major areas, like real estate or business or architecture, and then take a few courses that provide an overview of how the parts fit together?

To become an expert in every area listed by IFMA would require a lifetime's learning, but that is not what IFMA is proposing. Rather, it is arguing that facility planning and management is akin to city and regional planning, a discipline that draws on many others (economics, design, sociology, engineering). In both, students are exposed to relevant concepts, techniques, and theory. Specialization is declared primarily in the student's thesis, which explores a question or topic in depth. It also recognizes that learning is a lifetime project, and a good education should provide a foundation on which this learning can build.

There is another aspect to this: Specialized training in one of the established disciplines or professions, whether architecture or business or anything else, though helpful, does not (it is not intended to) address issues important to facility planning and management from the FM perspective. Architectural education, for example, emphasizes form or technical building issues. It is far less concerned with building maintenance and management issues or with how such forms will facilitate or impede organizational effectiveness.

The point is that the facility manager does not need the depth of the professional architect but does need to understand something about building design (and building systems, organizational behavior, business, etc.) so that the architect (or building systems engineer, organizational consultant, financial officer) can be directed to produce a building that supports the organization's objectives. Facility management education programs are designed to produce people who have a working knowledge of many different areas but, most importantly, have a vision and understanding of how these fit together and affect one another. This requires more than one or two courses, and it does not occur in architecture and engineering programs.

You, and a lot of others recently, seem to be stressing the value of contracting out not only services like cleaning, security, catering, and specialized design and engineering services, but I suppose eventually almost every aspect of facility management. How much of this current interest in contracting staff is just fashion, a device to look good by reducing headcount, as opposed to something that really lowers costs and improves service?

A good question. Unfortunately, I don't know of any research evidence that really answers it. IFMA's research reports indicate that contracting is becoming more common but make no attempt to determine its impact on costs and service. It is an area that needs some research. I do believe that some of the interest in contracting services is fashion, designed to improve profitability on paper by reducing the number of staff. But it also may make sense if it is viewed as a system.

The kind of training that IBM UK offers to its contractors, to teach them IBM's expectations of service and performance, combined with detailed performance assessment, goes a long way to protect service quality. Costs simply must be calculated and compared and should include the cost of managing the contractors, which is one reason that inclusive service contracts, which reduce the overall number of contracts, are attractive. One-stop shopping means fewer contracts to manage. Contracting also offers the potential for getting experienced people who know the most about their area, and it also enables greater flexibility in staffing levels, when fewer or more staff are needed. Thus, my sense is that contracting can have real benefits, but it must be viewed, developed, and managed as part of a total system including careful selection, training, and performance evaluation.

I know several facility managers who were educated and worked in fields unrelated directly to facility management, such as business, human resources, and computers. And they do an excellent job. The real issue, for me, is not specialized training but whether the person is simply a good manager. Good managers can manage anything.

It is true that many outstanding facility managers are simply good managers. It is equally true, however, that like most of us they cannot sit down at the piano for the first time in their life and play a Mozart concerto. But with some talent and a lot of hard work, and many mistakes, they can learn to play this and many other pieces over time. "Over time" and "many mistakes" are the keypoints. A general manager must learn much before becoming adept as a facility manager. And during this process, despite being bright and working hard, he or she will make mistakes, some of them costly.

Until quite recently, neither the general manager thrust into the facilities arena nor the organization that placed him or her there had much choice. Few seminar programs, let alone degree programs, existed. But this has changed drastically and will continue to do so. Programs like that offered at the Corporate Design Foundation in Boston promote the development of specific design management courses in graduate business schools so that general managers are better versed in managing design and facilities, in the same way that they have dealt with areas like finance, production, and marketing.

For organizations grappling with major facilities problems and concerned about using their resources effectively, the opportunity to hire someone with specific facility management training becomes very attractive. At Cornell, for example, the number of job opportunities offered regularly exceeds the number of students we graduate each year. Students with an FM education can get a fast start out of the blocks, and because of their specialized FM education they are likely to have a good sense of their role and how it fits into the organization.

You promote the idea of "targeted" workshops, but these seem to me to have at least two drawbacks. The first is that participants don't get the broad view of a problem area that they can get by participating in a seminar with facility managers from many different companies and industries. The second and related drawback is that the prime value of external seminars is the opportunity to meet other people and form an informal network, and if the workshop is restricted to a single company, this cannot occur.

Both drawbacks you mention are important. In fact, targeted workshops serve a different purpose than does a general seminar, and the two types of learning opportunities shouldn't be considered mutually exclusive. Attendance at general seminars can provide a useful background that makes it easier to assimilate the ideas explored in the targeted workshop. It is also part of the workshop leaders' responsibility to bring to the targeted workshop the broader perspective based on their work with many different organizations, and they often do this by introducing examples, anecdotes, and stories from other situations in which they have worked. Finally, the opportunity to make informal contact with peers at external seminars is extraordinarily useful. But you can also initiate these contacts yourself with a little effort. For instance, try calling up some of your counterparts in companies in your area and inviting them to an informal lunch. You can suggest the idea of an FM roundtable that meets once every month or three or four times a year, and because you are within reasonable travel distance of one another you can maintain face-to-face as well as telephone contact. You can also join local chapters of IFMA or other property related organizations where you can meet people and form a formal or informal network. Also consider participating in a college coop or internship program that places good quality facility management students in organizations for anywhere from a few months to a year.

PART 2

Organizing the FM Process

Planning Strategically

There is a wonderful, apocryphal story (Markoff 1989) about how Seymour R. Cray, the inventor of the Cray supercomputer, responded to a request by a vice-president at Control Data, which Cray helped start, to produce a five-year and a one-year development plan. Legend has it that the next day the vice-president found two three-ring binders on his desk, each containing a single sheet of paper. In the first binder Mr. Cray had written "Five-Year Plan: To build the world's fastest computers." The sheet in the second binder read: "To complete one-fifth of the five-year plan."

This story, which undoubtedly makes many strategic planners wince, underlines the need to think about why we make strategic plans and what value they have for organizations. Facility managers believe that they should be incorporated into corporate business planning processes early and in meaningful ways. Their involvement is viewed as fundamental to their being able to move from a reactive, crisis-ridden approach to facilities planning to a more thoughtful, proactive approach. The goal, of course, is to improve decision-making and response capabilities and to use the scarce resources of time and money wisely. The intent is to avoid situations like that of a major American computer manufacturer in which the facility management group worked for over a year to find new and better accommodation for a group. The only hitch came after the space was located and the FM team learned that six months earlier senior management had decided, for business reasons, to reorganize the group. The space was no longer needed. Another computer firm made a major financial decision to invest in a new manufacturing facility in Mexico. The decision was based on achieving a certain production rate in a given period of time. Unfortunately, no one had ever bothered to ask the facilities people to determine how long it would take to obtain a site and bring a new facility on line. The facility manager heard about the project only when accidentally bumping into a friend in the elevator. A little exploration revealed that the facility projections (and thus the business projections) were totally unrealistic.

The irony of facility managers' quest for improving the linkages between their own strategic planning processes and the organization's business strategic planning is that there is, I think, an implicit assumption by many facility managers that the organization is doing a good job of strategic planning but that FM is being excluded or brought in too late to participate effectively in the process. Perhaps, but more often than not, the strategic planning from which facility managers feel left out is not particularly useful in the first place. In many cases it is less an imaginative plan grounded in a rich knowledge base driven by a clear senior management vision and more a triumph of form over content. Too often the strategic plan turns out to be a bureaucratic shield, designed to persuade shareholders, senior executives, and the board of directors that the organization is a rational, forward-thinking body with a clear direction and sense of purpose (derived from a wealth of knowledge presented in impressive multicolored charts and tables).

Lauenstein (1986, p. 77) described the typical strategic planning process as follows:

The typical annual strategic planning procedure is managed by corporate staff executives, but the inputs come from operations. Top management assigns responsibility for designing and coordinating the process to a member of the corporate planning or financial staff. This person develops a questionnaire composed of two main parts. One calls for information relevant to strategy: "environmental analysis," the competitive situation, company strengths and weaknesses, industry trends, and perhaps an explicit strategy statement. The second section, which gets most of the attention, consists of financial projections for several years, usually five. The raw data are supplied by operating executives. Thus, it is in essence a bottoms-up approach.

The process is scheduled to begin some weeks before the preparation of the annual operating budget begins. The corporate staff sends its questionnaires to the divisions, specifying the date by which the forms are to be completed. The chore is an unwelcome extra burden to line executives, who become adept at determining the least amount of effort needed to satisfy the corporate office.

Answers to questions on strategic issues tend to be perfunctory. Line executives feel that this part of the questionnaire has little practical significance. The corporate staff is usually not in a good position to challenge the accuracy of what is reported. Even if they question some of the responses, there is inadequate time to develop more information. So, as long as all of the blanks are filled in with something plausible, the staff accepts most of what the operating people have prepared.

The planners do more with the financial projections. They combine them, add corporate income and expenses, and generate an overall company plan. Earnings shown for the first year or two are usually unacceptable. A series of hurried negotiations takes place between top management, the financial staff, and unit managers. Compromises are made. Ultimately, a consolidated set of projections emerges and is adopted as the official five-year plan. It is put into a fancy binder and distributed to senior executives and to the board of directors. The CEO keeps a copy conspicuous in his office to demonstrate to visitors that his company does its homework. The line managers find places for their copies where they will not be in the way.

The point, made by Lauenstein and other observers of strategic planning in American corporations, is that knowledge per se is not sufficient to create an effective strategic plan. As one analyst put it (Hoos 1978), "one cannot but acknowledge (1) the pivotal role of data; and (2) the weakness of this pivot." Lauenstein (1986, p. 76) likened what most U.S. companies do, focusing on number crunching, to "studying physics in order to learn how to pitch a baseball."

Strategic planning is a process whose most important product may be the process itself. It is the process, driven by a coherent vision, that determines what data should be collected and then sets up procedures for interpreting the data and transforming them into information that can help senior management weigh the risks associated with alternative courses of action. The latter part of this chapter will look at some techniques for identifying useful data to collect and ways of making sense of them, but first we shall discuss what strategic planning is and is meant to do.

DEFINING STRATEGIC PLANNING: UNCERTAINTY AND INTERDEPENDENCY

According to Lauenstein (1986, p. 76), "the function of strategic planning is to help executives evaluate the longer term implications of alternative courses of action to make better decisions." To be useful, he says, strategic planning should provide insights into:

1. The range of possible future developments and how best to prepare for them.
2. Where to allocate capital for attractive long-term returns.
3. What capabilities must be developed for competitive success.
4. How to design and organize the enterprise so that various activities support one another, including making sure that the facilities and over all business plan support each other.

Strategic planning is, at heart, concerned with resource allocation: How can the FM function best use its staff, knowledge, skills, equipment, and budget to advance most effectively the corporation's strategic business plan? Planning is forming a vision of how these resources can best be applied and includes establishing positions on such things as organizational structure (e.g., the location of the FM function within the organization and the functions it embraces), staffing (e.g., the role of contract versus in-house staff, the kind of staff needed), the role of resources in the organization (e.g., whether property should be managed as an asset, as part of a cost center, or as administrative overhead), and CAD and CAFM (e.g., the role of data and who should collect and maintain data bases).

Each of these aspects of FM must be examined in light of its ability to enhance the organization's competiveness: Is FM using its budget to maximum benefit? Are the FM policies and practices helping attract and retain the kind of qualified staff the top management knows it needs to remain competitive? Is there sufficient staff expertise and training to enable the FM group to produce and make sense of the data it collects to help the organization contain costs without undermining it flexibility or its ability to respond quickly to opportunities the market presents? Real strategic planning is thus much broader than what is typically described as strategic facility planning. For the most part, in practice this turns out to be some form of space forecasting, an important but just one small component of a strategic plan.

The frustration and challenge of broad-based strategic planning are doing it in the face of great uncertainty and great interdependency. Organizational theorists Richard Mason and Ian Mitroff (1981) argue convincingly that "every real world policy problem is related to every other real world problem." That is, solving one problem requires understanding the consequences of that solution for other problems. A simple FM problem sequence might be as follows: Solving wire management problems with raised-access floors means considering slab-to-slab height, which means considering higher overall construction costs, which may reduce the amount of funds available for lighting, furniture, or site improvements, which may influence employee satisfaction and performance, and so on. These are problems, according to Mason and Mitroff, of "organized complexity" or what Horst Rittle (1972, cited by Mason and Mitroff 1981) refers to as "wicked" problems.

Wicked problems are not evil, only immensely difficult to tame because of their interdependence. Rittle identified several characteristics of wicked problems, with which anyone involved with strategic planning will be familiar.

- *Interconnectedness.* Strong connections link each problem to other problems. As a result, these connections sometimes circle back to form feedback loops. "Solutions" aimed at the problem always seem to have important opportunity costs and side effects. How they work out depends on events beyond the scope of any one problem.
- *Complexity.* Wicked problems have numerous important elements with relationships among them, including important "feedback loops" through which a change tends to multiply itself or perhaps even cancel itself out. Generally, there are various leverage points on which analysis and ideas for intervention might concentrate, as well as many possible approaches and programs of action. There is also a likelihood that different programs (under the control of different departments) should be combined to deal with a given problem.
- *Uncertainty.* Wicked problems exist in a dynamic and largely uncertain environment, which creates a need to accept risk, perhaps incalculable risk. Both contingency planning and the flexibility to respond to unimagined and perhaps unimaginable contingencies thus are necessary.
- *Ambiguity.* The problem can be seen in quite different ways, depending on the viewer's personal characteristics, loyalties, past experience, and even accidental circumstances of involvement. There is no single "correct" view of the problem.
- *Conflict.* Because of competing claims, there is often a need to trade off "goods" against "bads" within the same value system. Conflicts of interest among persons or organizations with different or even antagonistic value systems are to be expected. How things will work out may depend on interaction among powerful interests that are unlikely to enter into fully cooperative arrangements.
- *Societal constraints.* Social, organizational, political, and technological constraints and capabilities are central to both the feasibility and the desirability of solutions.

There are several possible responses to such wicked problems. Like Seymour Cray, one can try to hold it all in one's own head and let one's actions reveal the strategy. Or one can ignore the longer-term picture and muddle through, a revered British planning approach. Another approach is to collect enormous amounts of data with the hope that, willy nilly, they will spontaneously combust into an integrated planning strategy. Or, as Mason and Mitroff contend, one can open up the planning process to the much broader participation of the affected parties, using "a wider spectrum of information gathered from a larger number of diverse sources" (1981, p. 13).

There are, in fact, many different approaches to strategic planning. Before looking at some of these, we shall distinguish between two different but related aspects of strategic planning: long-range planning and strategic development. Much of what the FM field calls strategic planning is, in fact, closer to long-range planning, and there is a difference.

Lauenstein (1986, p. 79) describes long-range planning's function as indicating "what specific actions need to be taken now to prepare for the future." It encompasses such things as creating scenarios, determining staffing requirements, and building a financial forecast under different market, economic, technical, and even political contingencies. Typically the long-range plan is modified frequently to adjust to changing conditions, and then this information is fed into each year's annual budget.

Strategies, according to Lauenstein (1986, p. 79), are "more general guidelines to allocating resources and developing capabilities. They represent management's approach to acquiring competitive advantage, they define the business, specify the markets to pursue, and identify the key resources to be developed to outperform others." The main difference between a strategy and a long-range plan is that the strategy should be pursued consistently, as it represents the vision to which the long-range plan is responding. One also would expect that the details of the long-range plan would vary from year to year, in response to changing conditions, whereas the strategy would be consistent. Lauenstein argues that the basic strategy should be reviewed regularly but changed infrequently. Maintaining a clear distinction between the overall strategy and the long-range plan or tactics for achieving the basic business goals helps keep attention on what one should be doing.

TYPES OF STRATEGIES

One theme running throughout this book is that whatever decisions one makes, they should be conscious, made after considering the consequences of different options. The role of the professional—whether an external consultant or an in-house staff person— is to help decision makers make the most informed decisions they can. This requires knowing what paths were not taken and why, as well as why earlier decisions were made. From this perspective, identifying options and their consequences is part of being professional.

Henry Mintzberg, a well-known organizational analyst who has spent much time studying how corporate strategies are formed (Mintzberg and Waters 1985), designed such a schema for thinking about strategic planning in general. It provides a useful benchmark for thinking about FM approaches to developing strategy.

Mintzberg defines strategy as "a pattern in a stream of decisions." He is interested in what organizations have to say about their longer-term objectives (their intentions). But he and his associates identify what they consider to be operational or realized strategies (what is actually occurring, not what is said to be happening) by looking at the organization's own pattern of actions. Too frequently organizations themselves pay more attention to what they say—their image of their strategy grounded in intentions—than they do to their own actions, which actually reflect their strategy (or lack of it).

Mintzberg positions alternative strategies along a continuum that ranges from "deliberate" (realized as intended) to "emergent" (certain patterns realized despite, or in the absence of, intentions). What are these strategies, and in what kinds of circumstances are they most useful? For the answers, see Table 5-1.

Mintzberg and Waters (1985) make clear that no single type of strategy is most appropriate to all types of organizations or to all types of situations. The *planned strategy*, for example, can work only in an environment that is either very predictable or very controllable. At the least, it assumes a stable environment. The *entrepreneurial strategy* typically works best in neophyte or small organizations in which personal control is feasible. This strategy often seeks out a specific niche (Steven Jobs's and Apple Computers' domination of the educational market, for example). Under crisis conditions, this strategy may also be found in large organizations, during which employees are willing to follow the direction of a single leader with a clear vision and the will to articulate and enforce it (Jan Carlzon and SAS airlines, for example). Because the entrepreneurial strategy is under the control of a single individual, it is actually highly adaptable, as it can quickly be changed in response to changing market conditions, new technologies, or a shifting regulatory climate.

Ideological strategies, in contrast, are less flexible because they are held fast by large numbers of employees who fervently believe in them as "the right way." Ideologues want to change the world, not bend to it. In unpredictable, complex worlds such strategies can become self-imposed strait jackets.

The *umbrella strategy* defines guidelines and outlines boundaries within which individuals can take action intended to move the organization in an agreed-upon direction. This strategy, one of the most widely practiced, works particularly well in larger organizations operating in complex and unpredictable environments in which "the patterns in organizational actions cannot be set deliberately in one central place, although the boundaries may be established there to constrain them" (Mintzberg and Waters 1985, p. 263).

The role of central management under the umbrella strategy is to develop and articulate a strong vision and the conditions under which strategies can emerge based on the actions and judgments of many different players. As Mintzberg and Waters (1985, p. 263) observed, "Those who have the vision do not control its realization; instead they must convince others to pursue it. The umbrella at least puts limits on the actions of others and ideally provides a sense of direction as well." Monitoring takes the form of seeing whether boundaries are being respected and the centrally dictated

Table 5-1. Types of Strategies

Strategy	Major Features
Planned	Strategies originate in formal plans: precise intentions exist, are formulated and articulated by central leadership, backed up by formal controls to ensure surprise-free implementation in benign, controllable, or predictable environment. These are the most deliberate strategies.
Entrepreneurial	Strategies originate in a central vision: intentions exist as personal, unarticulated vision of a single leader and so are adaptable to new opportunities; organization under the personal control of the leader and located in protected niche in environment; strategies relatively deliberate, but can emerge.
Ideological	Strategies originate in shared beliefs: intentions exist as collective vision of all actors, controlled normatively through indoctrination and/or socialization; in inspirational form and relatively immutable; organization often proactive vis-à-vis environment; these strategies rather deliberate.
Umbrella	Strategies originate in constraints: Leadership, in partial control of organizational actions, defines strategic boundaries or targets within which other actors respond to their own forces or to a complex, perhaps also unpredictable, environment; strategies are partly deliberate, partly emergent, and deliberately emergent.
Process	Strategies originate in process: Leadership controls process aspects of strategy (hiring, structure, etc.), leaving content aspects to other actors; strategies are partly deliberate, partly emergent (and, again, deliberately emergent).
Unconnected	Strategies originate in enclaves: Actors(s) loosely coupled to rest of organization produce(s) patterns in their own actions in the absence of, or in direct contradiction to, central or common intentions; strategies organizationally emergent whether or not deliberate for actor(s).
Consensus	Strategies originate in consensus: Through mutual adjustment, actors converge on patterns that become pervasive in the absence of central or common intentions; strategies rather emergent.
Imposed	Strategies originate in environment: Environment dictates patterns in actions either through direct imposition or implicitly pre-empting of binding organizational choice. These strategies most emergent, although they may be internalized by organization and made deliberate.

Source: Mintzberg and Walters 1985.

direction is being followed, not (as in the planned strategy) that predetermined action plans are being closely followed.

The point of Mintzberg's and Waters's research is to undermine the conception—the image if you will—of strategic planning as an a priori analytic process, rooted in knowledge and rational decision making and reflected in glossy binders filled with detailed plans, charts, trend projections, and so on. This is *an* approach, not *the* approach.

Equally important, Mintzberg's and Waters's interest in emergent strategies helps them concentrate on an important but neglected aspect of strategic planning: what they call *strategic learning.*

> Defining strategy as intended and conceiving it as deliberate, as has traditionally been done, effectively precludes the notion of strategic learning (learning from the experience of one's own organization). Once the intentions have been set, attention is riveted on realizing them, not on adapting them. Messages from the environment tend to get blocked out. Adding the concept of emergent strategy, based on the definition of strategy as realized, opens the process of strategy making up to the notion of learning. (1985, pp. 270 271)

For many organizations, and the senior managers who run them, the idea of emergent strategies is likely to cause heart palpitations. It seems messy, almost unprofessional, and even a dereliction of duty. But as Mintzberg and Waters noted,

> We wish to emphasize that emergent strategy does not have to mean that management is out of control, only—in some cases at least—that it is open, flexible and responsive, in other words, willing to learn. Such behavior is especially important when an environment is too unstable or complex to comprehend, or too imposing to defy. Openness to such emergent strategy enables management to act before everything is fully understood—to respond to an evolving reality rather than having to focus on a stable fantasy. (1985, p. 271)

IDENTIFYING EMERGENT STRATEGIES

For the most part, strategic planning, especially in today's (and tomorrow's) turbulent business environment, is a form of wicked problem: complex and complicated, ambiguous, uncertain, and full of potential for conflict. Wicked problems require emergent strategies, and both are more likely to be resolved effectively if they are rooted in processes that draw on the widest range of relevant information, ideas, and opinions. Like the elastic organization, whose goal is to collect not as many data as possible but as little information as is needed, good strategic planning hinges on the effective interpretation of information that diverse players in the process deem relevant. Good strategic planning is a participative process, not necessarily in terms of the grand vision, but in terms of feeding ideas into that vision so that it reflects the organization's best judgment about what world it is likely to operate in and what actions it needs to take to prosper in that world.

Fundamental to this view is the understanding not only that there are many players or "stakeholders" in the planning process and its outcomes but also that "contained in the minds of each participant in a wicked problem are powerful notions as to what is, what ought to be, why things are the way they are, how they can be changed, and how to think about their complexity. This represents a much broader class of information than is commonly used to solve problems" that are more simple or predictable (Mason and Mitroff 1981, p. 14).

It means, in fact, that the typical emphasis on trend data, competitors' positions and behavior, and so on, though necessary, is insufficient. A major objective of the strategic planning process becomes clarifying information and its underlying assumptions, that is, structuring an argumentative process in which contrasting and conflicting assumptions can be deliberately uncovered, discussed, disputed, and either resolved or—at the least—acted on while recognizing alternative consequences: in other words, risk.

The following criteria are based on this participatory view of the strategic planning process articulated by Mason and Mitroff:

1. *Participative.* Because relevant information is distributed among many individuals, the methods must actively involve important players or representatives.
2. *Adversarial.* To drive doubt to the surface where it can be publicly debated, resolved with more information, or simply acknowledged as unresolved differences, structured opposition must be designed into the planning process.
3. *Integrative.* Although participation designed to highlight opposition is central to the process, ultimately a unified set of assumptions and a coherent plan of action are needed to guide effective strategic planning. At heart this integration represents a vision of the future. As the earlier discussion about different types of strategies suggests, this vision may be strongly articulated in different ways and with different degrees of detail.
4. *Managerial mind supporting.* Good strategic plans require understanding the forces driving events. Managers must be actively involved in the process so they themselves can gain insight into and understand the rationale for various kinds of scenarios.

The model proposed by Mason and Mitroff essentially ignores approaches that are more centrally planned, whether by a small group of senior managers or a charismatic and forceful individual leader. Presumably the entrepreneurial and ideological approaches would conflict with a more bottoms-up, participative approach, but they need not. The point is to have a clear vision. The process advocated here can serve several purposes, depending on the culture to which it is applied.

In an organization with a strong, visionary leader, this process becomes a way of testing and validating a strong leader's position. The value may be less for the visionary and more for those who are charged with implementing that vision, because it is through this process that they will better understand the leader's underlying assumptions and therefore be more willing to support the actions needed to make it succeed. And it can help identify long-range plans, as defined earlier by Lauenstein, rather than guiding the basic strategy itself.

Used as part of long-range planning for detailed actions to support a broad vision, this participatory process can help pinpoint the reality to which the organization must respond. As Mason and Mitroff stated (1981, p. 18), "Complex problems depend on assumptions because it is not humanly possible to know everything of importance about a problem of organized complexity prior to the taking of action." Decisions often must be made in the absence of complete knowledge (not, it should be clear, in the absence of all knowledge!). For this reason the participatory process falls more into the emergent end of Mintzberg's and Waters's strategy scale. It is likely to work well in different-sized organizations, especially those without a single strong charismatic leader, in effort, most organizations.

STAKEHOLDERS AND THE DEFINITION OF THE PROBLEM

We create the problems we try to solve. Put in another way, our personal experience and background—everything from work history to education—guide the way we structure reality. Ackoff (1979, pp. 431–432) told a wonderful story to illustrate this point:

> The manager of a large office building received an increasing number of complaints about the elevator service in the building. He engaged a group of engineers to study the situation and to make recommendations for improvements if they were necessary. The engineers found that the tenants were indeed receiving poor service and considered three possible ways of decreasing the average waiting time. They considered adding elevators, replacing the existing ones by faster ones, and assigning elevators to specific floors. The latter turned out to be inadequate and the first two were prohibitively expensive to the manager. He called together his staff to consider the report by the engineers. Among those present was his personnel director, a psychologist. This young man was struck by the fact that people became impatient with a wait which seemed so short to him. On reflection he became convinced that their annoyance was due to the fact that they had to stand inactive in a crowded lobby for this period. This suggested a solution to him which he offered to the manager, and because it was so inexpensive the manager decided to try it. Complaints stopped immediately. The psychologist had suggested installing large mirrors in the walls of the lobbies where people waited for the elevators.

The point, of course, is not that engineering solutions do not work but, rather, that how one frames the problem (in this case as a people versus an elevator problem) guides the solutions one seeks. We spend too much time seeking answers to the wrong questions and too little time defining the problem. Assumption mapping is a device for making sure that there is some consensus on the nature of the problem before spending enormous time and resources looking for a (possibly useless) solution.

The remainder of this chapter looks at two phases of the overall strategic planning process: defining the problem and what Mason and Mitroff call "premising": choosing and communicating the particular set of goals, objectives, facts, assumptions, and hypotheses that will be taken as the "givens" in deriving any policy.

They list five phases of what they call SAST, or strategic assumption surfacing and testing (see Figure 5-1):

- Group formation
- Assumption surfacing and rating
- Debate
- Information requirements analysis
- Final synthesis

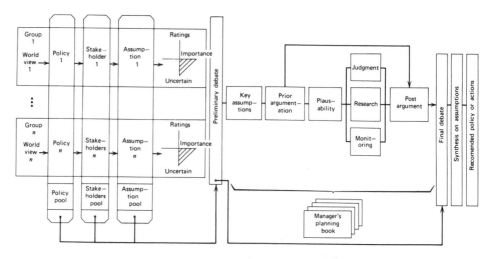

Figure 5-1. Overview of the strategic assumption surfacing and testing (SAST) process. (Source: Adapted from Mason, R.O., and I. Mitroff. 1981. *Challenging Strategic Planning Assumptions: Theory, Cases, and Techniques.* New York: Wiley copyright © 1981 John Wiley & Sons, Reprinted permission of John Wiley & Sons, Inc.)

Our purpose is not to discuss each phase step by step (see Mason and Mitroff 1981, who do do this); rather, it is to highlight some of the planning issues that can lead to effective SAST processes.

- The need to include individuals representing different experience and expertise (facilities and finance, human resources, marketing and sales, R & D, etc.)
- The desirability of creating small affinity groups of six to eight people with common values and viewpoints. This minimizes conflict within the group. The various groups, each with different values, experiences, and perspectives, can offer a diversity of views.
- The need to identify all the stakeholders who may influence (promote or undermine) and be affected by the policies adopted. The groups must consider how the stakeholders will respond to various proposals, if necessary by directly containing them or finding information that reflects their views and concerns (see Figure 5-2).
- The justification of a particular orientation or proposal (presumably drawn up by a senior management group before the process begins). In the Mason and Mitroff model, each group tests or validates different visions of the future (and perhaps in doing so proposes alternative visions as well). Another approach is to have each group create its own vision (proposal) and then defend it. This is a "bottoms-up" approach in which the vision emerges by consensus.
- The identification of the assumptions that underpin each group's strategy. In particular, the groups must determine both how important the assumptions are to their strategy and how certain they are that the assumptions are correct. This information generates a simple graph (see Figure 5-3). An assumption that is important and about which

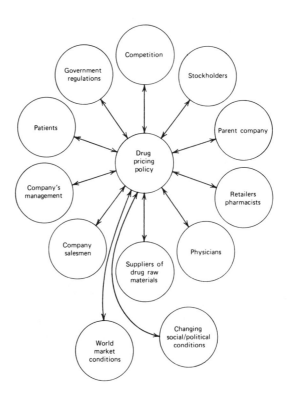

Figure 5-2. Example of a John Wiley & Sons, stakeholder analysis for a pharmaceutical company. (Source: Adapted from Mason, R.O., and I. Mitroff. 1981. *Challenging Strategic Planning Assumptions*: *Theory, Cases, and Techniques*. New York: Wiley copyright © 1981 John Wiley & Sons, Reprinted permission of John Wiley & Sons, Inc.)

the group is very uncertain calls for additional information, but an assumption that is both important and certain can become the foundation for the strategy.
- The presentation of the proposal to all the groups, who then discuss it. This is where the groups' different values, experiences, and backgrounds help uncover any relatively weakly supported assumptions. In effect, this is a form of group reality testing (see Figures 5-4 and 5-5).

At some point, when the different groups cannot agree on whether something is true or false, research may be needed to answer a question that everyone recognizes as critical to deciding how to proceed. This research may be market research, a postoccupancy evaluation, a financial analysis, or the development and running of a simulation model. It could also be a delphi panel, a focus group (with customers, or vendors, or technology experts), or a well-researched paper. Whichever, at this point information is being collected for a specific purpose and not because it might be useful at some time.

Senior management must still be responsible for creating the unifying vision. The preceding process is intended only to inform that process, not substitute for it. Following

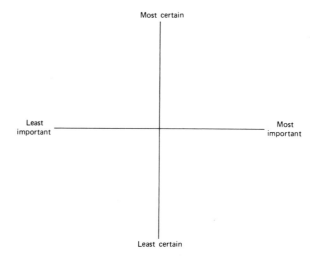

Figure 5-3. Instructions for identifying the assumptions underlying different strategic directions, and a graph for plotting these assumptions. (Source: Adapted from Mason, R.O., and I. Mitroff. 1981. *Challenging Strategic Planning Assumptions: Theory, Cases, and Techniques.* New York: Wiley copyright © 1981 John Wiley & Sons, Reprinted permission of John Wiley & Sons, Inc.)

it will not guarantee that the strategy chosen is the very best possible, but with it senior management can be confident of four things (Mason and Mitroff 1981):

- The widest possible range of knowledge was brought to bear on the strategic issue.
- Alternative proposals and visions and their underlying assumptions were subjected to a thorough, systematic, and critical examination.

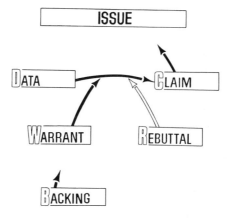

Figure 5-4. A model for structuring the arguments regarding the assumptions underlying different strategic options. (Source: Adapted from Mason, R.O., and I. Mitroff. 1981. *Challenging Strategic Planning Assumptions: Theory, Cases, and Techniques.* New York: Wiley copyright © 1981 John Wiley & Sons, Reprinted permission of John Wiley & Sons, Inc.)

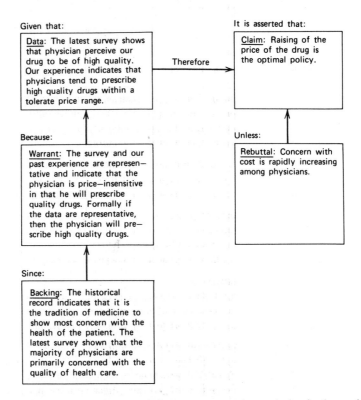

Given that:

Data: The latest survey shows that physician perceive our drug to be of high quality. Our experience indicates that physicians tend to prescribe high quality drugs within a tolerate price range.

Therefore

It is asserted that:

Claim: Raising of the price of the drug is the optimal policy.

Because:

Warrant: The survey and our past experience are represen—tative and indicate that the physician is price—insensitive in that he will prescribe quality drugs. Formally if the data are representative, then the physician will pre—scribe high quality drugs.

Unless:

Rebuttal: Concern with cost is rapidly increasing among physicians.

Since:

Backing: The historical record indicates that it is the tradition of medicine to show most concern with the health of the patient. The latest survey shown that the majority of physicians are primarily concerned with the quality of health care.

Figure 5-5.   Example of the framework for an argumentation analysis of a drug-pricing policy. (Source: Adapted from Mason, R.O., and I. Mitroff. 1981. *Challenging Strategic Planning Assumptions: Theory, Cases, and Techniques.* New York: Wiley copyright © 1981 John Wiley & Sons, Reprinted permission of John Wiley & Sons, Inc.)

• Everyone involved in the process understands, often for the first time, the rationale for selecting certain strategies.
• As much information as is needed has been collected and analyzed to shed light on high-priority issues affecting strategic decisions.

The process becomes the most important product, and there is now more likely to be wider agreement—or, at least, understanding—about why certain actions are being taken. As important, a collaborative working relationship among individuals from different disciplines, departments, and divisions—in which honest differences in opinion are not only tolerated but actively solicited—will have been established. This willingness to test assumptions, to seek feedback, and to collect information is found all too infrequently in even the best-run companies.

This process also reduces some of the distance between top and middle management. Receiving a glossy report written by staff people is far less likely to influence one's thinking about a problem than having helped write the report. The goal, according to Pierre Wack (1985a, 1985b), the retired chief financial officer of Shell Oil who has had extensive experience with the scenario approach to strategic planning, is getting top management to change their view of the world, their mental maps. "From the moment of this realization, we no longer saw our task as producing a documented view of the future business environment 5-10 years ahead. Our real target was the microcosms of our decision makers: unless we influenced the mental image, the picture of reality held by critical decision makers, our scenarios would be like water on a stone" (1985, p. 84). Top management's willingness to face uncertainty and to understand the forces driving it is, according to Wack, "an almost revolutionary transformation in a large organization" and is as important as the development of the scenarios themselves.

LINKING FACILITIES AND CORPORATE STRATEGIC PLANNING

The issues and processes discussed thus far pertain to strategic planning in any part of the organization. If it is any solace to facility managers who feel left out of the corporate planning process, human resources people often feel exactly the same way. The problem is not confined to facilities or human resources or to any other division of the organization but is essentially an outdated model of specialization, hierarchy, and the role of experts and managers. The Tayloristic model stressed separation, boundaries, status, exclusivity, and the narrow rather than the broad focus, and this worked— in a relatively stable, predictable environment. But it does not work now, as the Japanese have demonstrated brilliantly with their alternative model: job rotation, nonspecialization, and group-based work and decision making.

Paul Buller (1988) found several links between human resources and corporate strategic planning, and his analysis of these linkages and why they occur is equally relevant to facility management. In the following, I have substituted FM for Buller's human resources.

Types of FM/Corporate Linkage

- *Administrative linkage*, in which there is day-to-day operating support, but FM itself is relatively unimportant to the planning process.
- *One-way linkage*, in which FM largely reacts to corporate strategic initiatives. This is the most typical relationship and the one that facility managers would like to consign to the dust bin.
- *Two-way linkage*, in which there is a reciprocal and interdependent relationship between FM and the corporate strategic planning process. Here FM is viewed as credible and important. It is proactive and fully involved in helping guide the development of strategic plans. For example, FM would be asked to evaluate potential acquisitions and help plan their integration into existing facilities.
- *Integrative linkage*, the highest level of integration in which there is a dynamic, ongoing dialogue, both formal and informal, between the FM planners and corporate planners. At this level FM would be involved in all strategic business decisions, even those that do not directly concern the facility function.

Conditions for Effective Strategic Planning Integration

Having laid out this simple typology, based on detailed case studies of eight large organizations representing different business sectors (from computer and cosmetic manufacturers to insurance, financial services, and major retail), Buller then listed seven factors that are likely to lead to greater integration of strategic planning efforts.

1. *Business environment,* particularly increased competition, high levels of technical change, and changing patterns of labor market demographics (particularly a more demanding work force and one in which the demand of desired skills and experience exceeds their supply).
2. *Organizational history and culture,* particularly the realization that the "right numbers and kinds of people" cannot always be found.
3. *Strategy,* in which concentration on a core business is emphasized over diversification, which leads to greater decentralization and makes it more difficult to establish strong linkages among different units.
4. *Structure,* with more integration when the senior FM is on the management committee or is an officer in the company. More integration will be possible when the FM is formally designated as a business partner (creating a greater direct interest, responsibility, and authority related to business issues).
5. *Incumbent executives' values and skills,* including CEOs who believe that the FM function is important and FM executives who are able to understand the business and to participate constructively in the overall strategic planning process.
6. *Work force skills and values,* in which top management understands the importance of facilities and perceives the facilities group as having relevant skills and abilities to help the organization remain or become competitive.
7. *Management system,* in which senior executives, including FM, have a substantial percentage of their compensation "at risk" (tied to annual performance).

A thread that runs through much of the literature is that better planning, more integration, and access to higher-level decision making all are relatively unimportant in stable operating environments. Unfortunately, not many of these exist anywhere in the world today; instead, instability is the norm. Integration is often a by-product of organizational change efforts stimulated by the need to bring to bear as many points of view as possible to resolve complex, unpredictable, ambiguous ("wicked") problems. Flatter organizational structures and a culture that values diversity and information are not a substitute for a well-articulated management vision. But a management vision grown outside such structures runs the very high risk of misconstruing reality and, in doing so, making major resource allocation decisions that are, despite the best of intentions, counterproductive.

What this means for facility management, I think, is that although facility managers' ultimate ability to contribute to the organization's success depends in some measure on events outside their control, facility management can still improve its strategic planning and integration of its function into the corporate planning function. But it must:

- Take the time to learn the business. In part this is made easy because FM must regularly collect information from all components of the organization relative to staff projections, technology requirements, and so on. These contacts can be extended informally to ask questions about the business in general as part of the need of the facilities group to understand all aspects of the organization in order to provide the best service possible.
- Not wait for formal organizational structure changes. Facility managers should initiate informal contacts with other key players and functions in both facilities (e.g., tele-communication, MIS, real estate) and nonfacilities areas (e.g., human resources, finance, purchasing). Informal contacts provide an invaluable source of information quickly.
- Based on information from informal contacts and corporate documents, write brief assessments of how planned or existing corporate strategy will affect the facilities. Facility managers should circulate these reports through the organization (informally and often as part of informal meetings they initiate), simply offering them as a view they thought others might be interested in.
- Similarly, write brief assessments showing how certain FM initiatives could support corporate plans or exploit market opportunities.
- In informal meetings, offer insights into general planning and business issues, even when these are outside the formally defined facilities domain.
- Structure the facilities management planning process (informally, if necessary) to reflect an open, participatory process in which basic assumptions are tested. Facility managers should also invite "players" from other parts of the organization to participate in the process.

These suggestions are grounded in my belief—after working as both a consultant and a researcher in many organizations—that all of us too often erect self-defeating barriers and boundaries. We assume that others would not want us to contact them or would feel their turf is threatened or that we are wasting their time or exceeding our authority and responsibility. The success of extending the frontier, especially from a position of relative weakness, often depends as much on how one acts as on what one is trying to achieve.

Discussing with others how they view the world, what their understanding is of how the organization works, or what they believe would be the best way to achieve some outcome is often inherently flattering because it suggests (correctly) that the other person has something of value (insight, information, experience, access). It also implies a common purpose: to work together to help the organization prosper, to use resources effectively, to create a "win-win" situation in which collaboration benefits all parties. This means sharing credit (and occasionally giving it where it is not due, for the long-term benefits). It requires the confidence to say, "I don't know. What do you think?" and the belief that with good information you can actually do a better job.

Thus, in the end, strategic planning implies a vision in its own right, a vision of the kind of process that can move the FM function forward, the kind of participation that is needed to do that, and an understanding of how the process itself can become one of the organization's most valuable long term assets.

Skeptics Speak

The idea of emergent planning strategies sounds reasonable at first, but it seems to me that there is a real danger of the entire process's turning out to be like the aphorism that a camel is a horse designed by a committee. Everything is likely to end up as a compromise, with little likelihood of achieving a clear vision of where the company should be going.

Any participatory process can become a gooey morass, but if it is designed correctly it doesn't have to. It is important not to confuse the inclusion of multiple perspectives with infinite views, that is, with chaos. In fact, there are not likely to be more than two to four genuinely different visions (obviously, with the potential for lots of subthemes) for most situations. More to the point, the process can intentionally limit the number of options considered.

Remember that people can be reasonable. Most people will change their views in light of new information if it is presented in a way that helps them see how the overall scheme fits into their own vision. This often takes time, but if the information (which includes experience and insight as well as technical and trend data) is collected as part of a structured process in which those in doubt have helped identify the relevant information to collect, it is much more likely to influence strongly held views. The important point, as Pierre Wack noted, is developing a process and collecting information that helps reshape senior management's worldview.

Finally, an emergent process is not intended to substitute for management vision and direction, but to help shape it by testing it against a deliberately diverse community of opinion. In the end, it is still senior management that must determine the direction.

The kind of strategic planning process you are advocating seems as though it would work quite well in a small organization but would be difficult to implement in a large company.

Without doubt, all communication is easier in small organizations (although smallness per se is no guarantee of good communication). Yet there are virtues in larger size when it comes to strategic planning. One of these is that a wider range of views, experience, and knowledge are available that can be used to challenge and test assumptions underlying different policy directions.

Second, I am advocating a structured planning process, not a free-for-all in which everyone says and does anything he or she wants to. The idea is to develop teams with representatives from different disciplines, departments, or divisions that can either be asked to defend a particular position (with different teams defending different positions) or be charged with creating their own scenario and defending it against those created by other teams. If similar scenarios emerge (drawn up by teams with different perspectives and experience), then management can be confident that the strategy reflects reality as best as it can be determined. For different scenarios, there is a structured basis for testing the validity and accuracy of the assumptions underlying each. The likelihood is that parts of both are right and that some integration will be best. At points at which unresolvable differences emerge, then top management has the basis for making an informed judgment about which path to follow, with a good sense of the consequences of taking each path.

Our organization believes in a highly centralized planning process in which considerable attention is paid to collecting hard data on financial projections, market trends, developments in new technologies, and so on as a basis for developing a viable strategy. I believe this kind of information is fundamental to the planning process, and I don't see that it can help when the focus is on "different players' perspectives."

If the only basis for strategic policy were different players' opinions, you would be absolutely right: The process and plan would likely be disastrous. But the model is not "no information," it is—as I argued in talking about the elastic organization—collecting as little information as is needed to answer with reasonable confidence an important question.

The idea is to know why certain information should be collected and how it will be used to inform and influence the decision process. The idea of testing assumptions is to make explicit the assumptions underpinning a particular policy direction and then to look at the evidence supporting them. Too often, information is collected simply to obfuscate, to dull the mind with interminable figures and charts. But if information is deemed worth collecting by those both supporting and challenging a given assumption, it is much more likely to be heeded. Many of the same types of information are likely to be relevant whatever process is used, with the difference being in how participants view this information and whether they are using it to answer a question widely considered worth answering.

Your final arguments for what might be called "organizational self-help" programs, in which the FM takes a lot of initiative to get things done, sounds overly idealistic to me. The reality is much harsher, and people are more defensive and protective of their turf.

Taking the kinds of initiative I proposed will not work for everyone. It does take a high level of self-confidence, even brashness. But these qualities must be balanced with good people skills: being a good listener and being willing to learn, to modify one's own viewpoint, to admit one is wrong, and, more important, simply to admit that in certain areas one is ignorant. It also requires a thick skin.

You won't win every time. Some managers or technicians will rebuff you; some will patronize you; and some may even deliberately mislead you. But my experience, at least, holds that such responses are in the minority, not the majority. They are worth enduring (not necessarily repeating on a regular basis!) for the benefits of the learning, the greater credibility, and the greater effectiveness that are likely to emerge. I am not advocating butting your head against the wall; I am advocating that you see whether there is really a wall.

Centralization and Decentralization

Over the past several years I have been in dozens of organizations, in both Europe and North America, in which the question of whether to centralize or decentralize different aspects of FM structure, policies, and procedures was being hotly debated. Many firms are moving toward some form of decentralized organizational structure, usually to move facility decision making and support services closer to local area managers in identifiable profit centers. In CitiBank's new tower building in Long Island City, New York, for example, each of the occupying groups' considerable organizational independence is also reflected in its freedom to select its own furniture and develop its own approaches to space planning. From a facility viewpoint each department or division is essentially a separate company occupying a multitenanted office tower.

Yet for many organizations, organizational decentralization, in which more business decisions are delegated to local areas (whether a region, a subsidiary, a building, or a department) is being matched by more formal centralized corporate space and furniture standards that reduce local control over planning, design, and construction.

The reason that apparently contradictory tendencies seem so easily to coexist is that both decentralization and corporate space planning and design standards reflect two sides of a common theme: control. The issue is the level at which decisions can be made or need to be approved by some higher level before they can be implemented.

The principal concern is how and where in the overall system decisions are made and for what reasons.

Decentralization refers to a shift in organizational structure that distributes more administrative control to local centers or groups. Standards refers to a decision's conformity with a predetermined set of criteria. Both are different facets of the same issue. Standards are, in fact, a form of centralization, a device by which local control is reduced.

Centralization and decentralization are not so much polar opposites as different parts of a total system. They can and should complement and support not only each other but also the long-term strategic goals of the organization. The banking industry, for example, has changed dramatically over the past five years, driven by new technologies, changes in regulatory patterns, shifting customer expectations, and the frantic search for new financial products and services that can take advantage of these changes. From the epitome of the staid corporation, run by slow-moving staff working in marbled halls rising like a church dome to bless the handling of money, banks have become technological jet setters, computer addicts hooked to instantaneous transactions conducted not across a mahogany counter but across continents. Under these conditions, being fleet of foot and wit, with the ability to respond quickly to changing market conditions, makes a difference.

Realizing this, firms like Lloyd's Bank, with its headquarters in London, have moved to give local business area managers more authority over their basic business decisions. At the same time, Lloyd's bank has reduced some of the local area managers' control over branch bank facility design, by instituting corporatewide facility standards. By avoiding the time-consuming and costly custom design of each of hundreds of branch banks, Lloyd's has helped local area managers respond more quickly to changes in market conditions.

Both the centralization of facility standards and the decentralization of organizational control (seemingly contradictory policies) actually serve the same strategic objective: to be able to move quickly to exploit market opportunities at the lowest cost possible. The ability to integrate these (and other) dual tendencies is, in fact, a distinguishing feature of the elastic organization, as described in Chapter 2.

The most noteworthy aspect of the debate about the relative merits of centralization and corporate space and furniture standards versus decentralization is the dearth of published research, case studies, or conceptual analyses that discuss, let alone demonstrate, the advantages and disadvantages of different forms of centralization and decentralization of facilities decisions for different kinds of organizations. Examples of centralization and decentralization in firms like CitiBank and Lloyd's Bank capture intentions, not outcomes.

Like many fundamental FM decisions, the decision to decentralize or centralize FM functions is made more on the basis of logic or hope than on hard evidence. At least in my own dealings with different organizations, I have yet to see a detailed analysis (even rarer are systematic and comprehensive post-implementation assessments) of a decentralization program or policy that analyzes what should be decentralized and should remain centralized. What are the costs and benefits of decentralization in its different forms: organizational structure, policy and procedures, design and construction standards? Under what conditions is it likely to work best? Who, exactly, will benefit? What are its implications for staffing, for record keeping, for flexibility?

Organizations oscillate back and forth between centralization and decentralization, probably because as Brooke (1984) argues, the accepted wisdom (today) recommends delegating authority, whereas the threat of disaster urges centralization. Ironically, then, in many organizations, fad and fashion as much as data and logic are determining how to manage control.

Given the potential magnitude of the effects of creating facility standards or centralizing or decentralizing FM—which range from major shifts in staffing patterns and budgeting to redefining the role of the corporate FM function—some form of conceptual analysis seems worthwhile, if for no other reason than to stimulate discussion of an important issue. Clearly, some systematic research on this topic is long overdue. As a starting point, this chapter provides a framework for thinking about different forms of decentralization within the FM context.

CHOOSING WHAT TO CENTRALIZE OR DECENTRALIZE

In the facilities management arena, space and furniture standards, forecasting methods, project and construction management procedures, and the selection and purchase of products and services are often at the center of the debate about who should make such decisions and on what basis. The following is a list of these and other kinds of decisions that one can choose to centralize (standardize) or decentralize:

- *Organizational structure,* including formal reporting relationships and often the kinds of decisions and/or the approval of financial decisions that can be made at different job levels.
- *Planning processes,* including the processes (and information needed and means of collecting and communicating it) for making decisions about such things as site location, furniture layout, and building appraisal.
- *Operational procedures,* including procedures for space accounting and inventory, project and construction management, maintenance reviews, and database management.
- *Product selection,* including procedures for selecting and purchasing furniture, computer equipment, building systems, and finishes and materials.
- *Service selection,* including procedures for contracting staff and consultants.
- *Space,* including the amount, type, and distribution of space to be allocated to different kinds of job levels, functions, or facilities.
- *Quality,* including such things as the nature of finishes and materials, acceptable maintenance cycles for equipment and systems, and durability and life-cycle costs.
- *Work patterns,* including regulations concerning where and when employees should work, such as the movement between home and other remote settings and a central office.
- *Staffing,* including job descriptions, salaries, career steps, and awards.

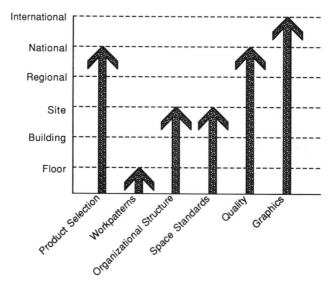

Figure 6-1.   A framework for thinking about the possible levels at which different aspects of the facilities management function might be centralized.

• *Graphics,* including logos, stationery, product packaging, trucking, and building signage.

This list is not exhaustive, and each of these areas may be centralized or standardized at different levels, as many companies obviously choose to do.

SETTING THE SPAN OF CONTROL

A 1985 survey by the American Society of Interior Designers for *Corporate Design and Realty Magazine* found that of 130 firms questioned, 70 percent had some form of corporate design standards program. Only 66 percent of these standards were written, however, and only 21 percent said the standards were obligatory. They were, in fact, guidelines rather than standards. And even these guidelines were often restricted to local conditions; that is, they applied to either one building or several buildings in a self-contained site or relatively bounded region such as a large city or metropolitan area. A major reason for those who applied standards only at the local level, or did not employ any standards at all, was the belief that the needs of different sites, buildings, or organizations were too diverse to be effectively standardized on a corporate-wide basis.

These findings underscore the fact that standards (one form of centralization) can be applied at many different environmental and organizational levels, from department, building, site, and city to regional, national, and international levels. As Figure 6-1 shows, what is centralized or standardized may, and probably should, vary across these different levels. A furniture, color, or even space standard is more likely to be applicable to a single building or similar building types (defined by age, function, and design) than to buildings in different geographical regions or nations in which building systems and modules, as well as culturally derived expectations about what is an acceptable working environment, vary enormously.

Thus even though IBM has strong national standards, they are different in the United States, Sweden, and Germany. Space and furniture standards based on open plan and systems furniture, which abound in the United States, are unacceptable in most European countries. A procedure such as database management might easily, however, be maintained at the regional or even national level. A policy to guide building design that simply lists a few criteria—for instance, that the building be simple, functional, and efficient— may be all that can be sensibly centralized across all levels, from the local to the international. Graphics standardization is more likely to be applicable across levels, whereas trying to standardize something as specific as bathroom fixtures across national boundaries often is an exercise in cost enhancement if not futility (Becker and Spitznagel 1986).

WHY CENTRALIZE OR STANDARDIZE ANYTHING?

The question lurking behind what to centralize or standardize is, of course, why standardize anything? What are the costs and benefits? First, the benefits.

Benefits of Centralizing Authority

The benefits and costs of centralizing and decentralizing authority in this and the next section are based largely on anecdotal evidence. They reflect anticipated more than documented benefits.

- *Greater efficiency.* Like the argument for economy of scale, centralization is believed to promote greater efficiency, in part by reducing unnecessary duplication. Presumably less time and fewer staff are needed to develop and then implement and monitor a single database system, space and furniture standard, or contracting procedure. Centralized support functions from reception to copying and food service should theoretically reduce the number of personnel needed to staff them.
- *Increased professionalism.* Although a region or site may not be able to justify hiring a highly qualified human resources trainer or automated building systems maintenance engineer because the workload is insufficient to keep the person occupied full time, a centralized function that serves as a resource to many different regions or sites can use such people full time, thereby justifying their salaries. This is one of the arguments for contracting out specialized labor. By having a single training function that serves many different groups, hiring better-trained and better-qualified teachers and providing more effective training materials and media can more easily be justified. Thus, the level of service and overall professionalism should be higher when they are centralized.
- *Less parochialism.* Decentralized decision making may encourage parochialism, in that local concerns and issues are likely to be considered more important than broad national or international concerns that appear to be weakly connected to daily ex-

perience. Centralized structures and policies intended to serve the entire organization, presumably have a broader vision and are more likely to consider the needs of the organization as a whole.

- *Uniform corporate image.* Most companies believe that a uniform corporate image strengthens customers' and employees' identification with the company. It presumably also maintains a certain standard of quality (whether in appearance, maintenance, or function) and helps reduce costs (because the cost of developing the base design is incurred only once). The primary question is what design features should be used to communicate the corporate image. Graphic standards may be a far cheaper and more feasible means of broad-based image standardization than are uniform building standards, for example. After all, it is much easier to put the same company logo on any building in any location than it is to put any building in any location.
- *Equity.* Centralized space and furniture standards are often justified in terms of equity. That is, giving employees who do the same job and are at the same level the same office accommodation presumably ensures fairness and reduces conflict or resentment among them.
- *Economies of scale.* Furniture, office equipment, building systems and materials, and even services such as space planning or consulting tend to be cheaper if they can be bought in quantity. Therefore, standardization, which makes national furniture contracts possible, for example, can help save considerable amounts of money. National contracts can do this not only because of lower costs per unit of product or service but also because a single contract reduces the administrative costs of procuring and monitoring several different contracts.
- *Independence.* Standardized procedures and space, furniture, and equipment standards may actually increase the organization's independence (and lower its costs) by minimizing its dependence on outside consultants and vendors. And there is less need for such services once a standard is in place and the in-house staff learn how to apply it effectively.
- *Common databases.* Centralized databases provide an organization-wide picture of performance that can be used to allocate company-wide resources. Collecting, monitoring, and servicing a database from a single location, with easy accessibility from local sites, can provide better overall control of progress and quality and lower the costs of maintaining and managing many incompatible databases.
- *Interchangeability.* Centralized standards permit interchangeable parts or modules. These in turn maximize compatibility and can decrease costs by making it possible to "mix and match" or replace panels, chairs, or computers at will, depending on what is needed and what is available. The cost and time spent in purchasing new equipment or in training people to install or use products with which they are unfamiliar should also be lower.
- *Security.* In order to protect databases, access to data in integrated files should be made more selective.

Costs of Centralizing Authority

- *Loss of innovation.* Centralized policies, procedures, and standards may retard the adoption of superior new approaches because they require the replacement or modification of a costly installed base of equipment or even skill and knowledge in the case of implementing new operating procedures or planning processes. If the standard adopted turns out to be ineffective, this can be a major problem. The organization may know that it is doing something below the level it could (and should) but cannot justify the expense of implementing a new procedure, creating or reformatting a database, or developing a different standard on a corporate-wide basis.

- *Loss of motivation.* Standards or central authority, in the form of review processes that give corporate rather than local staff the authority to make decisions, may undermine the motivation of local managers and staff who believe they understand their situation better than a remote corporate headquarters staff does. Centralization reduces what Tom Peters (1988) calls "chunking," in which small informal groups set their own goals in a highly fluid, action-oriented structure.

- *Delayed response time.* Centralized organizational structures that entail lengthy corporate review of local initiatives can seriously delay response time, resulting in lost opportunities dependent on quick response. Property decisions that exceed certain local approval levels and therefore require corporate approval often fall into this category. By the time a local area submits to headquarters a proposal for purchasing a site beyond the local approval authority, has the proposal reviewed, answers further questions, revises the proposal, and resubmits it, the property may have been sold to a competitor. The fear, of course, is that without centralized site acquisition criteria, drawn up by headquarters experts, money and time will be committed that might harm long-term corporate interests or strategy.

- *Avoidance tactics.* Central review processes that impose a dollar or square-foot limit on the size of the lease the local manager can make without corporate approval often result in decisions that always just avoid hitting the approval limit (such as with a 50,000-square-foot limit leading to hundreds of leases for 49,000 square feet). More flexibility might encourage a more strategic approach. At the minimum, the actual limit should be continually monitored to see whether it is becoming counterproductive.

- *Poor fit.* Organizational distance between those making decisions and those having to live with them often produces a poor fit or match between what the users believe they need and what corporate staff provide. Communication and coordination often become minimal, formal, and ritualized, leading to confusion, duplication, and conflict. Space according-to-rank standards, for example, may make sense intuitively as a means of ensuring equity. Yet in practice they may raise the cost of organizational change by forcing both people and panels to be moved every time there is an office reconfiguration. Uniform space standards also require people with different work-styles and work habits to operate in a similar fashion, possibly undermining their effectiveness.

- *Less leadership development.* Dependence on centralized authorities may discourage the development of local skills and talent. Employees who know they must, or simply can, call on headquarters staff before making a decision may invest less time and energy in acquiring new skills and knowledge.

This list reminds me a bit of the adage that "one person's trash is another person's treasure." The centralization benefit "less parochialism" is the decentralization benefit

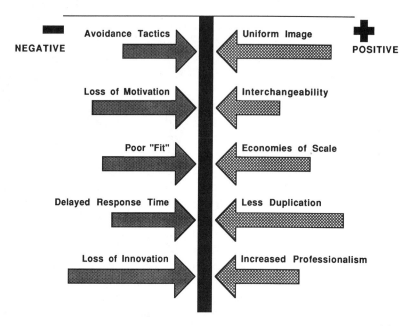

Figure 6-2.   A force-field diagram showing that in the abstract, the costs and benefits of centralization often cancel each other out.

"good fit." The same could be said of flexibility, response time, accountability, or even professionalism or expertise (e.g., local people understand local conditions better than does a staff at a distant corporate headquarters). Figure 6-2 shows a force-field diagram of the costs and benefits of centralization. It suggests at a general level that the costs and benefits neutralize each other (or that the positive and negative pressures would be reversed if the diagram depicted decentralization). The truth is that we have virtually no data to help us sort out what is myth and what is reality. It seems clear that there can be no simple answer to whether decentralization makes sense, for it depends on what is decentralized and exactly how the entire system is designed and supported.

For example, research in Britain on decentralization (Grant, Jammine, and Howard 1988; Hill and Pickering 1986), though not directly related to facilities functions, does suggest that higher profits are associated with a greater emphasis on decentralizing operating decisions to subsidiaries. Such operating decisions included those pertaining to purchasing, industrial relations, and personnel. But marketing and production seemed to benefit from more centralization, perhaps because they needed more specialized expertise and experience in these areas. Companies that had strong divisional offices and a major role in decisions that could have been decentralized further to operating subsidiaries tended to be relatively weak.

In another study of centralization in fifty multinational corporations (about half from the United States and half from Britain and the rest of Europe), the authors (Gates and Egelhoff 1986) found that decentralization increased with:

- the size of the foreign operation
- the amount of foreign product diversity
- the amount of outside ownership in the foreign subsidiary
- increased differences in local tastes and preferences

National differences were important as well. The authors argued that in the United States—with its emphasis on individuality and nonconformity, great racial and ethnic diversity—more explicit and formalized control is needed to manage competition among organizational members. In Japan with its greater homogeneity and stronger sense of conformity, subsidiary relations are characterized more by implicit social control than by explicit rules.

MAKING DECENTRALIZATION WORK

In general, what little research does exist (none of it directly related to FM) suggests that decentralization makes sense when there is considerable diversity within the total organizational system. It is likely to be particularly useful to operating decisions. In a sense, centralization should focus on the "what" (strategic orientation) and decentralization on the "how" (operational orientation). In facility management this might mean, for example, that a centralized policy or standard would be developed for the kind of information required for certain decisions but that local sites could determine the best way of actually obtaining that information. In terms of accountability, it might mean that headquarters would set an overall budget level but that local sites could decide how to use these resources to meet agreed-on targets. For space planning, it could mean that centralized standards generated by headquarters staff would define the amount of space per person and the type of furniture but that local staff would determine how the total amount of space should be distributed or laid out in their facility. Organizations would establish criteria for determining what to centralize or decentralize (Ahituv and Ronen 1985), which may include:

- *The relationship to other systems and structures.* The more directly a decision affects decisions in other areas, the greater the value of centralization will be.
- *Uniqueness.* The more varied or unusual the situation is, the greater the benefit of decentralization will be.
- *User diversity.* The greater the variety of users is in background, education, experience, and task functions, the greater the value of decentralization will be.
- *National contracts.* The more cost savings are generated from the economies of scale of national contracts, the more a centralized furniture standards may make sense.

Once one decides to decentralize, the issue, it seems to me, is obtaining the organizational support needed to make decentralization work.

The bedrock of decentralization is trust, discretion, self-management, judgment, and autonomy. Whether corporate staff are prepared to invest their trust in local managers and staff (or local staff in corporate staff) depends on a number of things. First is the available expertise, actual and perceived, at both the corporate and the local level. What evidence is there (and is widely known and accepted) to suggest that local staff and managers can or cannot make certain decisions? Related to expertise is training. Is it available in timely and sufficient quantities and forms?

Second is accountability. Are there clear consensus performance targets? Is the program being monitored in a manner acceptable to all parties, so that changes can be made if problems appear or expectations are not met? This presumes that the organizational structure or standard either can be modified relatively easily or, if it cannot, that considerable effort has been made to explore alternatives. Part of this process might be initially implementing the program on a trial basis to gain experience.

Third is sharing and coordinating information and experience. To avoid confusion or conflicting decisions, all parties must agree to share information on a regular basis.

Fourth are clear role expectations. Do corporate and field staff share the same views of what each is expected to do and what decisions each will be making?

Finally, fifth is a clear facilities philosophy. Strong philosophies and powerful corporate cultures reduce the need for detailed guidance by providing staff with simple but powerful guides for everyday decision making.

CENTRALIZATION AND DECENTRALIZATION

The issue is not decentralization versus centralization; it is knowing exactly what one wants to accomplish, which aspects of the overall FM function to decentralize, and which should remain or become centralized. Unfortunately, at the moment, there is little research to guide these basic organizational decisions. But facility managers contemplating some form of decentralization can begin by asking themselves the following questions before standardizing or decentralizing:

1. Who will benefit? Why? How will I know?
2. Is the cost of monitoring the program likely to be greater than the anticipated benefits?
3. Does senior management have confidence in local area managers and staff? Is such confidence justified?
4. What training and other forms of corporate support are needed to achieve acceptable levels of confidence and expertise in local managers and staff?
5. At what environmental or organizational level is it feasible to implement different forms of central authority or to provide local control?
6. What would happen if we did not decentralize (or standardize)? Are there other approaches?
7. If the standards turn out to be dysfunctional, how hard will it be to modify or abandon them for something more effective?

From a corporate viewpoint, decentralization will always be a risky venture. The organization risks spawning conflicting countercultures, as well as duplicating services, staff, equipment, and facilities, all of which can increase costs. The organization stands to gain, however, more innovation, greater motivation, more flexibility, and quicker response times, which may not only reduce costs but also offer unexpected learning opportunities and stimulate new procedures and policies that have broad application within the organization.

Decentralization is, in fact, part of a total system, which is why decentralized organizational structures can coexist and even flourish side by side with corporate standards programs. Moving financial control for facilities decisions to local area managers (decentralization) places responsibility for a business decision in the hands of those persons responsible for it. Creating corporate design standards at the same time (standardization and centralization) that remove local control for facility design decisions from the local area managers may be acceptable to them if there is a demonstrated reduction in response time and lowered costs (stemming from minimal custom designing and purchasing for each project). This, in turn, gains value only if a chargeback system is in place that gives the local area managers an incentive to lower their facility costs. To work, then, decentralization and standardization programs must be embedded in a systems design in which the self-interest of all parties is considered.

Skeptics Speak

After reading this chapter I still am not sure what I should be decentralizing. What is it you are actually recommending?

I would love to be able to make some blanket recommendations, but I just don't think there is sufficient evidence to do this with any confidence. Without general research evidence, I think it makes sense to collect some information about your own situation. This does not have to be time-consuming or expensive.

You might, for example, list all the things you already have decentralized. Because decentralization applies to the level at which decisions are made, you should record exactly what decisions can be made by headquarters staff, regional staff, and staff at a single site or building. You could then compare this list with a list of decisions that are typically made at each level. If there is a discrepancy, what is the reason for it? Explore with headquarters and field staff what they consider to be wrong with the existing decision structure and why they think such problems exist. At the same time, find out what kind of centralized support—whether training, access to experts, or ability to influence centralized guidelines, procedures, and standards—both groups consider most useful to helping the organization compete successfully.

This kind of simple organizational diagnosis can help identify misunderstandings and misperceptions and the kinds of adjustments to existing policy that might make them more effective.

Isn't it true that the very benefits you cite for decentralization, things like increased motivation and innovation, may actually undermine or contradict overall corporate goals and objectives?

Yes, it is possible, which is one of the reasons that some employees like being outside headquarters facilities. They feel less pressure to conform to corporate norms, whether in dress or behavior, and often create a subculture with values, practices, and policies that in some cases may diverge from what makes sense for the company as a whole.

I have seen this happen for systems development groups that, working in isolation from the groups for whom they are developing the systems, create systems that satisfy the developer more than the user. Or regional sales groups may design sales approaches and pricing structures that are at odds with those of other regions and national directives. It is also a reason that many companies, particularly in the manufacturing sector, have what they call simultaneous engineering or integrated product development processes. Their purpose is to bring together groups from marketing, sales, engineering, and manufacturing—each of which often has different values, priorities, experience, and information—from the beginning of the product development cycle.

The ability of decentralized groups to create their own culture is what makes effective decentralization so dependent on coordination, particularly the timely sharing of information about the effects of policies and practices at the local and headquarters levels on each other. It also underscores the importance of having clear and feasible objectives and performance targets. The proof of any policy, practice, or procedure should be how well it meets agreed-upon performance targets over the long run.

Also remember that circumstances change, and thus the necessary expertise to make decentralization work may disappear over time, as experienced staff move on. Or the level of expertise needed to make good decisions at the local level may increase, leaving people who were once capable of handling decisions at the local level less so. It is for these reasons that ongoing monitoring and feedback are so valuable.

In facilities organizations, centralization has often taken the form of explicit, written space and furniture standards. As computer-aided facility management (CAFM) becomes more common, will there be a shift in what is considered important to centralize or decentralize?

I think there may be. Without doubt, more effort is being devoted to constructing centralized databases. These take time and effort to construct, maintain, and use. Centralized FM groups are more likely, at least at first, to want to use these databases to help them monitor and control time, staff, and money on a companywide basis. At companies like Ernst & Young in London, however, databases residing on the mainframe can be accessed by local users through their own terminals to obtain information on the amount, location, and cost of the space they occupy.

In general, it seems to me that developing standardized procedures for reporting a limited amount of "core" data makes a great deal of sense because the form of such information is not greatly affected by differences in local conditions (the interpretation of standardized data may be, however, and should be analyzed with an eye to how local conditions—whether energy costs or task functions—may affect them). That is the "what" of centralization rather than the "how." It can be justified because of the high level of interdependence among different sites for access to scarce resources of money, expertise, time, and space. It also reflects the need for the whole organization to be able to monitor and control its resources.

A centralized database can also liberate local managers because they have ready access to their own (and possibly) others' records. By observing what others do and how their own operation stacks up against comparable units, they can increase their own experience.

CHAPTER 7

Organizing the Project

A former colleague of mine at Cornell invented a fascinating communication training exercise. Three people sat around a table with their backs to one another. In front of each of them were identical round playing boards with places for dominoes drawn on them. Each board had different dominoes glued down in the drawn boxes. The group's task was to discover, within three minutes, which dominoes were missing, so that by the end all the boards would have exactly the same pattern of dominos. Most of the groups failed, for a simple reason: In their rush toward efficiency they forgot to get organized. In this case, that meant asking a crucial question: How was the round board oriented? Where was the top? Groups that took the time at the beginning to organize themselves solved the problem in less than a minute, but groups that jumped to solutions never solved the problem.

How a project itself is organized is a major design task, and so spending time here can save time and money down the line. A well-designed project is likely to result in less duplication of effort; fewer misunderstandings and less resentment within the project team and between the team and users, contractors, and consultants; better decisions based on more accurate information (and therefore less time spent exploring dead-end paths); and better use of available and hired resources (internal staff, consultants, contractors).

Yet in the eagerness to get on with a project, it is not unusual for little time to be devoted to designing the project process. It is a bit like knowing you want to make a superb meal, ordering a lot of expensive ingredients, but then never taking the time to find a recipe. You might create something edible, with a lot of trial and error, wasted ingredients, lost time, and flared tempers, but probably the result will be more glop than gourmet.

In my experience, successful projects—ones that not only are close to budget and on schedule but serve their purposes well over time—have a common characteristic: an understanding of and a commitment to good communication. This means good communication within the project team; among the project team, senior management, and end users; and between the project team and its various contractors and consultants.

Good communication requires good information and a commitment and willingness to share it in a timely fashion. It requires understanding roles and role relationships and being sensitive to others' concerns, needs, and preferences. It means accepting responsibility and sharing credit. It requires confidence in the skills, knowledge, and experience of everyone involved, from contractor and consultant to secretary and senior manager.

Whether made explicit and publicly proclaimed or driven simply by a sense of what will work, the starting point for a successful project is an overall view, vision, or even philosophy of the project process. The trick is not to plunge ahead but to step back and discuss and gain some consensus on the philosophy underlying the process. What are some of the basic working assumptions and specific methods that will influence the overall approach? The type of project and the organization obviously color how any particular project will be organized, but the following working assumptions seem, to me, to be useful guides in almost any situation.

WORKING ASSUMPTIONS

The Process of Planning, Designing, and Managing Facilities is as Important as the Actual Physical Environment

This statement rests on my own experience and considerable research evidence that relates the employees' satisfaction with the work environment to the nature and amount of involvement they had in the planning and design process (Becker 1981, 1988b, 1988c, Brill, Margulis, and Konar 1984; DIO 1983; Froggatt 1985). It also is derived from the view that the planning and design process can act as a form of organizational development (see Chapter 8, "Managing the Briefing Process") which helps clarify and order business objectives, helps identify and address organizational conflict, discovers and develops hidden staff resources, and promotes collaboration and teamwork.

Good Design Requires Good Information

I should not be, but I still am surprised at how many projects proceed in an information vacuum. How people actually work, the percentage of people in the office on a regular basis, an accurate account of equipment, and an understanding of the organizational culture—any number of types of information—are often absent. This is all the more ironic in conservative profit-oriented organizations in which no financial decision would be made without very close scrutiny but in which facilities decisions that involve hundreds of thousands if not millions of dollars in direct costs, as well as affecting employees who represent a much greater and ongoing cost, tend to be ignored or looked at only perfunctorily.

Good Design Supports a Full Range of Human Needs, Values, and Activities

This principle reflects the belief that the built environment should support and enhance human dignity, comfort, and safety for its own sake. In one of the richest countries in the world, with one of the highest standards of living, there is no reason that we should tolerate or accept environments that dull the mind, cramp the body, cause illness, or deny individual identity.

Sweden, whose offices are among the most beautiful and functional in the world (see Chapter 9), provides its office workers with offices with windows and walls, high-quality wooden furniture, and generous common rooms and break areas—all without thought of conducting a study to demonstrate (and justify) how these design features would affect productivity or performance. Such offices are simply considered part of the cost of doing business in a society that prides itself on supporting human health and dignity. Attracting and retaining the kind of employees needed in today's organizations, reducing fatigue, and promoting various kinds of communication so that people can work more productively also are benefits of this principle, but such benefits are unlikely ever to be fully justified only on utilitarian grounds.

Good Design Emerges from Effective Collaboration

Projects, even relatively small ones, are too complex today to be effectively executed without some form of collaboration between users and providers, among different disciplines and departments, and among different kinds of expertise and experience. Collaboration can take many forms, from formal organizational structures that integrate functions like planning and construction with building operations and maintenance, to formally constituted project teams and work groups, to informal meetings called by FM to share information and discuss problems and opportunities with groups like telecommunications or real estate.

Good Design is Beautiful, Functional, and Cost Effective

Although some designers view function as at odds with beauty, many clients view beauty as at odds with cost and function. Neither is correct. Good design, by definition, should work at many levels simultaneously. It is not a question of making a choice but of being inventive under what are the usual enormous constraints of time, money, and staff.

To prevent these kinds of working assumptions from becoming empty rhetoric, they must be made explicit, widely and publicly discussed, and supported by senior management and the immediate project team. They should, in fact, guide the development of the whole project process. Taken seriously, these principles (or whatever ones an organization selects) can help the project team (and those it reports to!) avoid focusing only on one or two issues (e.g., cost or aesthetics) while neglecting others (e.g., attract staff, support desired types of communication). Working assumptions are useful as a benchmark against which specific proposals, activities, and procedures can be assessed as the project progresses: Are we getting the right kind of information? Are the right people involved, at the right times? Are we concentrating on only one or two important issues and letting others slide? As the day-to-day pressures of a project mount, it is easy (and understandable) to lose sight of the bigger picture. Having explicit principles that become part of ongoing working reviews can help resolve the project myopia that, like the fog along the coast, seems to roll in as the project progresses, costs mount, and time passes.

ORGANIZING THE PROJECT TEAM

At the beginning of any project, the first design issue is creating an effective project team. A number of questions need to be addressed.

Who Should be Involved?

Several different types of expertise are needed:

- *Content-based knowledge* associated with technical areas such as mechanical and electrical engineering, facility management, architecture and space planning, project and construction management, organizational ecology, human factors and environmental psychology, lighting and acoustics, and purchasing. The particular list of experts will depend on the specific project, and it can be very long.
- *Human relations skills* and knowledge associated with being a group facilitator and effective communicator, someone who can stimulate dialogue and critical thinking without causing conflict. In projects involving groups known to have difficulty understanding one another or when one group's expectations of its role are not likely to be shared by others (the project team's designers trying to design something for a group of staff designers, for example) incorporating this kind of skill can be critical to the project's success.
- *Project-based experience* gained from working on projects of a comparable size and complexity. Building a new headquarters or a $50 million computer operations center bears scant resemblance to the hundreds of thousands of dollars spent in renovating part of an office floor or the design of small branch offices. That is, experience with one type of project is not necessarily good preparation for another. It also does not mean that staff with experience only on smaller projects should not be involved with, or even lead, larger projects. But it does mean that some form of experience must be brought to bear on the project, whether in the form of training seminars, debriefings of project managers with the right kind of experience in other companies, or the use of outside consultants.
- *Knowledge of the "business"*. The methods described in Chapter 8 are intended to capture quickly and efficiently information about what the occupants of a facility do

and what kinds of people they are. Being familiar with job descriptions and task functions is essential but not sufficient. One needs to understand what different occupants care about, how they think (logical versus intuitive; experience versus numbers; objects versus people) how they like to work, what their professional identity is, and what aspects of the workplace they see as supporting or undermining their effectiveness. Having at least one member of the project team who has worked with and knows the kinds of people that will occupy the building can be an enormous help in getting answers to these kinds of questions early on. A project team that can demonstrate to its clients this kind of familiarity will be able to establish rapport and credibility much more quickly than one that cannot.

Defining the Core Project Team

A distinction should be made between the core project team and the overall project team. The core team, the group responsible for managing the overall project, must have easy access to and excellent working relations with a wide range of expertise, but the core itself should be small. It should include a project manager and one or two key staff representing two to three of the kinds of expertise just noted.

The key to the core team's effectiveness is the project manager. The ability to walk on water is a useful one for the project manager, but in its absence the following types of personal and organizational characteristics are important:

- A thorough understanding of the corporate culture, including the roles, attitudes, and biases of key managers and how (and by whom) decisions are made
- The ability to think conceptually and to be open to new ideas, matched by the ability to understand details and to make sure things will happen when they are supposed to
- A quick learner, unlikely to make the same mistakes twice and able to learn rapidly the basic concepts and language of many different expert groups
- A risk taker, willing to go out on a limb when necessary, to push the boundaries of acceptability without bursting them
- A strong personal and organizational relationship with at least one respected senior manager who can help run interference when needed, provide insights into and information about pending management directions, smooth out high-level conflicts, and deflect concerns and buy time to make high-risk decisions
- The ability to define objectives so that other players in the process know what they should be doing, what their roles are, and what they have to do in order to perform it well
- Good people skills, including knowing when to be tough as well as when to be flexible

It is this special combination of skills, rather than those of "engineer" or "architect" or "project manager" or the experience of projects of a comparable size (though that surely helps), that, in my experience, distinguishes a project that is not only well run, in regard to meeting cost and schedule targets, but is also likely to be innovative.

What Roles Should Different Players Take in the Process?

It is important to get real decision makers (people who have real influence and understand where things are going) rather than (or in addition to) people whose organizational position makes them the right players, but who may not get things done or do not really care about the project. Enthusiasm is critical; project players should actually want to be doing what they are doing.

Who will report to whom? Committee's roles and missions should be clear, and they should be given authority as well as responsibility for fulfilling their missions. A "users' committee" can be counterproductive if its members view their role as reviewing preliminary proposals while senior management or the core team view their role as conveying predetermined decisions back to their constitutents. Establishing subcommittees to investigate everything from lighting to new work patterns becomes empty symbolism if committee members are not given the time and resources to hire consultants, visit sites, or read the available literature.

It should be clear to all concerned who will make the final decisions (and preferably using what criteria), what kinds of decisions can be made by a committee, and which must be approved by some higher authority.

The Timing of Different Participants' Involvement

In general, it is better to involve people early rather than later in the process. The rugby model of the product development process (see Chapter 12) is based on the premise that getting different kinds of experts involved in the project from the beginning saves time and leads to more innovative solutions.

Yet not everyone needs to be involved at every stage of the process. Some consultants, for example, may be asked to stimulate thinking early on and then to review developments at critical junctures, but they do not have to be part of every project meeting. Similarly, at some points it makes sense to take the pulse of a broad cross section of employees, while only a small number might participate in regular meetings of a building committee.

Identification of Existing and Needed Resources

Are there hidden resources among existing staff? Are there people representing any of the three types of expertise listed earlier that are already on staff, possibly residing outside the departments that would be expected to house them? Are there people in mechanical engineering, security design, or human resources whose expertise and experience can be tapped (perhaps using them periodically, like an outside consultant, to review the project with a fresh set of eyes)? Are there people without formal credentials but whose experience has made them experts in managing information systems or computer applications, or in specialized environments such as computer centers or clean rooms?

Having located expertise in-house, the next question is whether it is unavailable because of time commitments. Absolutely essential to any large or long-term project is that those staff members assigned to participate be given time to do so; that is, project work cannot be done regularly on top of all other responsibilities. If staff cannot be given time to participate, then contract staff for the duration of the project should be considered.

Identification of Key Decision Points

When will key decisions be made (and by whom)? Important decision points are:

- Deciding whom to involve
- Determining structure and reporting relationships
- Identifying and communicating the project's working assumptions
- Identifying the data to be collected
- Collecting the data (cost, schedule, change orders, user requirements, etc.)
- Analyzing the data
- Developing explicit design requirements
- Circulating design requirements for discussion and approval
- Periodically reviewing schedule, costs, requirements, and consultant and contractor performance

A process rarely is (or should be) completely linear. Thus several of these steps will recur throughout a project. Any process will depend on the corporate culture ("how we do things here"), available time and resources, and the scope of the project. Yet these kinds of steps, and the decisions linked to them, must be taken regardless of project size. The main difference is likely to be in their scope and formality.

RELATING THE PROJECT TO THE ORGANIZATION'S CULTURE

When organizing a project, getting everything right means being as innovative as possible within the boundaries of what is organizationally acceptable. This often is not the "best" solution in a technical or even organizational sense. I have participated in several consulting projects in which the project team had made proposals, particularly for space planning, that were innovative but completely violated the existing culture; for example, they replaced enclosed offices for professionals with workstations and systems furniture. The directive often came from a senior facilities manager who believed that the open planning concept would use space more efficiently and thereby help meet the important corporate goal of containing costs. Invariably, the whole project would be driven by this top management directive, only to be abandoned months later when specific proposals were presented to user groups, whose own top management rejected them because they violated entrenched ways of communicating status.

Changing space allocation policies is changing the organizational culture, and you cannot sneak a culture change past managers and staff. Their eyesight becomes exceedingly sharp whenever their established prerogatives are threatened. Culture can be changed (slowly and with total commitment by top management), but it must be done in an open, planned fashion in which the costs and benefits are widely discussed and the implications clarified (for maintaining the status quo as well as changing things). Chapter 9 discusses organizational culture in more detail, but the point here is that the development of any project process is greatly influenced by the organizational culture within which it evolves.

The fundamental question is whether the proposed process supports the organization's current way of doing things or the directions in which it wishes to move. Does it reflect typical reporting relationships, departmental boundaries, implicit organizational values? Does this make sense, or is there a need to reconsider some of the more common approaches? For example, would the typical approach make it impossible to create a project team that crossed departmental boundaries, even if having this kind of information and experience represented in the core group would enhance the project's chance of succeeding? Is the kind of information considered useful, for example, to long-term business goals, thought by some as inappropriate for the facilities planning group to consider?

If the answer to these questions is yes, then some kind of culture change needs to be considered. The facilities group should then draw up a proposal that shows what the effects of maintaining the status quo are likely to be. Citing well-known past "failures" in which projects ran way over budget or produced buildings that were disliked and required immediate expensive renovation are likely to be powerful incentives to doing something differently. Even more effective is finding positive examples from competitors or other well-known companies who have already tried what you are proposing. Directly relating proposals to formal corporate objectives and philosophy, the kind often found in annual reports and strategic planning documents, challenges top management's commitment to these goals and shows that the project supports fundamental business objectives.

The point is to help management understand the consequences of various courses of action (both of doing and not doing something) so that they can make an informed decision about which way to proceed. Are they willing to accept the probability of higher maintenance and operating costs if the building operations and maintenance staff are isolated from the planning process? Or the cost implications and the communications consequences of fully enclosed offices? Senior management must understand what supplementary programs or actions will be necessary to support their decision. Will the building operations team be brought in before occupancy to explore the new building systems, to learn how to maintain them, and how the building operations may affect the kind of staff and training they need to be developing? Will there be programs put in place to counteract some of the social isolation of fully enclosed offices, and is there a department that will organize and fund these? In the elastic organization, with its emphasis on understanding the organization as an integrated system, the planning process for the building inevitably goes beyond bricks and mortar.

The project can be used as a deliberate intervention into the organizational culture, but not as a secret or subversive one. If top management's commitment to rethinking some of the ways of working and doing things is weak, then the design may have to be adapted to fit the culture better. Starting small and trying out an innovative approach on an experimental basis can be an effective way of demonstrating that something that few believe will work actually does.

Before reaching this point, an organizational diagnosis should be made. Table 7-1 is a chart developed by organizational consultant Fritz Steele that shows how changes in a proposed facility will affect management style and basic assumptions about how people

Table 7-1. Clarifying Confusing Facility Messages or Mixed Signals

Element	Old Meaning	New Meaning
1. Smaller personal workplaces	1. Decrease in organizational status	1. Different strategy on use of space (not related to status)
2. Large number of common spaces	2. These belong to no one and no one takes responsibility for them	2. These belong to everyone, need to design process to manage and to maintain them
3. Many places for informal conversations	3. Using these means you have nothing productive to do (and talking is not real work)	3. Using these means you are doing something productive (talking is part of real work)
4. Large, visible, central atrium space	4. Keep this space neat and "arranged," since it is public, front stage display space	4. Use this space richly, since it is part of the central backstage resources of the building
5. People not located right next to people and equipment that they see or use regularly	5. Low power people get stuck wherever there is any space left over, without regards to their needs	5. Functional inconvenience is a general principle (locate people to maximize informal, spontaneous contacts) not related to status
6. Styles of dress— jackets/ties versus more informal dress	6. The truly professional people dress formally to fit corporate culture	6. The truly professional people dress to fit the demands of their modes of work during the work day
7. Amount and style of furniture in one's workplace	7. The more and fancier, the more important you are to the company	7. More selectivity in the workplace to fit actual activities there with more alternative locations (amount of furniture is not important)
8. People talking in break areas, on terraces, etc.	8. Managers are not exercising the proper amount of control	8. Professionals are exercising appropriate tactical autonomy

should work in an organization. One needs to do diagnoses like Steele's (1986) to understand the assumptions, policies, and symbolic messages associated with various layouts and elements in the organization's settings and how those might be affected in a new or renovated facility. Once clear about some of these cultural implications, senior management can make more informed judgments about decisions that cannot be understood in purely financial, engineering, architectural, or construction terms.

Norms and Culture

A major factor in assessing the culture's impact on how a project is organized is determining whether the proposed organization will violate "the way we do things here." One way of beginning to understand corporate culture in relation to the project organization is to ask questions (particularly of senior management) like "Describe a successful (and unsuccessful) project." "What would happen if rank-and-file employees were allowed to participate in the planning process or if a special core building team that cut across departments were set up?" "What kind of information would help most in justifying a sharp departure in space-planning concepts?" "Who really will make the final decisions about this project, and what kinds of arguments does he or she find persuasive?"

Answers to these kinds of questions begin to clarify what is acceptable and what is not, which constraints to accept, which to try to change, and the best way of approaching change. In some organizations, computer printouts of data, showing actual versus projected staff in past space forecasts, comparisons of the number of square feet per person in different departments or in similar departments in competitor organizations, and the cost and speed of the project may be the most persuasive. In others, good anecdotes about successes and failures may be better. Some organizations put a lot of faith in outside consultants (even when the same thing could be and has been said by in-house staff), and so proposals are more effective from them than from staff members. It is a question not only of expertise or good ideas but also of being effective, knowing what kind of information (and usually combinations of information) presented by which people or types of people will get top management's most sympathetic attention.

ROLE MANAGEMENT WITHIN THE PROJECT TEAM

It is one thing to select the right experts to be on a project team. It is another to develop a cohesive team with a strong team spirit, comfortable enough with one another to be able to argue without becoming defensive or abusive, a group that actually enjoys one another's company, knows its strengths and weaknesses, and is committed to doing the best job possible with the available resources. Understanding the project team's roles is critical to the project's overall success.

Roles are the sets of expectations that people hold about someone occupying a social or organizational position (e.g., business manager, facility manager, maintenance engineer): that is, how he or she should behave. Misunderstanding and conflict occur when the people holding the position and those interacting with it do not share the same expectations.

As a professor, for example, some students expect me to provide more structured assignments than I believe are useful. When this happens, the students end up frustrated, angry, and disappointed. They feel I am not doing what they consider my job: giving a clear, explicit assignment that describes exactly what they should be doing. For my part, I wonder why students are so reluctant to interpret an assignment on their own. I become depressed, even angry, about timid, risk-aversive, bureaucratic students whose disappointment with me is matched by mine with them. No one wins. Role expectations must be mutually understood and, if not liked, at least accepted as governing the relationship.

Clarifying roles requires understanding *role constellation,* which refers to the other positions to which one relates (both inside and outside the team). One must identify the role constellation for a particular project (and how it may shift and grow over time as different players come in and go out of the process). How does FM relate to telecommunications, to human resources, to design and construction, and so on? Will the FM team's initiation of an "enculturation" program to help everyone from senior management to secretary understand the concepts underlying the building design and how these will affect management style and work patterns be viewed by human resources as a turf challenge? Creating an effective team means understanding linkages to other groups and departments, not just getting it right inside your own team.

Whether in relation to other groups and departments or within the project team itself, team building requires effective *role management.* In effect, team members (within the project team) and relevant departments contract with one another about expectations. Such discussions need to be a two-way process, and they need to be seen as an ongoing process, not something done once and for all and then set in concrete. Positions change, different people fill them, and the role boundaries shift in size and form over time.

All of these changes need to be monitored periodically. It may be nothing more than a half-hour of a regular staff meeting, or it may be a half-day retreat. The sooner and more often roles are discussed, the less likely there is to be a serious misunderstanding that requires a dedicated analysis.

Role conflict occurs when the expectations of those filling a role and those affected by it do not match. Role negotiation is intended to identify these kinds of role conflicts before they cause major resentments and disruptions.

Role ambiguity occurs when expectations are unclear for areas of behavior. Organizational consultant Fritz Steele lists "What I do," "How I do it," "How I'm measured for performance," and "What happens to my career as a result" as the four areas most likely to be murky. Muddied waters in these areas are inversely proportional to energy and commitment and so must be addressed before people will commit their energy and enthusiasm. Role ambiguity also refers to how the organizational pie is cut up, a form of boundary regulation. The more rigid the roles are, the more inflexible the team may be. Yet unless everyone is extremely confident about their position, without some reasonably clear boundary, it is easy to become threatened by other people engaging in activities you thought were in your bailiwick.

Both role conflict and ambiguity can lead to *role stress* and its consequences: wasted effort, energy drain, blaming, stereotyping, poor health, anger, deliberate lack of cooperation. Reducing this stress requires role management: disclosing problems, sharing experiences, negotiating and renegotiating, clarifying images of a role and achieving a better matching process. If not managed, role stress (which is embedded in the organizational structure) will be treated as someone's personal problems (the individual is perceived as being inadequate) rather than a consequence of how the process has been organized. This leads to people's blaming one another for their incompetence, but it does little to change the causes of the stress, which are built into the mismatch between role expectations and the situation.

INDIVIDUAL ASSESSMENTS

As part of managing roles within the team, the team needs to assess the people on the team in regard to their strengths, weaknesses, expertise, personal work habits, and so forth. No combination is perfect, and so part of a team's required working process is being able to determine its own patterns and to be able to discuss their conclusions openly, without embarrassment. Issues to address include educational background, work experience, personal styles (ways of working, use of time, pet peeves), strengths and weaknesses (good at details, lost in details, can see the big picture), and aspirations and concerns for one's own career.

There are lots of ways to do these kinds of analyses, but a simple approach is to gather the team off the site for a one-to-two-day team-building session. It is useful to have a group facilitator who is not part of the team to help keep the discussions on track and emotions within bounds. Each member might first begin by jotting down answers to the preceding questions, and then each person can talk frankly about his or her responses in a roundtable discussion. False modesty is no more useful to building an effective team than is unjustified chest beating.

This open discussion allows conscious team management; that is, choosing needed structures, ways of working, necessary outside resources, and the like to balance the skills, abilities, and work-styles of the team members. The challenge, of course, is to match the team's strengths with the demands placed on them by the project.

Information about team members must be shared within the team so that members can make choices based on realities, not fantasies or wishes. This is not just a management activity. Sharing personal views of one's strengths and weaknesses can be daunting, particularly if some team members feel that others have much more experience or many more skills. The group facilitator's role is to help people feel comfortable talking about themselves and reacting to others. Because this kind of discussion is so dependent on trust, it is likely to take some time to build up the team's comfort level, which is why these discussions should take place periodically.

SETTING GOALS FOR THE PROJECT

Having designed the process for forming the team and helping it evolve, the team must set its goals for the project by means of the following.

Identify Operational Goals

Once the project begins there will be hundreds of decisions to make, and so the principal goals should be identified first. The team must decide how to measure the achievement of goals throughout the life of the project. This is called *formative evaluation,* or an ongoing assessment that actually may change the activities and approach being used. The purpose is not to put a seal of approval on the project once it is over.

Identify Constraints

The constraints (such as time or budget) within which the project must operate should be established. What is or is not a constraint is a fascinating issue. In several projects I have seen an absolute constraint (thou shalt have open plan and systems furniture) imposed by top management wither away as the real consequences of the constraint began to emerge. Similarly, organizations often set unrealistic completion dates. Head-quarters buildings intended to open on twenty-fifth, fiftieth, or seventy-fifth anniversaries are good examples.

The team needs to distinguish between *fixed constraints* and *controllable constraints.* A controllable constraint is the management edict to use open plan concepts or to schedule completion of the building to coincide with the company's seventh-fifth birthday. Controllable constraints must be seriously considered, but they also must be seriously challenged if the project team and its consultants believe meeting the target (cost, time, scheduling, space planning concept) will undermine the project's overall success. The project team should marshal information and arguments that demonstrate to top management the consequences of accepting this "constraint" as an operational objective. Seventy-fifth birthday parties can be held two or six months after the actual birthdate without any significant loss. This demonstrates the hallmark of a controllable constraint, which is that the company can alter it if it wants.

Fixed constraints are those that the organization is unlikely to be able to change. They may range from interest rates and zoning laws to building codes and safety regulations. Although these limits may sometimes be influenced by the organization's activities (winning a zoning variance, for example), the company cannot act on its own to change them.

Gaining Consensus

There must be a kind of "bill of goals" or "ten objectives" against which daily actions, planning decisions, budgeting, and policy can be continually compared. The project team can construct an initial list of these goals, but they then must be thoroughly reviewed by top management, with participants encouraged to challenge and question them, so that doubts can be expressed and arguments and information collected to answer the concerns.

It is essential that top management believe in the project's goals. Proposed goals must be presented at the beginning to managers and occupant groups for review and discussion. Their commitment to the goals must be public, in the sense all other senior managers heard the same things and that at some point all signed a written statement of what these goals are. Publishing these in a company newsletter or having the senior managers announce these goals in meetings with their own managers and in a companywide forum (teleconferencing or meetings in a large auditorium, for example) underscores top management's commitment to the project's basic goals and purposes. Without this common ground, the project will begin to move in different directions, simultaneously and perhaps disastrously, as the project progresses.

Identifying Different Constituencies

Different groups are likely to have different goals, or at least different priorities for the project. Constituencies (e.g., disciplines or departments, senior management, rank-and-file employees, unions, consultants, stockholders) must be identified, and then representatives of these groups should review and respond to proposed goals and suggest others. The objective is to make sure all groups understand and are committed to the project's major goals.

Implicit and Explicit Goals

Some goals are widely accepted because they have great face validity (e.g., the need for more space or better HVAC or wire management). Often project teams have goals that are more controversial (e.g., more "efficient" use of space) because they require changes in the corporate culture and well-established policy and procedures (same-sized offices or the concept of shared offices and common areas). Such implicit goals are often hard to achieve and can generate mistrust and anger when they become apparent. For the most part, making goals explicit and testing their reception after they are explained are likely to result in greater support for the project and less anger, resistance, or apathy later.

What might be some of the goals for a major project? Examples are the following:

- More flexible building
- More humane working environment
- Better accommodation of information technologies
- More effective use of space
- Improved lateral communication across departments
- Acquisition of high-quality staff (clerical and professional)
- Better morale
- Greater employee commitment
- Clearer sense of mission

These goals should be ranked by different stakeholder groups so that when trade-offs occur, as they always do, there will be a basis for knowing what to sacrifice or compromise. The opinions of different stakeholders can be weighted differently (senior management given more weight than middle management or outside consultants, for instance) in order to reflect the decision-making structure. Formal and systematic procedures, such as ranking objectives that are then scored and analyzed, offer a more accurate and quantitative picture than do informal interviews or *ad hoc* meetings with individuals and groups. The number and size of the groups and the complexity of the project (with increasing size and complexity, more systematic and quantitative techniques become more valuable), as well as the organization's culture, will determine the techniques used.

Whatever technique is used, the point is to have some understanding of how different parties to the process rank various objectives, which can then be compared and analyzed. Those that all parties rank close to the top become consensus choices. Ones on which there is relatively little agreement should stimulate discussion about why that goal is ranked high or low and how its achievement would or would not enhance the organization's ability to meet its strategic objectives. Thus the process itself contributes to organizational development by helping uncover and address conflicts as well as identifying rallying points that diverse groups can and want to support.

COMMUNICATION STRATEGIES AND STRUCTURES

As should be evident by now, selecting the team and building its internal cohesiveness are basic, but the team's overall success depends on good communication outside the project team and even outside the organization.

Given the importance of effective communication within the project team, between the team and its constituencies (both end users and management), how the project team will handle communications should be treated as a design problem in its own right. Knowing why you are communicating, as well as the best way to do it, must be both planned and implemented.

Functions of Communication

The communication process is the glue that holds a project together. It serves several purposes: coordinating, spotting and solving problems, preparing people for tasks or changes, tracking progress, building team cohesion, monitoring costs, and making sure decisions fit the situation (and knowing whether the situation has changed).

An additional communication function, for groups outside as well as inside the organization, is marketing the project and the company. This means exploiting interesting and unusual aspects of the project to advertise the organization positively to all its constituents. Everything can be marketed, from the company's concern for its employees (e.g., briefing process, amenities provided, and quality of its facilities) and for environment quality (e.g., sophisticated use of new automated building systems technologies to conserve energy, site planning that preserves wetlands or protects scenic vistas, building that includes historic preservation) to concern for meeting customers' needs (e.g., a facility designed to stimulate product innovation, telecommunications and office automation that speed service).

Communication needs to be continuous and to spring from an understanding of how other participants in the process are viewing the process and their role in it. It must be a two-way process (within the project team and between it and others) and should include ideas, feelings, and reactions as well as facts. This is as true for communication with vendors, consultants, and contractors as it is with rank-and-file employees and management. The reason is simple: With an understanding of how others are viewing the situation comes the ability to anticipate problems before they erupt, and to initiate discussions to find mutually acceptable solutions at the point when emotions still can be controlled.

Many managers stifle communication for fear of opening a Pandora's box: If they pry open the lid on feelings, preferences, or ideas just a crack, they imagine a flood of emotion wrenching the lid from the box. So they hope that, by keeping the lid tightly shut, these feelings and emotions will vanish. They may remain publicly suppressed, but they rarely evaporate, and they can erupt when least expected, seemingly triggered by the most minor of problems.

The consequences of poor communication surface in resentments, in subterfuge, sometimes in deliberate sabotage, in reduced morale, and in apathy, perhaps most insidious. Whether from employees, managers, or contractors, the unwillingness to give one's best, to share ideas that could make things better, and help the organization prosper, are precisely what the organization wants most to avoid. What a waste of vitality, good energy, and goodwill!

It is true that some people who have had little opportunity to express their views will "vent" strong emotions when first given the chance. But many more will be delighted and surprised and a little skeptical about management's intentions and whether the process is "for real." The answer—and whether the project really succeeds—lies in whether ideas are acted on, responded to, and publicly noted by management. Communication is a two-way street; input is a one-way alley. Just as the project team wants and needs to share (give and receive) information, ideas, and concerns with the management to which it reports in order to be effective and to maintain its own motivation and momentum, so the people who are affected by the project management group want the same opportunity.

Choosing to Communicate

The project team needs to decide what it wants different players in the process to know, and when. A high-disclosure pattern leads to a greater sense of involvement and opportunities to help shape the project process, to learn from experience, and to test reality.

The first question is to decide with whom to communicate. Some likely sources are:

- Members of the core project team
- Senior management to whom the project team reports
- Consultants and contractors
- Management of groups that will occupy the facility
- Rank-and-file employees who will occupy the facility
- Vendors and suppliers
- Facility managers, architects, designers, engineers, and other professionals

- Customers
- Field sales force

The first few groups are probably taken for granted. What about the rest? The answer lies in knowing why you are communicating at all. For groups directly responsible for the project, the answer has to do with sharing information to make informed decisions and to test reality to make sure that decisions reflect it.

For projects that are significant because of their size, their complexity, or their innovation in design, process, materials, or construction, communicating with employees who will not occupy the building (like the field sales force or employees in other facilities or sites), vendors, customers, and the professional facility planning and management community (including architects, engineers, and designers) can become an effective and inexpensive form of marketing: keeping people informed about new ideas being implemented, new processes tried out, new materials being used. Communicating with these kinds of groups helps project the image of an active, evolving, innovative organization. It also says—merely by the fact the communication occurred at all—that the company is thinking about and is concerned about these players.

For organizational members who will occupy the building (regardless of its significance to the world outside the company), information helps control rumors, addresses concerns that reduce anxiety and resistance, and, especially early in the project, can help generate excitement and enthusiasm.

What to Communicate (and Solicit)

To employees, the most important information to provide concerns the nature and scope of the project and its schedule (see also Chapter 9, "Managing Environmental Change") and when employees will be directly affected; that is, will have to pack their offices, move to swing space, move to the new building, or receive new equipment or training in new procedures. As research we have conducted on office relocations has shown (Becker 1988b; Becker and Hoogesteger 1986), employees also want to know about their own work situation: what their own office will be like, where it will be located, where key people and frequently used equipment and supplies will be located.

Equally important, and relatively rare, is explaining why certain decisions have been made and how they are expected to benefit the company. Although employees will not like every decision, they are more likely to accept and support it if they understand how it benefits the company and themselves.

Sadly, too often things done well within a project are not effectively communicated to either management or employees. For example, organizations that have involved employees in the planning and design process, by having them participate in focus groups or respond to full-scale mock-ups of rooms and furniture, rarely tell employees how their feedback actually guided the project team's decisions. In one large project on which I worked, a full-scale mock-up of a corner of a new building was constructed to test furniture layouts, lighting, and fenestration. The windows were particularly important because they had been especially designed to allow employees to see outside without the bright daylight causing problems for people working with VDU screens.

The test facility showed that the window design was allowing in so much light that it was too bright on sunny days but was frustrating employees on cloudy days when the ceramic pattern in the window reduced visibility to what looked like a dense fog, with only the outlines of trees barely visible. The architect went back to the drawing board and redesigned the windows. The savings from not using the unacceptable glass was $3.5 million.

This firm did a good job of showing their employees how their participation in the process had affected the final design. Employees become disillusioned and apathetic if they feel their opinions are solicited but never used. Furthermore, many organizations fail to take advantage of the fact that their own employees' input led to different decisions than those the planners and designers might otherwise have made. It is equally important for management to explain why decisions that contradict employees' (or contractors' or consultants') feedback or preferences were made and how they benefit the organization. In the absence of feedback about how their input influenced (or did not) the decision process, people (rightly) become suspicious and resentful of the "participation" process and of management. Good intentions end up spawning bad relations, which is unnecessary and counterproductive. If management finds its rationale too embarrassing to proclaim publicly, then it should consider rethinking the rationale—and the decision.

From management, employees, and contractors the project team needs to know whether scheduling will cause problems or conflicts with other events, what resources will be needed (time, money, space, people) to help the project proceed smoothly, what procedures seem good or problematic (including why and what feasible alternatives exist), and what changes in organizational structure, staffing, and equipment uses will be needed so that the project team can plan realistically.

From outsiders, the project team needs feedback on how the project is being viewed by interested professionals, vendors, and customers. Is it seen as draining resources, as unnecessarily opulent, as a brilliant innovation, as business as usual? This kind of information can help in the design of marketing material and publicity campaigns, and it may also suggest different ways of doing things or the need to seriously rethink some parts of the project.

How to Communicate

Regular structures are part of a flow of communication: scheduled meetings, reviews, progress summaries, publicity releases. Designing such structures requires conscious choices that affect the quality and quantity of information sharing: whom to include, where to hold meetings (turf issues), when and how agendas should be set, whether advance materials should or should not be distributed, and if and how responses will be recorded and who will see them. A key issue, particularly given the range of people who may be involved in a large or significant project, is the media to use to communicate effectively. These can include:

• *Newsletters,* including articles in company newsletters (especially good for smaller projects whose audience is primarily internal). For larger projects, special newsletters devoted to the project can be distributed to both employees and outside groups, assigning the same costs to double duty (and allocating some of the costs as marketing, not project, costs). News items can be placed in newsletters of relevant professional associations and groups at essentially no cost other than writing the piece.

- *Magazine articles,* appropriate to significant projects and primarily useful for outside audiences, can be written by either in-house people or outside writers. This is the best form of free publicity. Widely distributing these kinds of articles within the company also helps build employees' pride and interest in the project.
- *Conferences,* at which project team members or consultants present papers or sit on panels, are an excellent way of communicating with outside audiences. Making time for staff people to participate in these kinds of events also increases the likelihood of informal contacts with peers with other experiences from whom they may learn new ideas and ways of doing things. Participation may be related to experience gained with a series of small projects as well as a single large project.
- *In-house forums,* in which project team members or consultants talk to large numbers of employees about a significant project. They can explain the ideas and concepts behind a project, answer questions, and at the same time get feedback on the general concerns. These sessions can be videotaped and then shown to management (to hear the concerns of their employees voiced to project team members) and to those employees (or possibly outsiders) who could not attend the live meeting.
- *Electronic mail and bulletin boards,* available to everyone in the organization and allowing regular, cheap, and widespread sharing of information about the project, both to and from the project team. Employees can be asked to respond to information in general; they can be queried about specific concerns of the project team; and they can address questions to the project team, with the answers being public to all. Obviously either employees must trust that their responses will not be used as evidence that they are troublemakers, or their confidentiality must be guaranteed.
- *Memos,* an overworked form of communication, through which the project team (including consultants and senior management overseeing the project) can present their views. Memos are not very useful for communicating with employees.
- *Meetings,* in which occasionally it is useful to have the whole core project team or the project leader and consultants meet with senior management or groups of managers who will occupy the building, so that they can learn how management is thinking and what their concerns are.
- *Wandering interviews,* in which project team members occasionally wander around and talk informally for a few minutes with their user constituents in their own workplace. They can be useful for discovering how the "troops" in the field view the project. It can be a rather jolting bit of reality testing, but the process itself—like many forms of communication—is as important as the information collected because it demonstrates the project team's concern about how its activities are regarded.

Developing Formats

Communication is ongoing, not an isolated event. To capture the opportunities in an ongoing communication process, one needs consistent formats for receiving and communicating information, for example management and contractor check-off and sign-off forms, and guidelines and checklists for design and planning. The idea is to transform both casual feedback and formal meeting notes into a database that can be analyzed and used, for both the existing and future projects.

Folding in New Participants

In small projects the number of players will likely be known from the beginning of the project. In large projects, lasting from six months to several years, natural attrition, promotions, and organizational change will invariably necessitate bringing new people into the project well after it is established. The first thing to do is to spend some time and conscious effort to bring the new people up to speed. Staff who do not share the same philosophical principles, who are uncertain about their role and how it relates to other positions, who are unsure what other team members' strengths and weaknesses are and how their own fit (or don't fit) in cannot be very effective. They need to be exposed to the kind of initial team-building exercises, described earlier, but in an accelerated time frame.

If communication has been multifaceted and broad based, the training should begin by exposing the new person to past newsletters, memos, and videotapes. The second step, which will also be easy if the team has been communicating with one another from the beginning, is to schedule a regular project team meeting in which existing and new team members explore the new members' role expectations, work-style, and so forth. The commitment to doing this is a positive message in itself from the team to its new members that they want them to be effective and are willing to spend some time to make sure it happens.

TRACKING AND MONITORING THE PROJECT

Tracking and monitoring the project are really just another form of communication, but with the information being intended primarily for project team members and senior management. The following need to be considered:

Responsibility for Tracking

Keeping track of information, decisions, and the like and making sense of them is a big job. One person should be responsible for collecting and analyzing information and making sure that it is distributed to the right people in a timely fashion.

Information to Track

Information to track may be expected versus actual progress and costs; type, number, and cost of change orders; information about changes in organization structure, size, style, or work pattern; and new developments in information technology and shifting conditions in unions. This should include information about anticipated change as well as existing conditions. Information is also needed about "how things are going" for different participants. A regular "check-in" procedure with contractors, trades, unions, and management just to see whether there are any problems makes it much easier to solve problems when they are small.

Penalties and Rewards

What are the incentives for participants to complete tasks on time and to provide information needed or requested in a timely fashion? What are the penalties? In a project with a large bank we found that the bank was unwilling to withhold payments to its contractors regardless of their performance. The bank wanted to avoid, at all (and great) costs, public disputes. The contractors knew this, of course, and used it to great advantage. Payment schedules must therefore be tied to specific performance targets and time frames. For example, asking graduate students to fill in time cards, as we have in the past in our own department, and then waiting to tabulate the total number of hours worked during the year until after the students have left for the summer, is a useless exercise if the intent is (as it was) to make sure that all the students are meeting their work obligations.

Formal Progress Reviews

Periodically the project team should review the progress of the project, comparing where the project stands at the moment in terms of cost, schedule, and direction with what was budgeted and anticipated. These reviews are a good time to look at how the project team is working and to check whether policies and procedures put in place earlier are meeting their intended objectives. These periodic reviews also can be a good time to involve outside consultants who are not caught up in the "culture" of the project. They will look with fresh eyes at what is going on and may be able to suggest better ways of doing things. It is important to think about where the project is headed and who needs to be informed about approaching events and activities. Are there sign-off procedures for changes in program, design, and construction documents and a mechanism for communicating changes back to appropriate groups for review? Are the relevant people being informed in what they (as well as the project team) consider a timely fashion?

SOME COMMON PROBLEMS

Based on my experience working with clients and running training workshops, the following common (and avoidable) problems often occur when organizing the project process:

- Insufficient resources (time, access to information, site visits)
- Overreliance on selected sources
- Ambiguous roles and tasks
- Out-of-date information
- Failure to obtain formal approvals at the right time

- Failure of communication within the project team and between the team and its constituents

These kinds of misunderstandings have real costs in time and money, and even greater hidden costs in terms of lowered morale, lack of staff commitment, and holding back of information and ideas. Deliberately designing the project process, from the structure and reporting relationships of the core team to the way it will communicate with both top management and employees, as well as relevant outsiders, will go a long way toward helping avoid these common problems. Such a process also can help the organization learn from its experience in time to help the immediate project become more successful. Finally, it can act as a form of internal and external marketing, at a very low cost and a potentially very high return.

Skeptics Speak

Who is going to run all these group sessions to help the project team work better?

There are usually two choices. One is to bring in staff from the organization's own human resources group. Depending on how internal service costs are charged, this can be a relatively economical way of running such sessions. If these staff members are trained as group facilitators, they can be quite effective. The drawback of using internal people is that team members may feel uncomfortable opening up and talking about strengths and weaknesses in front of an official representative from the human resources staff who, despite assurances of confidentiality, may be suspected of deliberately or inadvertently "leaking" information that may hurt the individual's future performance assessments. If team members express this kind of concern (and I think their views should be solicited), bringing in an outside consultant to lead the groups is a good alternative. Confidentiality is better assured, and with little previous experience with the team members the consultant is less apt to drag along preconceptions based on earlier work experience with the team members. The cost of a consultant for these occasional meetings is an insignificant percentage of the total project costs. In addition, the consultant can be hired with the understanding that part of the task is to enable the team to develop the skills required to take its own pulse regularly without outside assistance.

The idea of spending time helping a team work better together makes sense to me, but what you are proposing sounds like it would take a long time, especially on a major project. That would cost a lot and be hard to justify.

The cost of developing good communication is unlikely to be a significant proportion of a major building project. More importantly, the time and effort devoted to improving communication can be, if organized properly, a basic form of organizational development and an opportunity to market the company to the outside world at very little cost. Helping team members avoid conflict, having them identify goals that can be widely discussed, and so on are invaluable contributions to any organization. Not doing them, however, costs a lot of money. The beauty is that the benefit is gained as part of a process inherent in any normal facility program. In a sense, it is a kind of freebie because it is not targeted as a single-focus training program that pulls people away from their regular jobs to concentrate on organizationwide issues.

Second, several of the forms of communication, often initially targeted for outside groups, like magazine articles or presentations at conferences, can be used to communicate with internal groups at essentially no cost other than that of duplication and distribution. In the same way an internal newsletter can be sent to selected clients and act as a form of marketing, as I noted earlier. The real issue is where the costs of such programs are located. Because they relate to responsibilities of different departments (corporate marketing, administrative services, human resources, education and training), the costs should be shared by these departments. The goal of communication itself raises questions for the organization about the value of boundary maintenance versus collaboration, in both arranging programs and assuming their costs.

You may not like it, but I am one of those people who believe in Pandora's box. I don't think we should be telling the whole world what our strategic plans are or that every employee needs to know exactly why every decision is made. We pay some people to make certain kinds of decisions, and we should let them get on with their jobs.

I am not advocating telling "the whole world" your strategic plan. But I am suggesting that often you have more to gain by communicating realistic rather then false expectations. You may not want to tell employees, for example, that their function is going to be contracted out, but you should consider telling them that the company is thinking of doing this, why it believes this will help the company, and how the company is planning to help those employees who might be affected. If the actions you are taking seem incongruous (not moving a group to a new building that expects to be moved, because it will be contracted out), employees will invent reasons for the action that may be more damaging than the real ones. Staff who remain are also likely to become suspicious and will be skeptical about what is really driving decisions even when they get accurate information.

What kind of information the company decides to share reflects its basic beliefs about the employees' commitment to and trust in the company, as well as its understanding of the kind of information the employees want. You might try sharing some information and asking for responses from a small group to see what happens before creating a general company policy.

Managing the Briefing Process

At some point all organizations need to prepare a design brief. Refurbishment, occupation of new space, and purchase of new furniture and equipment all require that the organization determine what it is trying to accomplish with the design project before it seeks solutions to meet these objectives. Sadly, the truth is that many organizations jump immediately to solutions, following the current fashion of the day, be it raised-access floors, systems furniture, uplighting, or neutral and pastel colors. Or they concentrate on only one or two issues: lowest cost, possibly, or fitting the maximum number of staff into the smallest possible area.

Facilities decisions are made, in effect, in a way that no manager would ever manage the organization's financial resources: blindly investing without a detailed analysis of market trends, past performance history, projections of return on investment, and a thorough understanding of the investment vehicle. When done in facilities, as in purely financial situations, opportunities are missed and the likelihood of getting poor value for money is increased.

Note: I have used the English term *briefing* rather than the American term *programming* for the stage of the design process concerned with identifying occupant requirements because it is less likely to be confused with computer programming and the use of CAD.

Getting value for money in facilities requires getting a good design brief. This means understanding, first, individual and organizational requirements. What, exactly, is to be achieved by the new building, the refurbishment, the reconfiguration of furniture? The goal should be to avoid working nonsolutions.

WORKING NONSOLUTIONS

Working nonsolutions are suboptimal solutions. They are rarely sufficiently inappropriate to make staff quit or seriously ill, nor do they physically prevent the conduct of work. Instead, they are more subtle and insidious. They are solutions that sap productive energies, create tension and conflict, and promote pseudo-efficiency.

Examples of working nonsolutions are storage that cannot be reached without inconveniencing other staff; layouts with limited formal conference space and no provision for informal meetings in organizations whose success depends on frequent communication; furniture density and arrangement that makes conducting any form of telephone conversation difficult; shared storage, equipment, and work surfaces that require staff to wait in line to do their everyday work; seating that causes backache; lighting that causes eye fatigue; color schemes that depress and demoralize; layouts that are costly and disruptive to reconfigure; and heating and ventilation that make people shiver or sleepy. The list can go on and on. Each, in themselves, may have a relatively small negative effect. But in combination and over time their real cost is measured in lost personnel time, energy, and goodwill, the most expensive resources an organization has.

Like a dull saw blade, working nonsolutions are deceptive. Only when a sharp blade is substituted for the dull one does the inefficiency become evident. If you have never worked with a sharp blade, it is hard to understand the difference it can make. While not doing a thorough briefing process is often rationalized in terms of time and budget constraints, the fundamental issue is not time or money per se.

The process should be related to the size of the project and perhaps even more so to whether the process is likely to be recurrent. If it is, then it is easier to justify high development costs for a new approach that, once in place, may actually save time or substantially increase effectiveness over time.

The key to a successful facility design or renovation, whatever its scope, is collecting the right kind of information efficiently and having the imagination to use it creatively to solve problems.

THE DESIGN BRIEF

A good design brief guides the search for design solutions and provides an explicit basis for assessing their suitability. It identifies goals to achieve, problems to eliminate, assets to preserve, and opportunities to seize. Information about the organization and its operating environment; job function and work-style; and space, furniture, and equipment use both now and in the future are the foundation for statements about what the design should achieve. Done well, the design brief benefits the organization by shortening the time spent seeking solutions and reduces the likelihood of expensive mistakes. Even more important, by setting priorities it helps the organization determine where and where not to spend its limited resources.

The Design Brief and Organizational Development

Excellent briefing processes go beyond simply collecting information about user, equipment, or space requirements. They also can act as a form of organizational development. By involving staff in meaningful ways, the briefing process can generate accurate information and strengthen the staff commitment to decisions and the organization. These are issues that senior management understands and appreciates. Viewing the briefing process as a form of organizational development shifts facility planning and design issues from a narrow to a broad focus, from a concern for the physical environment per se to a concern for how the planning and design of facilities can contribute to employees' motivation and commitment, clarification of corporate goals and objectives, analysis of role boundaries and relationships, and rethinking of strategy and tactics. All of these are a form of organizational development that can affect an organization's ability to meet its objectives.

A project by an international team of researchers from Britain, the Netherlands, and Yugoslavia (DIO 1983) underlines some of the organizational benefits of understanding the planning and design process in organizational terms. The planning process can be viewed as involving decisions made at three phases: *identification* (recognition and diagnosis of the problem), *development* (the search for and/or design of solutions), and *selection* (the evaluation of proposed solutions and implementation).

The researchers found that the outcome for the organization varied depending on the phase in which staff and management participated. Participation by rank-and-file workers in the development phase significantly increased the employees' satisfaction with the process and the decision outcomes. Domination by top management in this phase decreased the chance of widespread satisfaction. The greater the participation by lower and middle management and staff groups in the implementation phase, the less efficient the process was. There was no relationship between the method of the decision making and the length of decision-making process, and more comprehensive employee participation did not cause time delays.

The significance of these findings for managing the briefing process is that rank-and-file employees typically have little formal involvement in the briefing process in the development phase, that is, in basic problem identification and diagnosis. They are, therefore, likely to be less satisfied with their participation and the final design than if they are involved from the beginning. This can have enormous financial implications, as illustrated by the Lloyd's of London building designed by the Richard Rogers Partnership.

An independent poll of the occupants of the new Lloyd's building (Becker 1988b) found that 75 percent of the occupants preferred their previous accommodation. An analysis I did of the Lloyd's briefing process (Becker 1988b) suggested that a failure to involve a full range of occupants and staff contributed to the building's current problems. This was not for lack of good intentions; in fact, considerable effort was made to involve staff and users. The problem was knowing precisely how to make the

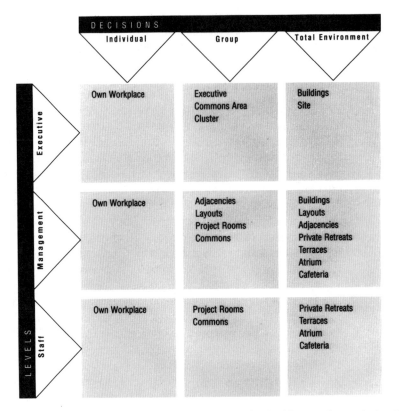

Figure 8-1. A design process matrix that identifies the decisions to be made by different players in the process in relation to different environmental levels. (Source: Steelcase, Inc. 1989)

most effective use of their involvement, especially at different stages of the project. Ameliorating problems with circulation, block planning, some interior finishes and materials, and the location of certain functions is now likely to cost upwards of $50 million, two years after the first occupancy of one of the most expensive buildings in Europe. Not good value for money.

This does not mean that all staff should be involved in all facility decisions, but it does mean that from the outset a clear conceptual structure should identify which decisions different groups in the organization should share.

Figure 8-1 shows a simple matrix that the project team working on the Steelcase Corporation's Corporate Development Center (CDC) developed. It suggests with what kind of decisions different-level employees, from executive to support staff, should be involved at different environmental scales, ranging from the workstation and the building to the site as a whole. The way in which one fills out such a matrix will depend on such things as the specific project, the organization's corporate culture, and the skill and knowledge of staff and employees.

This matrix reflected our recommendation that all employees be given the opportunity to influence some aspects of their physical surroundings, but that not every employee be involved in every kind of decision. Some are best left to technical experts (see Chapter 11, "Managing Space"), and some are the responsibility of management. (It is worth noting that the decisions that most American organizations would consider solidly within senior management's prerogative, such as decisions about site location, in countries like Sweden are strongly influenced by employee work councils. National culture as well as the more idiosyncratic organizational culture must be considered.)

Such decision matrices serve several purposes. First, they help separate strategic from tactical or operational decisions. Clearly, senior management should be more involved in broader, more strategic issues (e.g., should we have a new building, what form should it take, where should it be located, where does it fit into overall corporate strategy?) than in details about workstation design, furniture selection, colors, and finishes. Second, this kind of decision matrix helps set realistic expectations that give employees a sense of what kinds of decisions they will and will not be able to influence (Chapter 11 discusses in more detail some of the ways in which employees can be involved in the planning and design process). It also helps remind senior management what kinds of decisions they should not be making.

DESIGN PROCESS OVERVIEW

Once the project team has been selected and organized (see Chapter 7), they need to think about the briefing process itself, which is one step or phase in the overall design process. The following are characteristics of the design process that they should keep in mind:

Dynamic and Iterative

Even though the design process has stages and phases, from briefing to design development, selection of design, design implementation, and postoccupancy evaluation, the boundaries between them often overlap. The process involves constant input, development, review, revise, review, and approve cycles. To the frustration of many facility managers and designers, the project's goals and objectives shift as the project evolves. Few organizations stay frozen in time. Managers come and go, reorganizations occur, new technologies are introduced, and markers shift.

For large, long-term projects the only predictable thing is that what seemed as solid as rock at the beginning of a project often has the consistency of marshmallow by its end. The only way to cope with changing requirements is to collect information continuously so that decisions are not based on outdated information, to plan for contingencies from the beginning, and to plan in broad brush strokes rather than in fine detail until the last minute possible (see Chapter 11).

Phases and Stages

Each step or phase has many subtasks that need to be identified and planned. Implications for employees, management, maintenance, facility management, MIS, human resources, and the like must be considered, even for seemingly small decisions. This is one reason it is helpful to have a core project team that spans different expertise. Decisions should be reviewed at each phase. It is useful to keep track of the basis for decisions, not only to explain those that may not seem so wise six months or a year after the project is completed, but also so that there is a project history that can be studied, and learned from, for the next project.

Variety of Expertise

In general, decisions are sufficiently complex today to make it impossible for a generalist to have the knowledge and experience needed to make good decisions about all aspects of facility planning and design, even in subareas such as architecture, engineering, or telecommunications. To get the right information and to make good choices, many types of experts will be needed at different stages in the design process. Such experts include architects and interior designers, mechanical engineers, computer specialists, lighting and acoustic designers, human factors specialists, organizational ecologists, facility managers, and maintenance staff. For specialized tasks such as contracts, lawyers with special expertise in real estate or furniture or other facility-related areas should be consulted.

When hiring or selecting consultants, it is advisable to ask about their particular experience and exactly how they approach different tasks (not simply whether they will consider certain issues or have had certain experience). Experts in architecture and space planning, engineering, maintenance, organizational ecology, human factors, lighting, and acoustics should contribute to the design criteria and the review of decisions early in the decision process.

Managing the Change Process

Employees often are anxious about environmental change (our research also shows that employees can cope with office relocations and change without missing a beat, if they perceive the changes as enhancing their personal and professional identity and ability to work effectively, see Chapter 9, "Managing Environmental Change"). Typically, the environmental change effort concentrates on managing the physical move; the logistics of helping people pack their office contents and making sure these arrive at their intended destination on time; and scheduling movers, goods elevators, and telecommunications, and computer staff so that everything is in place and running when people arrive for work on Monday morning. This kind of logistical problem solving is fundamental to any successful move, but it should not be mistaken for the total move program.

To the extent they exist at all, programs for helping employees adjust to the change often are scheduled at the end of the design and construction process, just before moving. By this time, rumors, anxiety, and resentment may be rampant. It is thus more effective to view (and plan) the entire design process as part of the overall effort to reduce employees' anxiety and organizational disruption (see Chapter 9). Their involvement in the briefing process is, therefore, one facet of preparing them for the move. In general, the more information about the move that employees have, the better able they will be to prepare for it. The information should be realistic; that is, it should cover a full range of changes and their implications, not only those that management considers the most positive (see Chapter 9 for a fuller discussion of this issue).

After the Move

In many ways what happens immediately after the move is as important as what happens before. No matter how well the move is planned, little things still will not be installed or work perfectly. Therefore, it is useful to create a way to identify the glitches in the new facility and get them resolved quickly (or explaining to users why they cannot be and what will be done about it and when). This is one reason it is helpful to involve building maintenance and facility management from the beginning of the process and not only after occupancy.

STRUCTURING THE BRIEFING PROCESS

Several of the considerations mentioned in Chapter 7 for organizing the project are relevant to structuring the briefing process.

Top Management Support

The project team should make sure that top management understands and agrees with the basic briefing approach and the design requirements. Top management should establish and maintain strategic direction of the project, but should not get involved in day-to-day operational decisions. From a senior management perspective, the main concern should be how the decisions being made help the organization achieve its stated strategic goals. Management needs to know the implications of alternatives in regard to time, cost, personnel, flexibility, image, and so forth.

Clear Roles, Authority, Responsibility, and Accountability

To avoid wasted time, energy, and frustration, the project team responsible for organizing the briefing process needs to identify the classes of decisions to be made by different individuals and groups. The team should not second-guess delegated authority or tolerate second-guessing of its own legitimate decisions. It should have a good sense of what it needs to do a good job and then request the resources (time, money, expertise) needed to fulfill the team's responsibilities. If it is denied these resources, its responsibility is to inform management of the likely consequences. It should want to be held accountable; that is, to measure the extent to which it has achieved its goals in light of the resources and authority at its disposal.

Clear Philosophy

The project team should have a "big picture" view of the overall project and process. The team needs to think about the implications of its philosophy; for example, "doing it right the first time" may delay the project to make it better; it may require unexpected resources; or it may suggest the need to restructure role relationships or typical work patterns. Senior management must understand these kinds of organizational implications if their support of the "big picture" approach is not to be empty rhetoric.

Calculated and Controlled Risk Taking

Good projects often break the mold. The project team needs to be willing to take risks, but it should help others understand the benefits of risk in relation to agreed-upon project goals. Top management must buy into risk with the project team. Regular reviews and sign-offs in which the organizational implications of different choices are presented (e.g., the effect of a cutback of amenities on the ability to attract and retain staff, the impact of fewer common areas on informal communication processes, the increased response time and lowered cost and disruption if access floors are installed) are one way of doing this.

Tracking and Monitoring

The team should keep track of decisions made and stress the importance of identifying the effects of changes on other actions, players, and decisions. Team members should also identify the kinds of information they need to make good decisions (in a timely manner) and to sell the decisions to management and users after developing a clear view of the overall process and how stages and pieces fit together. Finally, they should anticipate consequences by team brainstorming, contact with others with similar experience and special expertise, and ongoing contact with a wide range of users and others involved in the process.

Procedures

Checklists and procedural guides help users and others provide programming information to review program materials, proposed designs, working drawings, and the like. Too often the project team assumes that representatives of occupancy groups or their managers know how to effectively solicit feedback from their staff or to explain proposed plans. But they often do not. Some simple tools, which may be no more sophisticated than a checklist of questions that should be asked of staff, can ensure better feedback and therefore better-informed decisions.

Involvement of Employees

Employees at all levels in should be involved in the project in some way, by completing surveys and participating in interviews, helping identify design requirements, and reviewing preliminary design proposals and policies for allocating and using space.

Time and Resources

The organization must make available the time and resources that employees need to make informed decisions and judgments. It is unfair and a waste of time and goodwill to create committees or focus groups and then not give the participants access to the resources necessary to do a good job. Such resources may include access to informed experts such as consultants, site visits to broaden one's experience and image bank of alternatives, and time to do one's homework.

Timely Involvement

Employee, consultant, and staff involvement should be timely, as the greatest gains are likely to be realized when people are involved at the beginning rather than the end of the process.

DATA COLLECTION OVERVIEW

Guiding the search for and evaluation of design solutions requires information about the organization; the operating environment; job functions and workstyles; space, furniture, and equipment; and building systems and equipment. Information about the number and type of employees, adjacencies, and existing space, furniture, and equipment standards—the typical approach to design programming—is necessary but not sufficient, not even in conjunction with information about mechanical systems, electrical power, HVAC, and information technology. Information should be collected about individuals, groups, and departments and their current and projected interaction, current and expected technical requirements, professional identifies and work-styles, and implicit goals and values. Good design is based on what works well (and should be preserved) and what needs to be improved (and should be changed). This means understanding the overall operating environment and organizational culture and identifying factors that constrain design options as well as those that might stimulate change and innovation.

This information must be collected for the current situation and for at least three to five years in the future. In general, a sensible approach is to opt for being approximately right rather than precisely wrong. In other words, there is little benefit from spending enormous efforts to be extremely precise about figures that can only be approximations. But for space-forecasting purposes, in particular, approximations can be useful in setting basic boundaries and identifying the magnitude of a problem (see Figure 8-2). Things change, and the lesson to be learned is not to abandon any efforts to understand future directions but to keep monitoring and updating one's information and the planning based on it.

When collecting data, the following points should be considered:

Use Multiple Methods

There is no single "best" data collection method. All have benefits and drawbacks. Every method can be done in an elaborated or large-scale fashion or quite simply, while still retaining the basic characteristics of the approach. How elaborate the method is depends on the time frame, budget, complexity of the problem, and the amount of familiarity or existing knowledge. Even the smallest briefing processes can, and should,

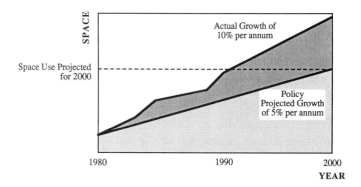

Figure 8-2. An example of a computer-generated graphic space forecast report.

use multiple methods. This may mean interviewing twenty people rather than two hundred or distributing a single-page machine-readable survey rather than a detailed ten-page questionnaire, running two focus groups rather than ten, or conducting observations over one rather than ten days. The overall picture of the organization's and its departments' and employees' requirements is likely to be more accurate and better understood using a range of these techniques, on any scale, rather than concentrating on a single technique used extensively.

Rank Requirements

Design means trade-offs. The goal is to make decisions that help achieve important design requirements. To do this, the project team needs to assign priorities to different organizational and occupant requirements to reduce the likelihood of achieving minor goals at the expense of major ones. Getting the colors right, for example, is a good idea, but research consistently shows that getting the HVAC, lighting, and seating right is more important to employees.

Requirements can be ranked by occupant groups, experts, and the project team, as part of focus groups or surveys. Setting priorities always involves someone's judgment, but the process can be systematic and quantitative (and still simple).

Separate Programming and Design

Designers should develop design solutions (and evaluate them) against a set of design requirements that define what the design is to accomplish. A design briefing, or collecting and analyzing information as a basis for establishing design requirements, feeds into the creative design process. Those who design should not be the same persons who are responsible for drawing up the program and using it to evaluate the appropriateness of design solutions. The potential for a conflict of interest is simply too high. Involving the designers in the briefing process does make sense, because they then will have a much better idea of how the information and design requirements were derived. Design requirements act as a kind of checks-and-balances system between designer and client intended to assure the client that their requirements are being met.

Thus an independent person or group whose role is to defend the design requirements and to determine how well proposed design solutions meet them is essential. By following the rugby team model (see Chapter 12), in which all players are present from the beginning of the process but the leadership roles vary with the different project stages, designers can help the project team understand possibilities that might not otherwise be considered.

Input and Review

Typically, users below the upper- to middle-management level participate very little in the design process. At most, they may be asked about their current work needs, often in surveys of narrowly defined functional needs at the workstation (e.g., amount of work surface or storage). Such users rarely have the opportunity to review how this information has been analyzed and interpreted and even less often to comment on how it has been translated into physical design solutions. Yet involving employees in this way helps build their trust and confidence in the process, as well as helping avoid obvious mistakes.

Dynamic and Collaborative Process

Organizations' goals, priorities, and constraints will change over the course of the project, and so mechanisms to anticipate such changes must be embedded in the process. The tendency is to blame the occupant groups for any changes or just to ignore them. In a review of the process used to renovate a major computer operations center for a bank, my colleagues found the architects chagrined to learn that their plan for accommodating information technology eighteen months before occupancy was made obsolete by new patterns of office automation. The problem was with the process, not that the bank refused to flash-freeze its computer applications at a given point in time. The project team thus must regularly communicate with informants and structure the planning process to reflect the totally predictable fact that during a long-term building project there will be changes. The old model of the briefing process as a discrete (and terminal) step before design development is simply obsolete today.

Variety of Media

Photographs, computer simulations, models, mock-ups, site visits, and axonometric drawings all are more effective, especially for communicating with occupants, than are working drawings or detailed plans. Most nondesigners do not understand floor plans or technical specifications, nor should they be expected to.

KIND OF INFORMATION NEEDED

This section looks at the kinds of information needed about the organization, the operating environment, job functions and work-styles, and the physical environment. In

Table 8-1. Information Needed in the Briefing Process

About the Organization	About the Operating Environment
• Goals and objectives • Plan • Constraints • Corporate culture • Organizational structure • Number and type of staff	• Business conditions • Law and codes • New technologies • Labor force patterns • Competitors' actions and plans
About Job Function and Work-style	About the Physical Environment
• Task analysis • Environmental satisfaction • Communication patterns • Adjacency requirements	• As-built plans • Space standards • Furniture and equipment inventory • IT take-up rate • Space, furniture and equipment • Amount, type and variety of IT • Replacement schedules • Demand for power • Amount of IT networking • Transportation and parking • Surrounding amenities

all cases, information should be collected about the current situation and about what various players in the process can best guess about how things will look in the future (see Table 8-1).

Goals and Objectives

What are the organization's strategic goals? This kind of information can be learned in part from annual reports, but more accurate and realistic are likely to be corporate strategic reports and business plans and interviews with influential senior managers.

Managers will not divulge this kind of information unless they know exactly why it is needed and also are confident that in doing so their trust will not be abused. There are no shortcuts to building trust. It takes time and is based on track records. A starting point is to take the time to explain why the facilities group, involved in a building project, needs to know about confidential business plans. For many business unit managers, this seems at first like an oxymoron, like the food service people wanting to know about how money market funds are performing.

Plans

What initiatives are already in place or about to start? Why waste time looking for better facilities for a group that top management decided to spin off six months earlier? The project team needs to be kept apprised of plans regarding such business objectives so that they can see whether their facility plans mesh with these and also determine whether they need to collect different or additional information to answer questions that arise as these plans are implemented. For example, will the marketing group's ways of working be accommodated in a building that was originally planned for data analysts? What are their special requirements, and how do they compare with the data analysts'?

Constraints and Givens

What are the fixed and controllable constraints (see Chapter 7), and are these expected to change (or could they be changed)? Will all the old furniture be reused? Will there be open planning? How many people will be allowed to occupy the building? Is the project time frame fixed in stone? Can a code height restriction be changed? Answers to these kinds of questions can help in allocating scarce resources (the time and money to collect information) by targeting the data collection effort to those areas that are most open to influence and are under the control of the organization itself.

Corporate Culture

Understanding the corporate culture is critical to an effective briefing process. Goals and philosophy proclaimed in annual reports, posters, and other corporate communication programs can be like frosting on a cake: beautiful to behold but difficult to swallow. The corporate culture is, instead, better reflected in the daily actions and activities of management and staff: how people interact formally with one another and management, how they dress, their use of time and space, the ways in which decisions are made, who makes what kinds of decisions, and the kind of information or evidence considered in decision making.

Asking different staff and managers to describe what the company considers a "good" manager or staff person, "persuasive evidence" or an "effective" presentation is a simple way to elicit lots of information about "the right way to do things around here." Observing how and where people interact, how presentations are made, how people are introduced to one another, how space and time are used, and so on provides invaluable clues to the validity of the interview data. It also can stimulate questions to ask: "Why is it done that way?" "Why couldn't it be done this way?" "What would happen if . . . ?"

Understanding the corporate culture also helps structure the type of information to collect (interview data and anecdotes may be useful in one company, whereas quantitative survey data may be considered good evidence in another), as well as helping identify the best people to whom to present the findings and the best way to do it. If decisions are made by a group, why waste time presenting the information to a single individual (unless the objective is to test the idea with a "friend of the court" before making the "official" presentation)?

Organizational Structure

Organizational structure influences adjacencies and determines, at least formally, reporting relationships and decision hierarchies. The project team needs to know how decisions are made formally and whether the existing organizational structure is likely to remain stable or change. This kind of information can determine from whom you collect information and about what. If, for example, two departments are to be merged, it will be useful to know how the new manager views the situation, as his or her views will drive the facility decisions.

Staff and Space

Headcount projections for a five-year period and and their relation to space requirements are probably the most basic information collected in any briefing process. But the issue is not just how many people, but also what kind of people: What kind of work do they do, and what are their expectations, their work-styles, and their communication patterns? Are they professionals for whom demand exceeds supply (and therefore have a strong bargaining position)? Are they the same kinds of people who have been hired in the past, or are they different: better educated, more professional, from different racial or ethnic backgrounds that may affect their work-styles and expectations or even their ergonomic requirements?

Information Needed for the Operating Environment

Business Conditions

What are market forces like? Where is the competition coming from now and likely to come from in the future? Is money tight or easily available? Answers to these kinds of questions affect the organization's attitude towards the nature, amount, and quality of space it needs. If more international firms will be competing in the same city, for example, then information about these firm's facilities should be obtained. Apple Computer consciously designs its facilities in Asia to a higher standard than is customary there as a way of differentiating itself from its competitors and attracting better-qualified staff. Office standards in London have improved dramatically in large part because of the influx of large American financial companies who imported higher American office standards. All these have raised expectations among the work force about what constitutes an acceptable working environment.

Law and Regulations

What are the tax laws, and how will they affect building form, or the decision to renovate an old building or build a new one? In the United States, one of the driving forces behind the success of systems furniture and open planning was the tax code, which treated panels as furniture, thereby allowing it to be depreciated at a much faster rate than conventional drywall construction. The provision of plazas (in name if not in ambience) in New York City is directly related to variances in height restriction if such amenities are provided at street level.

New Technologies

From computers to automated building systems, information must be collected about the nature, extent, and use patterns of existing information technology, as well as expectations about how it may change in the future. Union Carbide's headquarters building in Danbury, Connecticut, for example, was wired with fiber optic cable long before it could actually be used, based on the much lower cost of installing it during the original construction. Everything from workstation size to the size and location of electrical closets and rises and wire management systems will be affected by expectations regarding technology. For many organizations today the best approach is hedging the bet: putting in more than less. At the least, the decisions should be deliberate, based on the best information available and without believing that it comes with a guarantee.

Labor Force Patterns

Labor force patterns can now be predicted with some accuracy. There will be more women, dual-wage earners, older workers, and Spanish-speaking employees. Workers' expectations are rising with respect not only to pay but also to air quality, comfort and safety, time and spatial freedom, and the extent to which the environment supports their sense of personal and professional identity, their human dignity, and their sense of competence. These are not trivial issues in areas and industries in which the demand for well-educated, professional employees exceeds their supply.

Given demographic trends that show that there will be fewer qualified workers over the next two to three decades, understanding how shifts in the work force affect facilities decisions is essential. Information about these work force patterns have direct and immediate effects on both design requirements and design solutions (e.g., dual–wage earner families put increased pressures on transportation systems, day care, and access to shops and services; more women employees working at all times of the day and night increase demands for safety and security both inside and surrounding the workplace; age shifts in the work force lead to more concerns about health, fitness, and lighting and air temperature and quality).

Competitors' Actions, Plans, and Experience

Near London, the headquarters of a major manufacturing company—for over fifteen years considered the most prestigious building in the area—lost its luster (and its employees' sense of pride and accomplishment) when another firm built a handsome new headquarters building close by. We all measure our own situation by comparing it with others' situations, and so competitors' facilities can become a benchmark against which employees set their own expectations. The project team can also learn from its competitors' experience: How did they handle space planning or churn, and how did it work? What have been the benefits and drawbacks of a new automated building system?

Information Needed for Job Functions and Work-styles

Task Analysis

What exactly do different employees do? How do they work? Both written job descriptions and interviews are useful for understanding what different people actually do and how they relate to different jobs and parts of the organization.

Environmental Satisfaction

How satisfied are staff with their current environment, and how do they believe it affects their ability to work effectively and productively? Just because they have survived in their current surroundings should not imply that their current situation is satisfactory or should be continued. Interviews are effective for discovering how employees see their work environment affecting their performance. Surveys are an easy, cost-effective method for quickly obtaining large amounts of quantitative information. These data can be analyzed by department, discipline, age of worker, previous job experience, and sex of worker to find out how widespread opinions are and to target areas with special problems.

Communication Patterns

Who communicates, where, when, and how often now? Is that considered acceptable? Desirable? What are some of the problems within or among departments? Before changing the environment to support a new communication pattern, it is useful to see whether the problem is perceived or real and to distinguish among different types of communication (see Chapter 11).

Adjacency Requirements

Related to communication, adjacency requirements range from seating location and even orientation of workers within a team or group area to the relation of departments, buildings, and whole sites to one another. Most of the computerized adjacency software packages are based on the premise that people who have strong organizational relationships should be physically close to one another. It is more important, however, to know who should be communicating and who is likely to communicate. Then adjacencies can be designed to support groups that should communicate but, without close proximity, are unlikely to do so. In other words, spatial bonds can be used to overcome organizational barriers (see Chapter 11 for a "functional inefficiency" view of adjacencies).

Space, Furniture, and Equipment Requirements

How do people work, what equipment do they use, and how do they use it (in what way, sequence, combination with other equipment, other materials and resources, alone, together, etc.)? What kinds of furniture and equipment do they believe reflect their personal and professional identity or job status? Functional analyses rooted in ergonomics and human factors are important, but function goes beyond lumbar support, glare, and keyboard height and should include desired images of a functional and effective workstation.

Information Needed for the Physical Environment (Internal)

Information must be collected that describes clearly both "what is" and what is anticipated (in whatever degree of precision makes sense). Many organizations have no accurate report of the type or amount of equipment they have or its special environmental requirements. Many have not thought through what kind of electronic networking they want or expect and in what time frame. Although the accuracy of such information is often questionable, simply seeking it forces organizational players to share their (possibly conflicting) visions of the future. It is impossible to plan realistically or effectively without such information.

An inventory should be made of existing furniture, equipment, and support spaces like cafeterias and break areas, libraries, conference rooms, computer center, and project rooms that determines their condition, location, availability, ability to support technology, and flexibility and adaptability. The principal questions are what is available (or will be by the time it is needed) and whether what is available is suitable for its intended purposes (now or in the foreseeable future). This information is invaluable for determining whether new furniture or equipment will be needed, whether what exists can be used "as is," and what might be usable if it were refurbished or renovated.

Information Needed for the Physical Environment (External)

Information about the external physical environment will determine what services and amenities are provided on site and at what level. Again, it is important to understand how a site or neighborhood will be changing, and it also is important not to base amenities, such as dining or parking, on comparable services that will eventually be available. Knowing that something will be available can, however, justify a smaller investment and modest plans during the interim period.

Summary of Information Needed

Collecting and making sense of all these data can be a frightening prospect, so much so that it resembles the old tooth care and auto safety programs that tried to scare people into better health and safety practices but failed because the pictures shown were so horrific that people repressed the whole program. But remember: The objective is not to collect every conceivable bit of information but to collect as little as is needed to make an informed decision (a key principle of the elastic organization). For every piece of information collected, the project team should know in advance how it expects that information to be used in the design and decision process. If no reasons can be stated, then the data should not be collected.

METHODS FOR COLLECTING AND ANALYZING DATA

The following are some of the advantages and disadvantages of different data collection techniques. Detailed descriptions of these are beyond the scope of this book but can be found in a variety of other sources (Sommer and Sommer, 1980; Zeisel 1981). In general, a wide range of users and experts should be involved, but in different ways.

When the project team wants a representative viewpoint (generally a good idea) across user groups or types of employees, some form of random selection (e.g., every third person throughout the building) is appropriate. If it wants to gain insight into a particular problem or to explore future developments, then using informants who are known to be especially knowledgeable or experienced in a specific area makes sense. For committees and focus groups the project team can ask managers to select representatives to act as liaisons between the department or group and the project team. If the group affected is sufficiently small (fewer than thirty-five), then the whole group might be consulted.

Interviews and Focus Groups: Pros and Cons

Good for:

- Probing responses
- Following new directions
- Engendering goodwill
- Understanding complex relationships

Not good for:

- Developing quantitative data
- Quickly tapping a broad sample of employees

Interviews and their cousin, the focus group, provide a "gut feeling" about what people are thinking, feeling, and concerned, excited, or skeptical about. They are a good way of collecting anecdotes, which can be a persuasive source of evidence in some organizations. Because of their "hands-on," face-to-face character, interviews also tend to be highly visible and liked by employees.

Especially when employees are skeptical about whether management or the project team really cares, interviews are a better medium than surveys are, which by definition are remote and impersonal. What I call "pulse-taking" interviews, three-to-ten-minute random discussions with staff conducted in their own workplace, are especially effective in getting a sense of a place and generating goodwill.

The interview's greatest drawback is that it is time-consuming (in terms of the number of people who can be reached in a given period of time) and expensive (in terms of the time needed to conduct a large number of interviews). And although it is possible to obtain quantitative data from interviews, it is more difficult than from surveys. The focus group, in which five to ten people are brought together to respond to a specific proposal, and group interviews, which may be more wide-ranging, are a quick way of eliciting responses from many people. In efficiency, both fall somewhere between individual interviews and the survey. The group interview's main drawback is that one or two people can dominate the discussion, and if there are strong status differences among the participants, lower-level staff may choose to remain silent or mute their responses. The main benefit is that a range of opinions and views quickly becomes apparent, and group members may help stimulate one another, leading to new insights.

In conducting an interview, remember to:

- allow time for someone to answer; do not rush the respondent
- explain the purpose of the interview and who will see the results
- find a comfortable location with reasonable privacy
- explain how long the interview will be
- watch for confusion and repeat explanations if necessary
- write down key words and phrases; elaborate right after the interview ends
- probe answers; ask for more explanation
- do not "suggest" the right answer; do not become defensive

Done properly, the interview is enormously versatile and becomes even more powerful when combined with survey methods.

Surveys

Good for:

- Generating quantitative data
- Quickly tapping a broad cross section of employees
- Enabling a statistical analysis of subgroups
- Obtaining data cost-effectively

Not good for:

- Probing responses
- Understanding complex nonstatistical relationships
- Generating goodwill and confidence in the process

The surveys' strength is the interview's weakness, which is why a combination of the two is so useful. In organizations that value quantitative analysis or whose top management is skeptical of interviews as a technique, surveys, with their charts, tables, and graphs (numbers!) can be a more persuasive form of data analysis and presentation than interviews. The interview's contribution, used in conjunction with a survey, is the anecdotes that bring to life the numbers and charts, giving them a human face that helps fix in memory a particular point that may slip away if presented only in a chart or table.

Structured Observation

Good for:

- Raising questions to include in surveys and interviews
- Checking information given in surveys and interviews
- Generating visual evidence to support interviews and surveys
- (If systematic) Generating quantitative data
- Getting at issues that employees have difficulty verbalizing

Not good for:

- Understanding why something is occurring
- Getting at what "could be"
- Generating goodwill (unless coupled with interviews)
- (If short term) Getting a representative view of the situation

Structured observation can take many forms. One systematic and quantitative technique is called *behavioral mapping,* which uses predetermined codes to indicate where and when certain behaviors occur in a setting. Mapped over several times of day and several days or months, such behavior records build a picture of which areas within a building are being used by what kinds of people, in what ways, and at what times. This information can then be analyzed to identify the physical characteristics associated with different use patterns (e.g., lounges at the ends of corridors tend to be used less than do those near major circulation paths and activity nodes like mail rooms and coffee areas).

Less structured and quantitative, but quicker and still useful, are focused observations in which someone (ideally, two people who then can share their observations and check their interpretations) walks around a facility and observes certain behaviors and their residue: jury-rigged storage, lights brought in from home. Things to observe, each of which offers clues to environmental dysfunctions and actual (as opposed to expected or desired) behavior, include attempts to solve problems, typical and atypical uses, and inventive ways of using standard furniture or equipment.

In addition to noting observations on a recording sheet, under predetermined categories, a photo record of these findings is helpful for representations and for team meetings in which this "hard" evidence can be shared with people who were not present on the observation tour. Again, the value of such data can be enhanced by combining them with information from interviews and surveys, in order to explain why certain things are occurring, how these affect how people work, and so on.

Simulation

Good for:

- Exploring "what if" possibilities
- Eliciting responses to new designs or plans

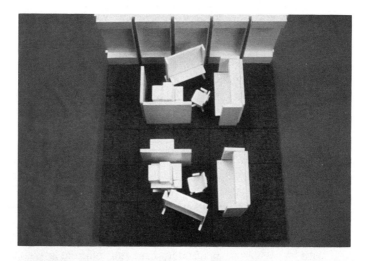

Figure 8-3. Different forms of simulation, ranging from abstract and detailed models to full-scale mock-ups, can be used to elicit feedback about proposed facility designs.

- Removing skepticism that something will happen
- Avoiding very costly mistakes
- Stimulating the imagination
- Generating enthusiasm and excitement

Not good for:

- Getting a completely realistic response

Simulations take many forms, including photographs, models, drawings, full-scale mock-ups, computer drawings, games, and video animation (see Figure 8-3). They are good for getting a sense of how people who are unfamiliar with a particular design or furniture arrangement might actually respond to it. Although some work is being done to make simulations more realistic, by adding sound, movement, three-dimensionality, and even smell to the experience and by increasing the detail in the simulation (especially in computer simulations), simulations are always just that: a representation of reality, but not the reality itself. The amount of time and the circumstances under which the stimulated environment is experienced inevitably fall short of the "real thing."

Yet by having intact work groups visit a full-scale mock-up of a work area equipped with different furniture systems, lighting, and seating and a working computer system, quite realistic feedback can be gained. The Sheraton Suite Hotels, for example, used a full-scale mock-up of a room to determine what size room, color scheme, and type of furnishings customers would like best. The point is that despite the limitations inherent in any form of simulation, the feedback is far superior to blind guessing about how people will respond.

Simulations also do not have to be enormously expensive. Simple working models with few details can be used for exploring different layout issues, and with computerized simulations different workstation or building layouts can be generated quickly and easily. The cost of simulation should be considered in relation to the cost of making a major mistake: Buying a million dollars of furniture that turns out not to accommodate technology or to meet employees' expectations or is much harder to assemble and disassemble than expected can make a fifty-thousand-dollar mock-up study (which identifies the dysfunction before the design is implemented), look like a very good value for the money. In this context the cost of even full scale mock-ups are by no means unrealistic.

Archival Records

Good for:

- Nonreactive information
- Inexpensive data collection
- A check on other sources of information

Not good for:

- An understanding of the dynamics of a situation
- An understanding of why something is happening
- A detailed look at an issue
- An accurate interpretation of data

The final technique of data collection is archival records, which have been collected by the organization as part of its ongoing record keeping. Records of exit interviews of people who have decided to leave the organization (did the facility in any way contribute to their decision to leave?) or of job recruitment interviews (did the facility influence their decision to accept the job?), medical and insurance records (complaints, visits to the doctor, prescription medicines), absenteeism, and turnover all are sources of data that facility managers almost never use well. Such data can be related to parts of the building (does an area with old, large-zone HVAC have more medical complaints or higher level of absenteeism?) and to planning processes (do projects in which employees are more involved have fewer change orders and higher levels of satisfaction with the workplace?).

ANALYZING DATA

Real skill comes in collecting as few data as are needed and in analyzing them as much as possible. Unfortunately, the reverse is often the practice. Collecting data is easy (although collecting accurate and valid information is more difficult). Analyzing information and and interpreting its implications for facility decisions often feel more like art than science. But they are skills that can be learned.

Simply counting instances of a given response can be very enlightening. How many staff reported (in interviews or a survey) air quality or lighting as poor? A more fine-grained analysis takes into account mediating factors. For example, do women, or older workers, or people who have come from another site report more or fewer problems than do men, younger workers, or people who have always worked in the same building?

In samples of up to a few hundred, if the responses are very simple (a checked box on a survey, for example), this kind of analysis can be done by hand very quickly. Many simple computer statistical packages are now available that are also very easy to learn and use. These are useful for larger samples, particularly if the project team wants to do more sophisticated statistical analyses. In either case, quantitative analyses can be done quickly, accurately, and cheaply—and often with impressive results in the form of computer-generated graphs and charts.

When interpreting results, whether from interviews, surveys, observations, or archival data, try to do the following:

Look for patterns of agreement

- across data sources
- by mediating variables
- with literature
- with experience

Look for contradictions

- across data sources
- by mediating variables
- with literature
- with experience

Try to resolve contradictions

- through alternative plausible explanations for a finding
- by reexamining the data
- by collecting specific data to test alternative hypotheses

Identify the most important findings

• by ranking and organizing them

Present the findings simply through

• charts and tables
• selected photos or videos that illustrate an important point

GENERATING DESIGN REQUIREMENTS

In my experience very few organizations, regardless of what kind or how much information has been collected or analyzed, write a proper design brief, that is, one that states, in order of their priority, what the proposed design is expected to achieve, what problems should be eliminated, and what the constraints are. In part, most organizations do not do this because there inevitably is not enough information to describe precisely such issues as how to achieve privacy or support different types of communication. But if the needed information has been collected and analyzed, it is possible to generate reasonable design requirements that can be used both to guide the search for solutions and to evaluate preliminary design proposals.

What does a design requirement look like? Here are some examples.

Privacy: Management offices and conference rooms should enable full conversational privacy; that is, conversations at a normal sound level should not be able to be discerned by someone in an adjacent office or passing by the office.

Lighting: General office ambient lighting should not create reflections on VDU screens.

Informal communication: Selection and placement of circulation, stairs, activity generators (e.g., coffee, copy, mail) should maximize the potential for unexpected face-to-face contact in which spontaneous conversations can occur without visually or auditorily disturbing people in their workstations or offices.

First, these specifications do not specify how privacy, lighting, or informal communication is to be achieved. They do not say to use a six-foot-high panel or uplighting or to create small lounge areas. The design solution should reflect the designer's creativity and inventiveness, based on experience and available information (while meeting the full range of design criteria). Second, they are not technical (though dB sound ratings could be specified, based on existing research and standards). Rather, the intent is to state what is to be achieved, in terms that designers, the project team, and users can understand. Third, the requirements are specific enough to enable them to be used to compare two alternative design proposals (open plan offices with five-foot-high acoustic panels and a sound-masking system versus a fully enclosed office with insulated drywall construction). Fourth, the likelihood that these requirements would be achieved by using different design alternatives should be reviewed by an acoustical or human factors expert and someone like an environmental psychologist who understands the design's social, psychological, and organizational implications. This kind of consultation acts as a "second opinion" to internal experts and experience, and it is likely to be grounded in a deeper understanding of available research as well as more experience with how similar problems have been addressed in other organizations.

Organized into a single briefing document, the design brief gives the organization, architects, designers, and project managers a constant reference point for keeping the project's goals in focus. It also helps guide the development, evaluation, and eventually the selection of a design that is likely to meet the organization's needs, not only at the moment, but over at least the next three to five years.

THINGS TO CONSIDER

The following are common issues that should be considered in various stages of the briefing process. They are intended as a easy-to-use checklist of things to think about when organizing and implementing the briefing process.

Data collection

- Has a single data collection instrument (e.g., survey or interview) been used?
- Are the informants not representative?
- Have too many data been collected (unable to analyze or use all of them)?
- Has there been a pilot test of data collection procedures and tools?
- Have responses been recorded accurately?
- Has the focus been on only a limited set of issues or problems?

Data analysis

- Have all the time and resources been spent on collecting data?
- Has the focus been on data that confirm biases?
- Have inferences been drawn from the data?
- Have overly complex techniques been used?
- Have multiple data sources been used together?
- Have patterns been sought (through a focus on elements and parts of the whole)?
- Have priorities been sought and assessed?

Design requirements

- Have selected data been used?
- Have the requirements been derived from experience or opinions, not data?
- Are the requirements not comprehensive enough?
- Are the requirements too general and so cannot be used to select from alternatives?
- Has the solution rather than what should be achieved been stated?
- Have data been used to set priorities and to identify trade-offs?

Generation and evaluation of solutions

- Have requirements or the brief been ignored?
- Has the focus been on certain requirements (and not others)?
- Has theory or research been used?
- Have the requirements been judged by how well they achieved the proposed design?

- Have alternatives been compared systematically?
- Have established priorities been used to guide the design?

BENEFITS OF STAFF INVOLVEMENT

Throughout this chapter, a recurrent theme has been the importance of involving end users directly, both to provide information to guide the design requirements and to review how preliminary design proposals meet these requirements. The reason for this emphasis is simple: How the employees' involvement in the briefing process is resolved will influence the amount and quality of the information collected, which will influence the nature and quality of the solutions proposed and accepted, which will help determine the employees' satisfaction with the process, which will color their view of the final outcome.

The management of the briefing process is a *metamessage*. Conceived strategically, the briefing process can become a form of organizational development and can contribute to the employees' enthusiasm, understanding, and acceptance of the final design or to their hostility, rejection, and apathy.

As a form of organizational development, the briefing process helps meet individual goals of personal recognition, sense of competence, and sense of responsibility. And it helps meet organizational goals of motivated and committed staff. It also helps lower costs by making it more likely that there will be fewer change orders before the building is completed and by eliminating serious problems that could have been identified and resolved through a more effective process.

There is no such thing as a perfect briefing process or design. But by thinking of facility planning and design within the broader context of organizational development and by spending the time and resources to collect the necessary information and involve staff in a meaningful way, it is more likely that any new design, whatever its cost, will support the organization's objectives.

Skeptics Speak

I do not see why it is worthwhile to try to involve a large number of rank-and-file employees. Everybody has a different opinion, and you will get as many answers as the number of people you ask.

Employees are different and their preferences vary, but common educational experiences and job functions generate considerable consensus, as the research by Brill (1984) shows, for not only basic design considerations but also individual preferences like color. Research I did several years ago on housing preferences had similar findings. The interesting aspect of this research was that I found a number of housing images that experts (i.e., architects) favored but that users hated. The reverse was also true. An unexpected finding was that there was a middle ground, with housing images that both the expert and the layperson liked equally well. We then used that insight in another research project, which was the planning and redesign of a hospital nursing unit. Rather than having either the experts or the users select colors and wall coverings for the corridors and lounges, we ran workshops in which we tried to identify the middle ground, images that both groups could accept. It was not only possible but relatively easy.

These research studies demonstrate that there are more alternatives than either chaos—everybody doing his or her own thing with complete disregard for how it affects those around them—or systemwide uniformity in which everyone (at least at a given job level) receives exactly the same furniture, arranged virtually identically. As I noted earlier, there are a wide range of acceptable options and techniques that balance the individual's and the group's need for control with that of the organization's.

Employees constantly come and go. Therefore, planning environments based on the specific requirements of particular individuals makes no sense, as different users are likely to occupy the same space at some point in the near future.

One way to think about this is in reference to the difference between custom or bespoke clothing, which is tailored specifically for an individual, and ready-wear apparel that one chooses off the rack, often making minor adjustments to a basic size to accommodate individual differences within a common category. Although all people are different in some respects, people doing the same job tend to have a lot in common based on equivalent job requirements, similar education, and also an informal common learning process that socializes the individual to what is acceptable behavior or ways of working. This is what we call *normative behavior,* or the learning of the corporate culture.

Thus, although some of the detailed preferences of different users may vary, at the level of basic work functions people doing the same job often share common concerns and preferences. The Union Carbide Corporation found that when employees were permitted to select one of thirty different office furniture and amenities packages, five of the packages accounted for almost 60 percent of the choices. And with only a few exceptions, most of the designs were acceptable. The best approach, it seems to me, is therefore not bespoke design but ready-use design, in which one might mix and match from an easily available and interchangeable kit of parts.

Isn't involving users not only more time-consuming and therefore more expensive than relying on experts, who have broad experience and specialized knowledge, but also less likely to result in good decisions?

It all depends. Even the experts have to talk with somebody in the organization about the organization's goals, its ways of working, and so on. Senior executives and other managers are the appropriate source for information on strategic direction. But relying on senior executives to explain ways of working and the functional requirements to support them in regard to people lower in the hierarchy is risky, as the recent Harris Steelcase Office Survey (1987) showed. Senior managers' and, in fact, facility managers' concerns about the environment differed significantly from those of rank-and-file workers. The technology of work has changed enormously with office automation, and workers' basic values and expectations are formed during specific stages of the life cycle, which usually are different from those for people in senior management, who are older. Accordingly, the typical manager probably does not understand in great detail how workers do their work or what resources they believe are necessary for them to work productively.

The goal should not be to eliminate all experts but to use them skillfully so that their contribution fits a strategic development effort. Part of the experts' role can also be to help create awareness of options and their consequences to people actually making the choices, at whatever level in the organization. In a project I did with the World Bank, in which hundreds of employees were given the opportunity to respond to different furniture and lighting mock-ups in a special facility, the first part of the experience was walking around an educational display describing in easily understandable terms a variety of ergonomic issues. The idea was that when providing feedback, employees should have some of the same information in hand that the experts and managers had in their own decision making.

In some cases, employees will simply not have the requisite knowledge to make informed decisions. In highly technical areas such as the selection of computer equipment, HVAC systems, or lighting design, for example, the kind of brief information overview the World Bank provided will not be sufficient. But are these the kinds of decisions most employees want to make? The answer is no. Most employees are concerned about their own workplace, including its furniture, lighting, temperature, and ventilation; access to windows; the layout of their own work groups; and amenities such as parking, cafeteria, and fitness facilities. These are areas in which employees are likely to have strong opinions and considerable experience. They are interested in those aspects of decisions that affect them directly, and they can often articulate what their design requirements are for such areas. These are very different from technical specifications, which require special expertise. The objective is to use the different kinds of managers, employees, and technical experts to their best advantage. Consultants should not be telling the organization what its goals or design requirements are, nor should managers or employees be making decisions about technical issues about which they are uninformed.

The underlying principle of most of the choices described earlier is that there is a need to balance corporate and individual needs for control. Rather than losing control, management increases it by focusing more on strategic than tactical decisions. It does so by constructing decision framework within which employees can make choices that do not undermine broad organizational objectives. With respect to facility management, this may be having professional engineers design and select a HVAC system that is intended to give individuals a choice of ventilation, cooling, and heating. Or it may be lighting designers or ergonomists helping the facility manager select furniture systems whose components—no matter how they are arranged—can meet requirements for comfort, safety, and durability. It may be facility managers who draw up basic space-planning guidelines within which individuals and groups can plan their own work areas.

Professional expertise does not have to be sacrificed to offer individuals and groups meaningful choices and control over their own work areas. Successful choice programs give employees adequate resources to make good, informed decisions. "Adequate resources" may mean attendance at seminars given by experts on selected topics, time to visit other sites using innovative approaches, and discussions with senior management concerning problems or opportunities faced at the company level about which individual employees may be unaware. The point is simple: If people are asked to make judgments without the relevant information, they are likely to make poor ones. The problem is not the judgments, or those making them, but those responsible for constructing the framework within which such judgments are solicited.

Managing
Environmental Change

People resist change. Right? Not necessarily. Holiday travel would not be choking airports; the DIY ("Do It Yourself") home improvement business would not be surging; and real estate offices would not line the streets of every trendy neighborhood if people always resisted change. The truth is that people resist some kinds of change.

Given the choice, most people resist unfamiliar situations that they fear will be uncomfortable, unpleasant, and dangerous. Few people rush to embrace situations that lower their self-esteem, undermine their sense of competence, sever treasured friendships, or make it harder for them to achieve desired objectives. The challenge is to understand better the conditions under which people will or will not resist change, and what organizations can do to lower their employees' resistance to change, when it does surface.

This is not a trivial issue. "Churn" rates (calculated as the number of offices that are reconfigured each year as a percentage of the total number of offices) in many large organizations average about 30 percent annually and may in some cases reach 70 percent or higher. A large American study of office workers by Michael Brill and his associates (1984) found that 37 percent of corporate employees are relocated within their company annually; 9 percent of them relocate three to nine times a year. The need to accommodate new and more information technology and organizational change in the form of everything from new management styles and organizational structures to acquisitions, mergers, retrenchment, and the spinning-off of parts of a large company all are driving this physical change. Minimizing the disruption to work and the length of time that employees need to adjust to changes in their surroundings can have significant financial implications. Because organizational change and technological advancement is unlikely to slow anytime in the near future, what can companies do to manage environmental change effectively?

UNDERSTANDING RESISTANCE TO CHANGE

In thinking about how a change such as an office relocation, renovation, or just a small reconfiguration of workstations will affect employees, it is useful to distinguish between what actually is driving the change and what is publicly proclaimed as the rationale. The former are factors that management considers acceptable or legitimate reasons for the proposed changes, such as reducing costs by making workstations smaller or by increasing the percentage of open versus closed offices. The latter is what rank-and-file employees typically hear as part of an orientation program, such as that the new workstations will be ergonomically better, safer, and more comfortable.

It is not so much that facility managers or other change agents lie to employees; it is more a case of what remains tactfully, if purposely, unsaid. The audience makes all the difference. It takes enormous confidence and a clear sense of purpose to tell the same story to audiences with different expectations. Justifying smaller or open-plan offices as a way to improve space use efficiency in order to reduce costs or to accommodate more people in the same amount of space, is not likely to be a rewarding experience when told to employees. It can feel a bit like paddling upstream with a pitchfork.

Management assumes (hopes?) that employees will consider justifications like improved ergonomic conditions as positive, or at least as legitimate. After all, they do speak to employees' concerns about health and comfort. True, but so do operable windows and individual light, temperature, and ventilation controls, human factors about which employees care more than an adjustable chair or work surface but that are much less frequently provided. Employees usually view proposed changes in the workplace within the context of subtle social and organizational implications. (Is my status affected? Am I further from my friends?) Yet ways in which employees will interpret proposed changes are, in my experience, rarely considered in planning either what to change or how to help employees easily cope with whatever changes are made. The financial consequences of ignoring the social and organizational underbelly of change can be very high.

One example: Several years ago a local hospital installed a nurse-dispatching system intended to increase efficiency (and patient service) by reducing the nurses' travel time. Devices electronically linked to a central monitor were placed at regular points along corridors. As nurses passed these "check-in" points they were supposed to engage the device briefly, which then indicated to a central dispatcher where all the nurses were at any give time. The dispatcher then could "beep" any nurse and tell him or her which room to go to without the nurse's always having to return to the nurses' station first. Great efficiency. Utter failure.

Nurses would not check in. Why not? To keep costs down, the central dispatcher had no medical training, and the nurses, being professionals, refused to be told where they should go and what a priority was by someone who was not a professional peer. The nurses' professional identity was embedded in their being able to judge by themselves where and what they should be doing at any given time. The system cost several hundred thousand dollars plus the salary of the dispatcher. But it was never used and caused enormous resentment among the professional staff.

Employees, whether nurses or claims adjusters, are not inherently opposed to efficiency. Like many people, occasionally including senior managers, they tend to be fully supportive of others increasing it. To understand people's response to environmental change programs, it helps to keep in mind that, like a diamond, any change has many facets. Which side is turned to catch the light depends on who is holding the gem. A good change program, like a good-quality gem, sparkles from any angle.

A FRAMEWORK FOR CHANGE

A useful framework for studying the implications stemming from even a seemingly minor environment change is one developed by anthropologist Amos Rapoport (1970). He divided all work-related activities into four components: the activity itself (e.g., communication), the specific way in which the work is done (e.g., by means of writing, telephone, word processor, face-to-face meeting), associated activities (e.g., listening to music, eating, looking out a window), and the symbolic meaning of the activity (e.g., its implications for personal and professional identity or status). How can this framework be applied to understand employees' responses to changes in the office environment?

The main idea is that any change must be analyzed in terms of its effects on employees at all four levels. Movement from a typewriter to a word processor may engender little resistance, for instance, if it has relatively few effects on associated activities that employees value, if, perhaps, the work is still performed in a location that does not prevent the chance to break the monotony of work by chatting occasionally with friends or coworkers or looking out to a pleasant view. If employees view the change as lowering their professional status (the symbolic level), by making them mere "machine operators" for example, they are likely to resist it. But if they view the change as enhancing their professional identity, by making the employees feel more like "programmers" or "professionals," then they may embrace it. Similarly, if they view the change as enabling them to work more effectively, they are unlikely to resist it.

Management's responsibility is to understand themselves and then to help employees understand the full range of implications across all four levels. Management needs to make sure that valued activities and symbolic meanings are preserved, if not enhanced, when the change takes place. Because all changes are multifaceted, generating both positive (e.g., better lighting and more pleasant surroundings) and negative outcomes (e.g., smaller space and more restrictions on how to use it), any planned change must be viewed in terms of its overall response profile. It is the total package that counts, not any individual element. That is why employees, often to management's consternation, can appreciate new ergonomic seating and still resist a move or, conversely, complain about poor lighting but not want to move.

Management programs to help employees prepare for a move that begin when all the decisions about the change itself have been made are, from this perspective, often too little and too late. They are, in terms the Reagan administration made famous, means of damage control. Well-managed employee change programs should be less like a coating sprayed on rough construction to conceal from building inspectors the real material and workmanship and more like a continuous inspection. The overall project process should be explained not only in regard to materials and building techniques but also in regard to labor relations, economics, employee supply and demand, scheduling, politics, law, and psychology.

SMALL WINS, REAL PROGRESS

For many facility managers the problem with large environmental changes that require significant rethinking about how space is planned, designed, allocated, and used is that the organization is so massive, intractable, and daunting that they despair of solving it. The magnitude of the change required to gain acceptance for a new building design or a different furniture standard can intimidate and overwhelm anyone. The mere prospect of such change can sap energy and discourage actions and initiatives that are needed if any progress is to be made. According to social psychologist Karl Weick (1984) these are big problems, and that's the problem.

People often define social problems in ways that overwhelm their ability to do anything about them. Weick argues that a first step in solving big problems is to redefine the scale of the problem to make it more manageable. In doing so we generate opportunities for "small wins," which are more likely to motivate and stimulate us than trying to tackle huge problems that are immensely difficult to solve. Small wins individually and cumulatively can make a difference. The small wins approach also makes good sense when applied to facility management.

Being made responsible for managing hundreds of properties about which sometimes almost nothing is known—including the location of the deed or the expiration date of the lease—may not qualify as a world-scale problem, but it can still be rather frightening. The same is true of a management edict to reduce space occupancy by 50 percent over the next five years, or the FM's operating budget by several million dollars. Asking an existing FM staff trained in the trades and hired when the primary FM activity was maintaining what now seem (and were) simple buildings and building systems to think more like managers and less like handymen is no less daunting. These are real, not hypothetical, examples, and they multiply endlessly. Trying to solve them in one massive effort is unlikely to succeed; redefining the scale of the problem to enable small wins makes more sense.

Small Wins

There is something attractive about solving a big problem, until you try to solve it. Then it becomes frustrating. Weick contends that, ironically, people often cannot solve problems unless they think they are not problems. When the magnitude of the problem is scaled upward in the interest of mobilizing action (think how good you would feel if you solved world hunger!), the quality of thought and action actually declines, because processes such as frustration and helplessness are activated. Recasting larger problems into smaller, less arousing problems can help people identify a series of smaller, controllable opportunities that produce visible and positive results: small wins.

The key to the small wins philosophy rests on some strong psychological evidence concerning the effects of arousal on human performance. Basically, big problems tend to be very arousing; smaller ones less so, and that is their strength. Considerable psychological research shows that performance is best under moderate levels of arousal. Either too little or too much arousal lowers performance. The optimal level of arousal for performance is also affected by the difficulty of the task.

The more difficult the task is, the more that very high levels of arousal will impair the performance. In particular, at relatively high levels of arousal, coping responses become more primitive. For example, those patterns of responding that have been learned most recently are the first ones to disappear. This means that skills, knowledge, and techniques that one may have recently acquired at FM seminars, for instance, are likely to take a back seat to more familiar "rule-of-thumb" practices that one has used (perhaps not very successfully) for a long time.

When highly aroused, people also treat new situations as if they were more similar to older and more familiar situations than they in fact are. This means that such people are likely to misinterpret the current situation. For example, using the same shovel you have always used successfully to dig a new hole is not very effective if what you think is sand turns out to be concrete.

For all these reasons, redefining a big problem into a series of smaller ones is likely to lower arousal and improve coping. Separating a problem into more manageable chunks reduces the interference of high levels of arousal into new ways of thinking about a problem or into applying recently learned skills and techniques. It means looking for small wins rather than large victories.

Small Wins and FM

What does this all have to do with facility management? It offers, I think, an interesting way of conceptualizing and then tackling big facility problems like the ones noted at the beginning: dealing with cost-reduction edicts and major space efficiency improvements, with the seemingly insurmountable problem of organizational churn, and with raising the competency of FM staff, and so on. Weick (1984, p. 42) cites the example of William Ruckelshaus, a past director of the U.S. Environmental Protection Agency, who was charged with cleaning up all aspects of the environment. But he went instead for a small win:

> He discovered some obscure 80-year-old legislation that permitted him to go after some cities on water pollution. He took advantage of the legislation, effectively narrowing his practical agenda for the first year or two to "getting started on water pollution." On day one of the agency's formal existence, Ruckelshaus announced five major lawsuits against major American

cities. The impact was electrifying. The homework had been meticulously done. Noticeable progress was made quickly. It formed the beachhead for a long series of successes and distinguished EPA from most of its sister agencies.

What might some similar "small wins" tactics look like in the FM arena? Integration of FM-related functions like MIS (management of information systems), telecommunications, or the design and construction of new projects or large renovations with basic FM activities often proves elusive, in part because of organizational structures that formally separate these different functions into different departments or divisions. Going for an organization restructuring is a big win approach, and a big win for one group generally means a big loss for another (for whichever group ends up reporting to the other in this case). Big win strategies generate lots of emotions and a lot of resistance.

A small wins strategy might be to start inviting people from related but structurally separate departments to lunch or to an internal seminar to discuss informally some of the ways in which decisions in each department affect the other. This is a way of getting started quickly. Acceptance of this kind of invitation is very likely, and it begins to build an informal bridge and establish personal contacts that underlie and promote trust and understanding.

This kind of low-key, low-risk effort can begin immediately, requires no formal approvals, and is usually satisfying to everyone. And it can have real benefits. It makes it easier and more likely that people will call up and just ask what is happening or is planned or even volunteer information because they now understand better the implications of their decisions on other departments and activities. This kind of informal cooperation tends to be reinforcing in its own right when it results in facilities designs and policies that work more effectively. All groups are likely to be encouraged to continue looking for ways to foster the integration.

Senior management's demands for huge increases in space efficiency or reductions in operating expenses are another big FM responsibility (problem?). These kinds of demands seem to call for a big wins strategy to match the magnitude of the problem. But if one tries to impose in a single swoop significant across-the-board cuts in office standards, the response will be predictable: fury. Such a strategy, even if successful in its immediate objective of increasing space efficiency, raises the larger question of whether this contributes in any way to the organization's overall ability to meet its basic business objectives. A big win for efficiency in the short term may be a big loss for effectiveness in the longer term if efficiency is bought at the expense of hundreds of hours of collective complaints, resentment, and simple inability to do one's job because of insufficient space or inappropriate environmental support.

An alternative, small wins strategy, would be to target groups like sales representatives, auditors, or management consultants who are expected to spend most of their time in the field with clients and customers. In one computer company, this was done by initially involving a small group of sales representatives in a project in which their individual desks were replaced with a single large table equipped with computers as well as outlets to plug-in the portable laptop computers that they used in the field (see Chapter 9). Given the time out of the office their jobs demanded, the logic (at least) of scaling back their space was evident. All sales persons had an assigned rolling file cabinet stored nearby that they could roll under the table next to wherever they were seated at the moment.

By starting small, some of the inevitable problems were identified (insufficient storage space), and better solutions were sought. The FM group had at least secured a toehold on increasing space efficiency without generating enormous resistance. As staff became familiar and more comfortable with this new way of working, they could help sell the idea to others in the organization based on their own experience.

At Shell Oil in Houston, Texas, the standard way in which the FM group tries out everything from new space standards to new technologies is to use their own department space as a living laboratory, to which they routinely invite people from around the organization to come, see, touch, and discuss new ideas the FM group is exploring. Many of these become accepted practices after people from other departments have had the opportunity to see how something looks and works and to talk with people who have used it.

The same approach has been used at an American utility company to introduce more systematic computer-aided property management monitoring and tracking procedures. The software and training were sold, internally, to one site at a time, with each site then becoming an advocate of the process which they helped sell to the next site. No amount of effort to introduce the new procedures to all the sites at once would have been successful.

Small wins may not have the glamour of big wins, but they are more attainable and therefore more motivating and less intimidating to tackle than are big problems. For facility managers they represent a useful way of resolving problems, pressures, and demands that often seem to pound on one's doorstep like waves in an endless winter storm. The key is finding pockets of receptivity and then exploiting these as a means of getting started.

WHAT CAN MANAGEMENT DO?

My own research on employees' reactions to office relocations indicates that people have little difficulty coping with a change in the workplace when those changes are perceived as an improvement over their current situation (Becker 1988b; Becker and Hoogesteger 1986). Unfortunately, employees often have only a hazy idea of what their new workplace will be like, and it is this ambiguity that spawns rumors and anxiety. Employees need to understand why the change is being made and to receive detailed information about the move and what their new work situation will be like. Inviting employees to help plan the change removes the mystery and makes them change agents, not pawns in someone else's chess game. To avoid unnecessary employee resentment and anxiety or even just apathy—all of which can only make adjustment to the change difficult and undermine work performance—management can take specific actions, including the following.

Focus Groups and Committees

Getting employees involved from the beginning in the actual planning can help build realistic expectations about the project. Focus groups in which small groups of employees provide feedback about specific proposals can help identify problem areas and stimulate the search for mutually acceptable solutions for everything from physical design to policies for how space will be used. The more specific the proposals are to which employees are asked to react (whether a physical design or a policy or procedure), the more specific the feedback will be. This is why many organizations now use some kind of full-scale mock-up to elicit employees' responses to planned workstation designs.

Building committees with employee representatives serve a purpose similar to that of focus groups, but they usually meet continually. It is important that representatives actually communicate with their colleagues and report this information back. But they often do not, in part because they have not received any training or help from the project team in how best to communicate to and solicit this kind of information from their peers. It is the facility management group's responsibility to provide this kind of support, whether they do it themselves, enlist the help of the human resources department, or hire outside consultants. One danger of standing committees is that their members lose sight of their review role and begin to act as advocates of the plan. This is one reason that focus groups, whose members can easily shift over time, are so valuable.

Management Briefings

A common approach is for the facility management project team to communicate its ideas, plans, and proposal to group or departmental managers. They expect these managers to communicate with their staff and to then report back on the feedback they receive. The problem is similar to what happens with employee representatives: Managers' commitment and willingness to communicate this kind of information to their staff vary enormously. Some view it as a waste of time ("We pay these people to work, not to play designer."). Others, view it as unnecessary ("I know what my people need. I did that same job once.") To some, this kind of involvement may threaten their definition of the management role ("I am the manager and I get paid to make these kinds of decisions.").

In one study (Becker 1988c) we separated departments in the same division into high employee involvement or low employee involvement, depending on the management style of the group's senior manager. We found that the managers of low involvement groups did not believe it was important to share with their staff information about an upcoming relocation. Managers in the high involvement groups tended to share more information about the move and talk more with their employees about how they felt it would affect them. The result was that employees in the high involvement group were more satisfied with the move and with their new environment, rating twenty-eight of thirty-two issues higher than did the low involvement groups. The high involvement groups also reported less difficulty adjusting to the new move (although in this case the overall adjustment was easy for most employees).

Open Houses

In the same study of environmental change, we also interviewed employees before and after the move and asked them what information provided by management was most helpful. Memos were the least helpful, and although many remembered the orientation meetings on safety and telephone use, the open house (for the employees and their families) was by far the most successful effort.

Because the open house included the employees' families, it did much more than just provide factual information about the new offices. For many spouses and children it was the only opportunity to actually see where their spouse or parent disappeared to every morning, and it also gave them the chance to connect names with faces of colleagues often mentioned but never met.

Some organizations delay their open house until just before the move, when the offices are completely ready for occupancy, whereas others hold theirs much earlier. Earlier tours can help employees ask timely questions that staff responsible for planning the move can address in other types of premove activities. During the tour, employees should be shown their own work location and its relation to associated services and people, as well as being given a general tour of the facilities.

The open house should be a real event: a party, fun, lively, with food or refreshments, perhaps even some entertainment or quirky awards ("Asked the Most Question" Award), and speeches from top management and other key players in the change effort. The scale of the effort will obviously vary depending on the scale of the change, but the principle of an open house as a recognizable (and memorable) event can be applied to changes both small and large.

Pulse Taking

Organizations often plan premove programs for employees without trying to understand what the employees' actual concerns are and how these change over the course of a project, from early in the planning stages until after the move. While planning the Steelcase Corporation's Corporate Development Center (see Chapter 10) my colleague Fritz Steele and I conducted several "pulse-taking" exercises to identify the kinds of information employees wanted (and what rumors were circulating) several months before the move. This information helped guide the premove orientation programs, making it more likely that time and effort intended to help employees prepare for the move would address important issues.

There are lots of ways to "take the pulse" of an organization. In the case of the Steelcase Corporate Development Center project, we did wandering interviews. Steele and I roamed the existing facility for a day, talking with employees at random, depending mainly on who had a few minutes to spare. The only prior arrangements were an electronic notice on the IBM PROFS electronic mail system from the project team letting managers and employees know that we would be walking around and asking some questions about people's expectations and concerns about the upcoming move and building and that this information would be used to help prepare the orientation meetings.

Having two of us to do the mini-interviews allowed us to get together afterward to compare notes and to see whether we shared the same sense of the mood of the place. Based on our interview notes and discussion we then made recommendations to management about the kinds of issues and information that should be included in the various orientation programs.

There are other methods that one can use as well. Brief surveys can be sent to staff asking them to list or just check off items they would like to see addressed in the orientation programs. Or this kind of survey can be conducted through an electronic mail system. Surveys have the advantage of eliciting the opinions of many people, but their disadvantage is being unable to follow up answers, to see what lies beneath the surface, and to get a good sense of priorities or the level of emotion driving them. Departmental discussion groups or other informal groups can also be used to get good feedback economically from quite a large number of people.

Realistic Previewing

Many organizations try to "sell" their employees on change by highlighting only positive aspects of the change. They fear that talking about negative aspects of the move will open a Pandora's box, inviting complaints and causing stress and anxiety. But research in medical and organizational settings suggests the contrary, showing that realistic previewing, in which people are told in advance what to expect, good and bad, lowers stress and helps set expectations that are likely to be met.

Patients preparing for major surgery, for example, experience less stress and pain if they are given accurate information about how painful and how long the recovery period will be, rather than being given bland assurances that everything will be all right or being told just to concentrate on how much better they will feel after the entire healing process is completed. The organizational behavior research (e.g., Louis 1980) shows that recruitment programs that focus on the sunny side lead to more dissatisfaction and higher levels of turnover once on the job than do more balanced and realistic views of what the overall job will be like. This research underscores the fact that the change does not end the minute it occurs. Like an oil tanker that takes five miles to come to a standstill after its engines have stopped, a change has momentum that takes it beyond official stopping and starting points. In the context of environmental change, this means that the goal is not only to keep anxiety down before the move but also to ensure that postmove feelings are and remain positive.

Realistic previewing in regard to a reconfiguration might mean showing to the staff floor plans or, even better, models of the new office layout, with each individual's location clearly indicated. It would mean discussing all the reasons behind the change, including concerns for containing costs and using space more efficiently, as well as the desire to provide a healthier, more comfortable environment. Employees will notice, at speeds approaching that of light, conflicting or inconsistent explanations for change: things like their own spaces shrinking to something roughly the size of a medium-sized rabbit warren (justified because there is such a shortage of space and cash) even though managers' offices (in the same company) are twice or three times the size with nicer furniture and better views. In my experience most employees are quite reasonable. They will accept some decisions they do not like if they believe they are valid. They have a harder time accepting decisions that maintain the status quo (including all its perks and perquisites) at management levels while asking rank-and-file staff to sacrifice for the good of the company.

Facility managers thus must be prepared to justify their policies and plans. In one company where I was doing research the facilities manager had his staff (popularly known as the "midnight gestapo") routinely rearranged furniture occupants had shifted from the original layout. If someone moved a desk before lunch or at the end of the day, after lunch or the next morning it magically reappeared in its original position. He gave no real reason for this action, which caused enormous resentment. It turned out that he simply believed that some office layouts were more "professional" than others. It would have been hard to argue this point successfully in public (he did not try) in the absence of any specific supporting information. Pressures to maintain certain layouts because of health or safety reasons such as loose wires or overloaded circuits are much easier to explain and are more likely to be accepted.

Ongoing Outreach

In many organizations, management begins to think of preparing employees for an environmental change a few months before the change actually occurs. All too often these preparations take the form of outlining to employees precisely what they will not be able to do in the new environment: drink coffee or eat at their desk, rearrange their own furniture, hang posters on the walls or panels, store personal goods in their desk. Although there sometimes are good reasons for these kinds of policies (like keeping the cockroach population down or avoiding damage to certain kinds of panels), the underlying rationale is often communicated poorly or not at all. By the time such regulations appear, virtually all meaningful design decisions that might have influenced the policy (the purchase of panels, for example, that would not be damaged by pins) have already been made.

Continuous communication with rank-and-file employees starting very early in a major design change is more effective than a single orientation meeting. In effect, the environmental change program can be integrated with the architectural programming effort. Employees, or often employee representatives, are then prepared for environmental change by participating in it: learning why a change is proposed, what it is intended to accomplish for the organization, understanding the roles of different internal groups and outside consultants, and acting as a conduit for information and feedback between their own work groups and departments and the project team. This integrated change model leads to few surprises and has a good chance of helping employees understand the larger organizational context in which the proposed changes are occurring.

Viewing an employee change program as part of the basic planning and design process is relatively unusual, however. To the extent it is done at all, a common form for continuous (unidirectional) information about the project are newsletters written specifically to help inform and prepare employees for a major move. All kinds of information can be included: stories about players such as the architect or project team; discussion of innovative planning and design concepts and processes; a "hot line" number that employees can call if they have questions or want information about the building and moving schedule, special materials, or building systems. These newsletters should continue some time after the move to help employees know how different problems are being addressed and who is responsible for resolving them.

More effective are small, face-to-face meetings with departments and work groups in which move spokespersons, department managers, or department representatives (if there has been some type of broad-based participation) discuss the move both before and after it occurs. The organization should be prepared to explain why certain decisions have been made and how they will benefit the organization and, ultimately, the employee.

Troubleshooting Teams

No move, of whatever scale, is likely to come off perfectly. Some furniture will not be right; some lighting will not work; there will be problems with heat. Getting these kinds of things right quickly is important. As part of the planned move to the new NMB bank in South Amsterdam, the Netherlands, a team of troubleshooters composed of an electrician, an engineer, a carpenter, and a furniture installer roamed the building at the time of the move and right afterward to identify problems with furniture, telephones and computers, and heating and cooling. If possible, they fixed them on the spot. If that was impossible, they let the employees know that the problem was officially logged and would be monitored on a computer punch list until it was resolved. The presence of such a team is itself important to communicate to employees that the company cares and is doing all it can to make the move as easy as possible. It is good to have a single telephone number for employees to call for any kind of facility-related complaint. This should reduce the employees' frustration at having to make many calls to find the right person, and give the organization a mechanism for systematically tracking problems and monitoring how fast they are being resolved. Employees' should be guaranteed a response within a given time period (e.g., forty-eight hours).

Symbolic Gestures

Particularly for a relatively small reconfiguration, employees may feel that they are being treated a bit like a file cabinet, something that is just rolled into its new place, unlocked, and used. A simple, inexpensive gesture such as a flower on a desk, some candy, a box lunch, or a friendly note from a senior manager (not a list of "Don'ts") are the kind of unexpected but appreciated ways in which management can acknowledge that it understands that even small reconfigurations or relocations are irritating and disruptive. For major renovations and new facilities, a well-designed occupant manual that explains some of the concepts underlying the design, how the building can be used to its greatest potential, and who to contact if there are problems can be of both practical and symbolic value.

One of the more innovative approaches to helping employees cope with a new office environment I have heard about falls somewhere between a "gesture" and an "environmental design." It was proposed and implemented by Jerry Jensen, facility manager at Louvre Drapes, a subsidiary of Beatrice Foods Corporation. Jerry was a bit dismayed to find that two hundred employees who participated in an office renovation that included new workstations costing several thousand dollars each were mildly disgruntled after the move. To help the new offices feel a bit more comfortable and personalized, all employees were given $100 with which they could buy virtually any kind of office accessory they liked: wastebaskets, storage bins, task lights. In relation to the overall project budget, the $100 was small peanuts, but the effect was tremendous: enthusiasm, excitement, a positive attitude. Not every organization can afford this type of program, but it helps put into perspective the fact that in some cases spending a little more money may be the difference between getting a lot or a little value from an expensive project.

LIFE AFTER INSTALLATION: SETTING USE PATTERNS

Getting right the design of a new layout, a renovation, or a new building takes time, and most organizations accept that. Fewer spend the time (and money) to determine how the new facility or area will really be used. Yet, in a study we did of a major office redesign and relocation in the U.S. Treasury Department, we found that policies governing how the new environment could be used contributed significantly to dissatisfaction with the environment. For example, rules against eating at one's desk and about what and how much employees could affix to their panels became much more stringent after the move. This was understandable, but to a point. Few people want to see a brand-new environment become a pit, but neither do most people want to flash-freeze their surroundings, like green beans or peas, so that those who harvested them can claim that they have not lost any of their original flavor. Approaches to the problem of managing "appearances" or the extent to which employees can personalize their environment vary greatly. Two examples help define opposing corporate mind-sets.

The first example was in the headquarters of a major American insurance office. As a colleague and I walked around the office as part of an informal POE to see how employees were responding to their furniture and workstations, we noticed how well the office was "wearing." It looked, in fact, brand-new. We mentioned this and found to our surprise that this was by design and not by chance. This organization actually had a "clean office" awards program. The facility manager periodically inspected different departments and awarded the cleanest a trophy that was kept in the winning department until the next judging. The award obviously meant something, as several employees kept spray canisters of Lysol detergent in their desk drawers to wash away smudges and dirt from their off-white desktops.

The second example comes from a place we stereotypically expect to be fastidiously clean and orderly: Germany. (Stereotypes are so reassuring that it is a pity when reality renders their preservation so difficult.) Here, too, a contest was held to determine the most beautiful office. But in contrast with the American insurance office, the criterion here for winning was not that the offices looked as though they had been occupied an hour earlier but that they had been the most transformed with posters, plants, and other decorations. The bank had even invited a local florist to display and sell its wares in the lobby to make the beautification effort simpler for the employees.

The idea that "beauty is in the eyes of the beholder" could not be better illustrated by these two examples. The actual benefits of these kinds of management programs are hard to gauge, and in fact most organizations neither develop such programs nor judge them on the basis of hard facts. Rather, they do what they believe will have a positive effect, sometimes perhaps more from the organization's than the employee's perspective. These kinds of environmental use decisions are, however, not trivial to most employees.

Conflict among employees and between employees and facility management staff can become rather fierce over issues of personalization and what is deemed (and who deems it) acceptable. One person's trash heap is another person's treasure trove, which can be a problem if you believe your house is near the dump. One approach to solving this problem is for the facility manager simply to issue edicts. Another is to design a process which allows representatives of different departments and groups, including user groups, facility management, and unions, to consider different options that would work reasonably well for everyone.

One example of how this can be done comes from the Steelcase Corporation's new Corporate Development Center (CDC). Here the need to have a mechanism in place to monitor continually how well the facility was working from the occupant's viewpoint and to use this information to create policies and practices that would help create a good and dynamic fit between the facility and those using it was met in three ways. The first was to establish a services council composed of all the groups who provide CDC occupants with services: facility management, catering, security, telecommunications and computers, and business services (e.g., supplies, word processing). This group meets frequently to discuss problems and propose and then implement solutions to them. The services council then pushed for the establishment of a tenant's council, composed of representatives from all the major CDC occupant groups. Its role is to identify problems with how the facility is working and then both propose solutions and work these out with the services council. To serve all users of the CDC, a CDC newsletter produced by CDC occupants was also begun.

Another approach is to run workshops that bring together management, unions, and employees to discuss policies regarding how the facility can be used. In one workshop I ran for a federal agency, we began by defining just what an "appearances program" was: a set of policies and procedures designed to accommodate differences in individual and group preferences. The basic premise was that "small things matter." (This could be seen as a user-oriented version of the architectural aphorism that "God is in the details.")

What should be included in the definition of "appearances"? It can be everything from color, lighting, finishes, plants, and pictures to accessories, furniture, smoking, eating, and use patterns. It is really a framework for thinking about what kinds of decisions employees should make over time (not just at the time of a major renovation or new facility). It defines the character of the building in use.

A second working assumption was that "one size does not fit all." If people are different, which even indifferent observation can easily confirm, then it seems sensible to ask whether the environment cannot be made malleable enough to reflect some of these differences. Adjustable, ergonomic seating does this, but its acceptance by management is more a function of the belief in its effects on productivity than a commitment

Table 9-1. Advantages and Disadvantages of Involving Staff in Decisions About "Appearances"

Advantages	Disadvantages
• Increases staff commitment	• Threatens some managers
• Increases staff satisfaction	• Appears too comfortable
• Raises staff productivity	• Creates greater resistance to change
• Requires less administrative monitoring	• Leads to occasional excess by employees
• Provides stronger individual and group identity	• Produces stronger commitment to group than to organization
• Attracts independent staff	• Weakens unified corporate image

to supporting individual differences in work-style or preference. But why not? What, in fact, are the goals of the new design or reconfiguration? How might more choice for employees affect staff commitment, satisfaction, productivity; the attraction and retention of staff, administration of the facility, equity among employees, costs, corporate image, flexibility and adaptability (see Chapter 11)? What are the pros and cons of opening up some "appearances" decisions to rank-and-file employees?

One way to start analyzing the pros and cons is to make up a simple table that identifies what different players (facility managers, employee or union representatives, the architect, business group managers) believe will be the outcome of giving employees more choices. It might look like Table 9-1.

There is simply not enough research available on the effectiveness of these kinds of programs to be confident that all of the outcomes listed would actually occur. In practice, they depend on the specific appearances program and how it is introduced. Given the paucity of data to guide decision making in this area, the best tactic is to work with representatives of different groups to develop mutually acceptable policies.

A group facilitator seen as knowledgeable and with no particular axe to grind can help the group sort out conflicting opinions and beliefs. Such a facilitator can also keep the group from being dominated by one person and help it honestly address both the advantages and disadvantages of the policies being proposed. These policies can then be tried on a pilot program basis, which creates the opportunity to learn what works well and what does not for a particular unit, without committing the whole organization to a policy that no one can be sure will work.

Creating a mechanism to capture and exploit the experience of a pilot program is as important as the initial trial program itself. There is no point in setting up an experiment and then never looking through the microscope. Part of the responsibility of the team developing the policies should be to devise ways of deciding how well they work. This might include some random interviews with employees, discussions with managers, focus groups with employee representatives, a simple survey, or an analysis of formal complaints. The idea is to decide as much as possible in advance what the criteria will be for keeping, eliminating, or modifying the program.

In general, alternatives with more choice require, from both managers and staff, more tolerance, compromise, commitment to individual and group differences, faith in the reasonableness of staff and management, and individual and administrative flexibility.

THE BENEFITS OF GETTING IT RIGHT

The simplest way to avoid employees' resistance to change is, not surprisingly, to provide work environments that actually help them get on with their work comfortably and efficiently and enhance their sense of competence and personal and professional identity. The more that environmental change does this, the fewer planned change programs are likely to be necessary. For employees who are likely to react negatively to the change, planned change programs are useful to help reduce employee anxiety, retard the spread of debilitating rumors, reduce disorientation and downtime both before and after a move, communicate a caring corporate image, and lower direct costs by making it more likely that whatever programs are planned will be on target. In a real sense, everyone will gain.

The scale of the change programs should be linked to the nature of the change project. The key is not the overall size of the change in square feet or dollars but the extent to which the new situation will affect valued behaviors, communication and social relationships, and traditional or conventional ways of working. Ironically, organizations often fail to use good opportunities to ease adjustment processes. That is, they may not explain how employees' feedback actually influenced design, planning, or policy decisions, leaving the erroneous impression that the employees' needs were given short shrift. Or they may spend the time and effort to obtain feedback from employees but then not use the information. People do not blindly resist change, nor should organizations blindly introduce it.

Skeptics Speak

Don't these kinds of change programs take a lot of money and time? How can you justify their cost?

The cost and time to develop a change program should be related to the difficulty of the planned change. Changes that are relatively minor, not only in physical scope, but also in the extent to which they are likely to affect valued ways of working, cause little adjustment difficulty and therefore need no elaborate premove or postmove change programs. It is important to do some checking ("pulse taking") early on to see whether what you consider "minor" is shared. Make sure you consider the effects on employees doing different jobs or at different job levels. The boss may have no problems with the move or change, as little will change for him or her, whereas the technicians or clerks may be very apprehensive because, in fact, new space standards will change significantly their personal work environment.

When thinking about the cost, it is always easier to calculate the visible, direct costs of mounting a program (e.g., time to develop the training program, time to participate in it, costs of training materials) than it is to measure the costs saved or other benefits (e.g., time not spent complaining or looking for misplaced items; less irritability, frustration, and resentment; greater cooperation that may spill over into activities unrelated to the move itself).

It is possible to calculate and derive cost savings from these relatively invisible benefits by assuming some minimum time lost and multiplying it by the average cost of labor for that time, and then multiplying that times the number of employees involved. But this really misses the point. It makes more sense to think of the costs of the change as a part of the total project costs. Enormous effort and money will be spent trying to get the building or renovation right, and so it makes no sense to spend all this money and then undermine the effort by asking people to occupy and use it who may not understand the basic concepts or who have no positive way of interpreting and responding to a change that appears negative to them. Remember that salaries and wages, and the people who earn them, are the organization's most expensive and valuable resource.

In the case of new facilities or major renovations, it may also be possible to fold internal change efforts into external marketing programs. For example, at the Union Carbide Corporation a videotape about the new headquarters building and its planning and design concepts, originally made as part of an employee orientation program, has been and continues to be shown to thousands of visitors to the building as well as new employees. The videotape, a one-time expense, has been marketing the company— as progressive, forward thinking, technologically sophisticated, concerned about its employees—for many years.

People will complain at first, but they quickly adapt and get on with their work. Why bother with expensive and time-consuming change programs?

I don't accept that people always complain. Rather, they complain if they feel abused, left out, uninformed; or if what is proposed threatens their personal and professional identity, their dignity, or their ability to work effectively. If I offered you an office twice as big as your current one, you probably would accept it. But if that office were in a building less conveniently located, you might think twice. In effect, you would consider the trade-offs. We all do. Part of the purpose of a management change program is to help employees understand what the trade-offs are, from a departmental or organizational view as well as from an individual view.

People adapt, but at what cost? Our own research shows that once people have moved into a new facility and become familiar with it, many of their concerns do evaporate. But planning for such projects can take many months and, in major projects, years. Addressing employees' concerns and anxieties, and just simply telling them what is happening, and why, can garner enormous goodwill. It will also contain (but not eliminate) a rumor mill. In one company where we were doing a study of the relation between new lighting and employees' health, performance, and satisfaction, we were dismayed to find that a rumor had started that the reason for all this research and the tearing up of the ceiling was that there was a major health problem in the building, which was not true. Tracking down these kinds of rumors (pulse taking, again) and having simple mechanisms to explain what is being done and why can help prevent a small rumor getting out of hand or, better, ever starting.

It seems to me you are coddling employees. Change is a part of today's work world, and people must just accept it as part of the job.

If the supply of employees you need greatly exceeds your demand for them, this kind of attitude can survive. But if demand exceeds supply, as it does increasingly for not only highly specialized technical workers or seasoned managers but also motivated, conscientious employees who are capable and willing to read and write and follow instructions, than just trying to "tough it out" and exhorting your employees to shape up is courting disaster. Employees' expectations about all aspects of their working life are increasing. They want good pay and interesting work, and they also want safe, comfortable environments that help them work productively. People want to be recognized as individuals with feelings, concerns, anxieties, ideas, and energy. Environmental change programs can help achieve this. As such, they are really a form of ongoing comprehensive organizational development efforts, not just a temporary antidote to an unsettled situation.

I don't see how you can measure the benefits of these programs. And if you can't measure them, how do you justify them and remain accountable, which you argued in earlier chapters was important.

Measuring the benefits is difficult, but there are ways. You can, for example, work with departmental managers to identify those attitudes or behaviors they consider valuable and believe might be affected by the planned change. These might range from tardiness and willingness to cooperate to irritability, belief the company cares about them, morale, and commitment and motivation. The purpose is to discover what managers actually care about. This list can be made into a brief survey or set of interview questions, which can then be administered a few times over the course of the project. It might even be part of a study that analyzes similar projects, some of which do and do not use a planned change program.

More informal, but still structured, techniques such as focus groups with managers and with employees can be used to explore reactions to the change programs, and to identify those aspects that seem most valuable, why, and so on. Part of these group meetings might include an effort to capture interesting anecdotes from participants that illustrate how the planned change effort has helped employees adjust, increased their commitment, or improved their attitude and morale. These kinds of "stories" are often powerful indicators in organizations, especially when compared with other change efforts that may not have gone as smoothly.

Because cost is always an issue, is there a stage in the process at which benefits are maximized and therefore to which efforts should be targeted?

That's hard to say, but my general feeling is that the most important stages are during the initial start-up and definition of the project, just before the move, and right after the move. During the long period when work is just going on, occasional missives— in the form of a memo or an article in a regular newsletter—may be enough to keep people informed and enthused. If the situation that people are leaving is valued for some reason, perhaps because the building is an old historic building or was the company's founding location, then you might want to stress and create a "leave-taking" event, something that helps people collectively share their grief, in effect, while at the same time generating enthusiasm for the next stage in the firm's evolution. Just after the move it is very important to have a mechanism in place, such as an environmental "swat team" to seek out and correct building problems. This is when people are most anxious but also most eager to get settled and get on with their work.

PART 3

Planning and Managing Workspace

Defining Office Quality

Office quality is in the eyes of the beholder. For the user, it may mean glare-free lighting, a spacious office, good ventilation and clean air, daylight, an operable window, close parking, and a safe location. For the developer, it may mean a rapid sale or early leasing at good prices; for the architect, professional recognition among peers; and for the community, an attractive facade in harmony with the residential neighborhood. Quality is, in fact, defined largely by self-interest, but any facility must serve these different masters. Office quality, then, can be viewed as the search for common ground (mutual self-interest) among different constituencies, each with its own axe to grind.

The American Express Company describes this search for common ground by groups who often see one another more as adversaries than as partners in joint ventures. The First National Bank of Chicago, for example, convened a consumer advisory panel at which new product ideas were tested. Based on customer feedback, the bank introduced a twenty-four-hour automated audio response system that gives all depositors routine information about their balances and allows money transfers among accounts via a telephone computer hookup. With this, the bank met customer expectations for quick service while extending service availability. In another "joint venture," the Royal Bank of Canada invited members of the low-income community to serve on its advisory groups for branch offices. Feedback from the advisory groups led the bank to change its hours of operation, set aside rooms for community gatherings, offer bank-run seminars, and provide counsel on financial management. These kinds of efforts benefit both parties, and they evolve out of an understanding of what the end users need, not what the provider thinks they should want.

Major developers such as Rosehaugh Stanhope Plc., in London, have over the past several years entered into comparable kinds of partnerships with their facility constituents: accountancy, legal, and financial services firms. They have sponsored a series of ongoing focus groups and postoccupancy evaluations with representatives of these business sectors to learn what their office needs are and how well the buildings they have developed are meeting them (DEGW 1985, 1987, 1988). This is a far cry from the speculative developer mentality that provides buildings with glitzy-looking facades and photogenic entrance lobbies that will sell or lease a building quickly but may do a miserable job of actually supporting the diverse needs of the tenants or owners.

WHAT OFFICE QUALITY IS NOT

When thinking about the physical characteristics of office quality, it is easier to say what office quality is not than what it is. Certainly for the rank-and-file employee, office quality is not synonymous with new or expensive buildings. The dowdiest-looking buildings, safe enough but sagging with wear and age, often are for users a better working environment than is a modern office block with its new carpets exuding gases, its windows locked shut, its air conditioning system set at a centrally determined setting, and its systems furniture lined up like field artillery to support the uniformed soldiers of the information army. For the workers in the trenches, the greater freedom to adapt their space to their own requirements can outweigh a visually attractive facility (see Figure 10-1). But the executive, the developer, and the architect gain little satisfaction and garner even less attention from such comfortable but unpretentious, media-dull workplaces.

Office quality cannot be determined by either glancing at a balance sheet or describing an office's aesthetic qualities or technological capabilities. These are important building blocks of office quality. But it is the pattern and arrangement of these building blocks in use that define office quality. That office quality is, like most kinds of quality, both in the eyes of the beholder and more than skin deep is beautifully illustrated by the Lloyd's of London building designed by the Richard Rogers Partnership (see Figure 10-2).

As I have written elsewhere (Becker 1988b, p. 55): "Like few buildings and all great architecture, the new headquarters for Lloyd's Corporation—popularly known as Lloyd's of London—makes the blood run. To approach it through the 19th century arcades of Leadenhall Market or to view its blue cranes and stainless steel superstructure from across the Thames River framed by the Tower of London quickens the pulse. But how does it work?" The answer is "it depends," and what it depends on is one's perspective.

Sociologist Robert Gutman makes the useful distinction among three types of "programs" that both guide the building's design and can be used to evaluate its success. The *architectural* program defines the building's form, and its primary audience is the architecture community, the architect's peers. The architectural program is driven by the desire to do something visually stunning and inventive or playful, to stand out in some way from contemporary buildings. Architectural awards, notoriety, fame, and

Figure 10-1. Looks can be deceiving: Older facilities can do a good job of supporting informal communication.

attention are the rewards, and they most definitely are not based on how well the buildings work in use. They cannot be, for by definition, such awards are almost invariably decided before or immediately following the building's occupancy and are based on how architectural critics and peers judge the building, not on how those using or operating judge it.

From the architectural perspective, the Lloyd's building must be judged an unquestioned success. It is widely regarded by architects as a brilliant example of what a modern, but not postmodern, building can be. This does not mean that all architectural critics love or even like the building but simply that it is recognized for being highly inventive and unusual, an architectural idea pushed near to its limits and valued precisely for this reason. It has catapulted Rogers to personal fame, become a tourist attraction, and can be found in every book or article about modern office architecture. The architectural program has been well met. But what about Gutman's other two types of program?

The *user* program refers to how well the building works from end users' point of view, in this case the people working in and using the building. Here, not novelty but comfort, human dignity, and the enhancement of personal and professional identity are the principal criteria. And the building has fared less well. In a survey of all the building occupants by an outside survey organization, 75 percent of the occupants indicated they would prefer to return to the 1928 building across the street that they had previously occupied. Complaints about the lighting, vertical circulation, some of the finishes and materials (rubber floors and exposed concrete block in some support areas), and the organization of the different insurance groups within the building underlay the reported dissatisfaction (see Figure 10-3).

Figure 10-2. The Lloyd's of London building did an outstanding job of projecting corporate identity. (Photo: Lloyd's of London)

It would be easy to lay all the blame at the architect's feet, too easy and wrong. Ultimately, all the decisions were approved by Lloyd's, including the black color of the ceilings, the blue rubber floors and exposed concrete block of the members' cloakroom, and the location of the marine and auto insurance groups. And this brings us to the third program, the builder's or *facility management* program.

In the construction phase the governing criteria for the facility management program often are cost (though not in this case) and schedule. After occupancy, building operations and maintenance—everything from energy efficiency and ease of cleaning the inside and exterior of the building to servicing building systems and equipment—are the focal points of the facility management program. The "good" building is defined by how well it works in use from an operational viewpoint.

From this perspective Lloyd's is a mixed success. Flexibility was a major criterion, and in many ways Lloyd's is flexible. As planned, the insurance market has expanded from the second floors to the fourth floors with relatively few technical problems in terms of wire management or power capacity, areas that received enormous attention in the planning process. The automated HVAC systems linked to a computer-controlled system that tracks direct energy costs (by area occupied) on the floors above the insurance market have also worked very well. At the same time cleaning costs, especially for the stainless steel exterior, are very high, and the rubber floors, concrete

Figure 10-3. The Lloyd's of London high-tech interiors were less successful in supporting members' personal and professional identity and the nuances of social intercourse so important to the Lloyd's insurance market.

block walls, and exposed overhead pipes and ducts in the members' cloakroom have proved to be so unpopular with members that they have been replaced with more traditional carpeting and paneling.

So is it a good building? It depends. The factors that can contribute to office quality are many and interdependent. The likelihood of organizing them into a single predictive model is not great, but practice continues with or without theory. It is possible to describe ideal office scenarios with regard to space requirements, for specific segments of the office market, as DEGW's work (1985, 1987, 1988) for Rosehaugh Stanhope has shown. Yet at the moment such work is limited largely to the professional and financial market sectors. By focusing on the space requirements of professional offices, such work also slights an important lesson learned from the Lloyd's experience: A good facility cannot be defined entirely by its shape, size, planning grids, and building systems. A good facility requires the balance and integration of the architectural, the user, and the facility management programs from the inception of the building project.

FACILITY QUALITY AND THE ELASTIC ORGANIZATION

Chapter 2 described the three types of facility organization: the loose-fit, tight-fit, and elastic organization. Each of these types suits organizations at different stages in their evolution, operating in different types of business environments (from relatively static to highly turbulent). The elastic organization seems best positioned to meet the challenges of the next decade: the rising cost of space matched by rising employee expectations about what constitutes an acceptable work environment; continued organizational change, in regard to both internal organizational structure and new work patterns and management styles; mergers, acquisitions, and divestitures; and new information technologies. Like a rubber band, capable of maintaining tautness while assuming an infinite number of shapes, the elastic organization balances the need for organizational control with the individual's and group's need to be able to influence aspects of their work life and workplace.

Thus hallmarks of the elastic organization include more emphasis on guidelines and decision frameworks, many drawn up jointly by management and staff, within which employees have more freedom about how and when and where to work. The result is predictable: a strong distinction between front and backstage areas and more physical diversity and more visible (and acceptable) variation in work-style (see Figure 10-4). The focus in the elastic organization is on performance, not on the appearance of being busy. Being physically present is not confused with being productive.

In a sense, process is the elastic organization's most important product. Fewer data but more information is entered into planning decisions. How space is used, managed, and allocated, as well as its physical characteristics, becomes an important component of facility quality. Innovation in policy, procedure, practice, and design becomes part of the culture and is not considered an aberration. The facility is truly viewed as a system and not as a series of independent elements. Any decision, whether office size or the location of the conference rooms, makes sense only when viewed as part of the overall facility design.

Given these aspects of the elastic organization, one can think of a high-quality facility as having a number of characteristic space planning and design features as well as distinct approaches to the planning process. The next two sections outline some of the facility planning, design, and management characteristics of the elastic organization.

Related to Space Planning and Design

- *More centralization and decentralization.* For example, a centralized facility management group draws up corporatewide space and furniture guidelines, which are likely to allow individuals and groups more choice within a management-determined framework: selecting from different furniture styles and function packages, choosing different components from a given furniture system, creating different layouts in an area assigned by management, and purchasing furniture within a management-determined financial limit (see Figure 10-5). Although the facility framework is likely to be determined centrally, the business decision about whether or not to make a physical change is likely to be made by the local business manager.
- *More localized environmental controls.* Continuing a rapidly spreading trend, individuals will be given more control over heating and ventilation. A good example is the hotel room. Like hotel guests, employees will have limited control, enabling them to raise or lower the room temperature by four to six degrees, to choose one of three fan speeds, and to select the direction of the lighting and the number and type of lights on at a certain time (see Figure 10-6).
- *Automated building systems.* Local control at the level of the individual office or project room will be designed as part of a totally automated environmental control system. Sensors will continually monitor overall air temperature and flow—in response to

decisions by individuals and groups—and regulate building and floorwide HVAC systems in order to maintain conditions at predetermined levels.

- *Smaller offices and less variation in size.* Rising space costs have put a premium on using space efficiently. In response, support and professional office workers' offices have shrunk in size, and managers' offices will follow. The enormous cost of reconfiguring workstation panels and walls to accommodate differences in office size linked more to the support of status distinctions than to communication or task requirements has also led to fewer differences in office size. Ultimately, as is already true in Sweden,

a

b

Figure 10-4.   Front stage public areas convey the corporate image; back stage private work areas reflect individual work-styles and personal preferences.

c

d

Figure 10-4. (*Continued*)

Figure 10-5. At Union Carbide (a,b) the fit between employees and their personal workplaces was enhanced by permitting every employee to select from fifteen different furniture packages (each of which came in two colors) which varied greatly in function and image. In Sweden (c) it is not uncommon for work groups sharing a commons area to be given a furniture budget to use to select furniture that they feel supports the way they work best.

many offices, including those for support staff, will be the same size, somewhere around 100 to 120 square feet. Same-sized workstations also make it easier to move people rather than panels.

• *Shared work areas.* Smaller offices will be complemented by more unscheduled shared office space such as dedicated project rooms, shared storage and informal meeting areas adjacent to small groups of work areas, and break areas. These shared areas,

c

Figure 10-5.   (*Continued*)

Figure 10-6.   A fixed service wall gives every employee individual control over lighting, temperature, and ventilation and forms a planning grid to help control unnecessary reconfigurations of workstations.

in which some functions typically housed in an individual work area are now placed in a common area, are part of the system of space that allows individual work areas to shrink in size. In conditions of extreme density and high space costs (e.g., Tokyo) and where employees are expected to be out of the office much of the time (e.g., field sales reps, financial auditors, management consultants), the nonterritorial or free-address system (see Chapter 11) is likely to become the norm.

- *More amenities.* In addition to the standard amenities such as vending machines, break areas, and cafeterias, organizations will increasingly provide banks, cleaners, convenience stores, and child care and fitness facilities. From dual–wage earner families on tight schedules and employees working around the clock to a more demanding work force, more and better amenities will be necessary to attract and retain the kinds of workers desired as well as to allow them to work effectively while maintaining other family and life-style commitments (see Figure 10-7).

- *More natural environment.* The concern for environmental quality, which until now has concentrated mainly on furniture ergonomics and air quality and temperature, is likely to expand to a host of other issues, including direct access to daylight (as is happening now in northern Europe), more natural finishes and materials (e.g., wood, wool, cotton, plants) that do not exude gases and can contribute simultaneously to several senses: visual, tactile, olfactory, auditory, and, in some cases, taste. (For example, the herbal gardens at the NMB bank in South Amsterdam, the Netherlands, supplies daily ingredients for the cafeteria menu.)

Related to Process

- *More preliminary design planning.* More effort will go into preliminary processes for planning and designing building (see Chapters 7 and 8): Who should be involved, when, and how? What are the conditions for a successful project? For an effective project team?

- *More user involvement.* From detailed preprogramming to systematic postoccupancy evaluation, the successful elastic facility will depend on good information based on employees' reviews and feedback about not only physical designs but also policies and procedures for allocating space.

- *More integrated facilities structures.* To avoid the kinds of mistakes made at Lloyd's of London (and many other places), facility managers and building operations experts will participate in planning stages, and they will have a stronger voice. Design and construction will be combined with facility management, and both will be more tightly linked to corporate planning. More effort is likely to be spent working to find solutions that work both aesthetically and operationally, as opposed to championing one and sacrificing the other.

- *More consultants.* The amount of specialized expertise required to create a high-quality facility is enormous. In addition to traditional skills in architecture, engineering, and interior design, highly specialized skills in mechanical engineering, security, telecommunications, office automation, lighting and human factors, space planning, environmental psychology, and organizational ecology, automated building systems have become common requirements. Because in-house teams cannot justify maintaining

Figure 10-7.   The workplace is more than the personal workstation or office. It is the total office environment, from cafeteria and library to fitness facilities and informal break areas. (Photo a: AV dept NMB Bank Amsterdam 1988; Photo b: SAS Airlines 1988)

the necessary level of expertise in all these areas on a permanent basis, consultants and contract professionals will become part of a good facility.

- *Greater accountability.* Chapter 14 looks at FM performance assessment in detail. The good facility will be one in which cost containment is viewed in light of acceptable service levels.
- *More teamwork.* Just as many organizations today are stressing greater collaboration and teamwork among their business units and line functions, facility management also will be forced to work together to provide a seamless facility, one in which, in the users' experience, there is no boundary or disjunction in the service they receive to

Figure 10-7. (*Continued*)

enable them to work effectively. In effect, facility management will coordinate virtually all services provided in a given facility.

- *Training and education.* High-quality facilities require high-quality staff. More specially trained facility planners and managers, made possible by both full-time and professional education programs springing up around the world, will be a hallmark of top-quality facilities, and more effort will be made to identify the skills, knowledge, and personal qualitites needed to succeed as a facility manager (see Chapter 4, "Staffing the FM Organization").

It is the integration of facility planning and management processes and physical design that produces successful facilities. No one element by itself is sufficient. There is no single, magical combination of elements—size, materials, shape, location—that guarantees a high-quality facility. Asking the right questions is often more valuable than constructing a set of specific and easily outdated design criteria. The right questions should identify facility characteristics associated with quality by the many different players judging it: management, employee, architect, developer, and financial institution. The right process seeks to find common ground among the players, to show how certain features can satisfy each one's requirements. The following questions suggest a basis for seeking this common ground:

1. *Safe, healthy, and comfortable environment.* Does the environment provide thermal, auditory, and air qualities that are perceived by users as acceptable as well as meeting existing health and safety standards? Do the furniture, equipment, and space minimize staff and customer fatigue, discomfort, and stress? Are the site, building, and the internal work areas safe for occupants whenever the building is in use?
2. *Social integration.* Are there opportunities for both small-group contacts and privacy?
3. *Adequate and timely feedback.* Does the office facilitate direct feedback from supervisors as well as indirect feedback gained from observing the results of people's actions on others or on products and facilities?
4. *Adaptability.* Does the facility allow staff to influence their micro-environment? Does the shape of the building, its building systems, electrical capacity, partitioning, cable management, and circulation facilitate internal reorganizations of work groups and departments?
5. *Image.* Is the office environment congruent with the staff's professional identity and expectations? Does it enhance the organization's standing with its staff, clients, community, and competitors?
6. *Site.* Is the site safe and accessible to affordable, comfortable, and convenient transportation or parking? To clients and services? Will it be attractive for renting, lease back, or sale in the future?
7. *Efficiency.* Does the building and its space, furniture, and equipment minimize wasted time, energy, and materials? Do they reduce operating and maintenance costs without sacrificing performance on other criteria?
8. *Technology and construction.* Can the building accommodate new technologies? How much effort in time, construction, and disruption would be needed to accept new technologies?

Facility Quality and Diversity

Office quality speaks to diversity, not uniformity: diversity to accommodate individual differences in staff and customers, technological change and unpredictability, and shifts in organizational culture and patterns of work. A good office provides a rich and varied opportunity structure, for both those managing the building and those working in it. It views cost in the context of individual and organizational performance and draws on others' experience wherever it can be found to broaden horizons. Increasingly, this means a careful look at the international scene.

Table 10-1. Thorny FM Issues and Unconventional Solutions

How to Cope With	Solution
Computer cable morass	Use batteries
"Hot spots"	Use portable HVAC units
FM viewed as a resource drain	Become a developer
Adjacencies in large departments	Create small departments
Unpredictable organizational change	Design fixed service spines
Incompatible computer systems	Use integrating software systems
Lower space-planning costs	Use fewer design experts
FM invisibility to top management	Package and sell FM internally

Source: Becker 1988e.

INTERNATIONAL FM: TAKING OFF THE BLINDERS

Anyone working in facility management for even a short while runs up against some thorny issues: managing adjacencies in large departments, dealing with information technology "hot spots" and a morass of cable, convincing management to view FM as an asset, coping with constant and unpredictable organizational change, and reducing costs while improving service. The list is not short, but perhaps our ways of resolving them are few.

I once read a wonderful book, whose title I have forgotten, that boiled down whole "How To" books to a few words. Those intended to help fat people lose weight, for example, were condensed to "Eat less!" So easy to say (and true) and yet so hard to do. Table 10-1 tries to do this for some thorny FM issues. Each solution listed has, in fact, been used by real organizations to solve these problems. Their beauty lies in the directness and simplicity with which they define, and then attack, a problem.

It is not simple! I wonder, however, whether we do not make the FM world even more difficult than it already is by looking at a long list of thorny issues through the wrong end of the telescope, that is, from the narrow perspectives of our own culture and our even more limited personal experience. Is there not a risk, a real danger, that by always looking inward we might miss or take longer to uncover innovative solutions to FM issues?

THE JAPANESE MODEL

Over the past several years I have hosted, in the United States and England, Japanese FM study tours. Often comprising senior management from Japan's most prestigious companies, universities, and government agencies, these tour groups are dedicated to learning, in as short a time as possible, as much as they can about FM in England and the United States. They identify experts and innovative companies in the FM field and then examine everything from their strategies for organizing the FM function and space planning, and design to computerized facility management software and creating and managing FM databases.

Why? They know they might learn something new. Or, increasingly, given the speed with which the Japanese are able to assimilate new ideas into their own culture, they can confirm that no one actually has a better FM mousetrap. The Japanese are remarkable, among other reasons, for being able to combine what seem to many people as contradictory tendencies; that is, confidence (if not superiority) in their own ability and an unabiding curiosity in learning from others a better way of doing things. Statistical quality control, now almost universally associated with the Japanese, is an American idea generated by William Demming, an American professor from Michigan. American manufacturers were not interested. Today, Japan's highest award for manufacturing excellence is the Demming Award. But the Japanese are not an isolated case. The Dutch, rapidly developing FM in the Netherlands, are also mounting study tours of the United States and closely watching FM's development in Britain.

THE "NOT INVENTED HERE" SYNDROME

The traffic from the West to the East and even across the English Channel has, until quite recently, been very slow indeed. Things are beginning to change, however. The International Facility Management Association has consistently reached out to Britain, Japan, Canada, and recently Australia and New Zealand, to help them establish and promote their own FM.[1] These efforts are helping increase the awareness of FM around the world, but they often feel more like state visits than working parties. They serve a useful purpose, but they should not be confused with detailed site visits and focused small-group discussions. To a certain extent sporadic official international visits can mask, in fact, resistance by many rank-and-file facility managers to study seriously other countries' approaches to FM.

General xenophobia apart, slides showing densely packed Japanese workers in austere surroundings seem to cloud for many the possibility that one might learn something from what may appear to be a rather primitive approach to office planning and design. Many aspects of how others plan and design their offices will not be applicable. The idea, however, is to be selective and to emphasize planning and design concepts that, though not directly translatable to a British or American context, could stimulate new approaches that would better fit our own cultural patterns and work practices. We might be surprised by the ease and efficiency with which Japanese, the Dutch, and the Germans hold informal meetings in offices without partitions, for example. Organizations concerned about costs but realizing the need for ever-increasing amounts of staff training might profit from a better understanding of how new employees casually learn the "right way" of doing something by informally observing a more experienced worker in an adjacent workstation, thereby reducing the need for formalized training that too often is disconnected from the demands of daily work patterns.

The off-hand dismissal of things foreign is by no means only applied to things Japanese. Often when I show slides of British, Swedish, Dutch, or German offices to audiences

---

[1]It convened in 1989 the First International Facility Management Symposium in Washington, D.C. Leaders of fledgling facility management associations in the Netherlands, Germany, Japan, and Canada joined the United States delegation in sharing recent FM developments in their respective countries.

in the United States, the general reaction is, "That's interesting, but that is Germany" (or Sweden, or Holland, etc.), as though that is sufficient reason for dismissing other ways of doing things. Can we afford such attitudes? I do not think so, for several reasons.

LEARNING BY OSMOSIS

There are lessons to be learned from how others do things, and to some extent, we learn by a kind of visual osmosis. The quality and nature of facilities for London's financial services community have, for example, been rather dramatically transformed, not only by the direct demands of information technology, but also by the example of how American multinational firms located in London design their facilities.

One problem with learning by visual osmosis is, of course, that much of great value cannot be directly observed. An organization's cost control procedures, staffing policy, CAD programs, or property management analysis procedure, for instance, simply cannot be observed in the same way as can architectural or interior design. A second problem, which is even more acute, is actually determining, even after discovering how something is done, whether what seems like a good approach actually works in practice. There is only one solution to this problem, and that is to conduct systematic research.

AN INTERNATIONAL RESEARCH MODEL

The Japanese have the right model for systematic research. First, they conduct rather probing site visits and office tours. They do not blindly imitate everything they observe, nor are their surveys of the office planning, design, and management random. Rather, they are carefully structured, sometimes to identify innovation; as often, to understand typical approaches. They then are willing to go the next step: to fund research that will systematically explore an issue in more depth. The Japanese have done this with a survey of the Japanese office sponsored by the Japanese New Office Promotion Association, and through research projects sponsored by individual companies and working parties composed of people from government, industry, and academia. This research is often international in its scope and thrust, but its real significance is the willingness to cooperate.

International Lessons

What might we learn from a more focused analysis of international FM practices? As Table 10-1 suggests, we might learn whether the British, the Dutch, and Swedish reliance on work groups to plan their own work areas, using some simple guidelines, rather than the use of professional interior designers and space planners typical in the United States, produces more efficient workspaces or ones better matched to the organizational culture, or simply costs less. We might learn whether Japan's use of battery-operated laptop computers plugged into a mainframe do not have some advantages, for at least certain kinds of work in particular types of organizations, in terms of lower costs and easier wire management. We might learn whether some American firms' commitment to developing facility management as a profit center—in the form of an in-house property development group—raises the quality of facilities, the time and cost to bring them on line, and their ability to respond quickly and cost effectively to organizational expansion, shrinkage, shifts in market location, or changes in business direction. We might learn whether the American model of locating members of a department together in one area, regardless of the size of the department, actually enhances communication, compared with the Swedish and Dutch practice of creating smaller areas for from five to twenty workers, even when this requires splitting up subgroups within a large department.

We might, in fact, learn how to improve facility management faster and more economically, and we might increase our understanding of the conditions under which innovations in one country can be used in another. We might avoid stumbling down blind alleys that others have already tried. Facility planning and management, like all other forms of business and management, operates in an international arena. To serve its companies well and to continue to grow as a professional discipline, it needs to develop not only an interest in FM policies and practice around the world but also a strong research tradition that generates a solid knowledge base built on the systematic testing of its working assumptions.

THE VALUE OF GOOD FM

Facilities can be a significant organizational asset. At a minimum, well-designed and well-managed facilities are likely to reduce direct operating costs through more efficient monitoring and control of everything from energy use and maintenance costs to construction budgets and staffing levels. More importantly, whatever resources the organization allocates to its facilities are likely to be spent to better effect. Good databases and internal benchmarking can help identify trouble spots at early stages so that management can explore why certain regions, for example, seem consistently to be over budget, behind schedule, or overstaffed. Good initial planning can speed the construction process and lower its cost by reducing avoidable change orders. Facilities designed to accommodate new information technology and unpredictable organizational change save time and money in refitting costs, in less downtime, and in less disruption to highly paid employees. Other benefits are more subtle: layouts that promote desired forms of communication among staff, architecture and interior design that help attract and keep qualified staff who may be in short supply, and ergonomic and buildings systems design that improves air quality and lighting and helps reduce employees' fatigue and medical complaints while raising their satisfaction.

Skeptics Speak

If office quality is "in the eyes of the beholder," how in hell can a designer or facility manager ever hope to provide a quality environment to an organization with more than one employee?

Saying that quality is "in the eyes of the beholder" does not necessarily imply that everyone sees the world differently. Most people would agree, for example, that a

Rolls Royce or Mercedes is a high-quality automobile, that Thomas Jefferson's Monticello home is a magnificent residence, that a Mont Blanc pen, a Georgio Armani suit, Ferragamo shoes, a Rolex watch (the list is endless, alas) are quality products. Few people I know would find it difficult to live with walnut paneling, leather chairs, and oriental carpets in their offices (or anywhere else, for that matter). As a culture, we are exposed to common media, educational systems, and advertising that shape our tastes and values in remarkably similar (but not identical) ways.

My point is that, with regard to large components of the office environment, there is likely to be remarkable agreement about what constitutes quality (even though our culture is). In part this agreement stems from a shared culture, in part from socialization processes that take place once people join firms. We learn quickly what IBM or Apple or 3M or Moe's Grocery considers acceptable, not only in work behavior, but also in terms of office provision.

Yet at some levels, there are differences in work-style, and they are important (just as they are to life-style). Chapter 11 addresses some of the ways in which "functional diversity" can be built into facility planning, design, and management.

A lot of what you says makes sense, until you begin to think about cost. I would like to have a Rolls Royce, but I can't afford it, and likewise most organizations can't afford to meet the "quality" expectations of their employees. All you are doing is falsely raising people's expectations.

I hope not. The issue, as I see it, is not simply spending a bundle of money. It is using to their fullest potential whatever resources are available. This may mean buying ergonomic chairs instead of new desks, or worrying less about the lobby's color scheme and more about glare-free lighting. It may mean spending money on good lighting in the workstation rather than on walnut paneling in the lobby. It does mean taking the time to understand what people really care about, rather than assuming that you know or are presuming to tell them. The issue is sensible resource allocation, not unlimited expenditure.

Most organizations are concerned about competing successfully. What's the lesson that we should learn by looking at Japanese offices? They have been frighteningly successful in global competition, and yet their offices are among the most cramped, poorly lit, poorly furnished, and uncomfortable in the world. At the same time we have poured literally billions of dollars into improving the American office. Why bother?

Because you don't have any choice. Just as a Swedish office worker would find most American offices intolerable (no windows, no privacy, synthetic finishes and materials), American office workers would simply refuse to work in the typical Japanese office. U.S. government agencies like the Internal Revenue Service and the Environmental Protection Agency, whose offices sometimes bear an uncanny resemblance to the Japanese office, are finding that people are turning down jobs or leaving the agency because they do not want to work in dreary, uncomfortable offices. The rapid increase in the number of foreign firms with offices in Japan is having a similar affect there. Japanese office workers are beginning to see that our firms provide much higher standards of office accommodation, and they are beginning to be more vocal about wanting improved conditions. The emergence of the New Office Promotion Association (NOPA) and JFMA (Japan Facility Management Association) reflects and is stimulating this heightened awareness of office conditions. Thus improved offices become, over time, less tied to demonstrations of employees' increased productivity at their workstation and more to the ability to attract and keep the kind of staff that organizations know they need in order to compete successfully.

CHAPTER
11

Managing Space

Space is a precious commodity. It costs money, a lot of it, particularly in major international locations. Few organizations have enough of it, and even fewer have enough of the right kind for what they would like to do. They try to get by. And increasingly, in the face of the twin pressures to keep costs down while improving the quality of the space provided, they are beginning to innovate: same-sized offices, smaller offices, fixed service spines, fewer status distinctions, computer-aided inventory tracking, chargeback systems, and other space management policies.

These innovations have less to do with new social and organizational fashion and ideology than they do with hardheaded financial considerations and the need to meet a variety of organizational demands. Although organizations differ and the same organizations change over time, the following issues are faced by virtually all at some time:

- Cost containment
- Organizational change
- Informal communication
- Privacy
- Attracting and retaining staff
- Image and identity
- Individual control
- Information technology

SPACE MANAGEMENT AND INFORMATION TECHNOLOGY

Considerable technical information is now available about how to plan technically to accommodate computers, office automation, and automated building systems (Butler Cox 1989; Duffy, Cave, and Worthington 1976; Eastman Kodak 1983; Worthington and Konya 1988). But from the viewpoint of managing space to meet the kinds of organizational demands just listed, the challenge is inventing space-planning concepts that lower costs and increase flexibility while improving the quality of the environment. This can be done in part by exploiting the characteristics of information technology, especially its capacity to support remote work and mobile workers through its ability to:

- *Bridge distance and time.* The electronic transmission of data is so fast that for all practical purposes it is instantaneous, without respect to geographical distance.
- *Store enormous amounts of data.* Millions of bytes of information, representing thousands of pages of printed material, can easily be stored on even personal computers. These data can be retrieved, processed, and transmitted electronically or via hard copy to multiple locations almost instantaneously.
- *Stand alone.* Smaller equipment, including personal computers, terminals, and printers, can easily be connected to conventional or dedicated power outlets in virtually any building.
- *Easily link terminals, computers, and peripherals.* Through systems such as AppleTalk, Ethernet, and other local area networks (LANs), it is becoming easier to hard-wire computers to one another so that data can be transmitted easily among people physically separated without tying up telephone lines using modems.
- *Support mobility.* Increasingly lightweight and more rugged equipment that can be connected to conventional power outlets permits individuals to carry computers with them from setting to setting, within the office or to other sites, cities, countries, and continents.
- *Allow virtually simultaneous input.* Computers have sufficient capacity to allow many individuals to participate at almost the same time in creating documents and processing information; that is, equipment can be designed to support group work (very little of it is, but the potential exists).
- *Provide graphic, number, written, and oral capacity.* The original focus on number crunching has evolved to the point that sophisticated graphic displays, ranging from freehand drawing (using digitizing pads) to optical scanning of existing visual material are widely available at increasingly lower costs. Voice input/recognition devices that allow people with limited writing skills or restricted physical abilities to create and manipulate information are well along in development.

Issues of churn, informal communication, attracting and retaining staff, even cost reduction, will never be solved entirely by technology. To exploit information technology to meet these goals requires fundamental changes in management style and organizational culture (see Chapter 12. "Space Management and Organizational Culture"). It requires an elastic organization committed to expending energy and taking risks to find a better way of doing things.

There is no single right answer, no single "best way" of doing something for all organizations. The following approaches to fulfilling the organizational demands just listed, both through space-planning and design concepts and policies and procedures for managing space, represent not final answers but interesting attempts by elastic organizations to push the boundaries of the acceptable a little further out, sometimes with information technology and sometimes without.

ORGANIZATIONAL DEMANDS AND INNOVATIVE PLANNING AND DESIGN SOLUTIONS

Cost Containment

Although nearly all organizations are concerned about cost, for some this is the single driving force guiding space planning and design. In what I call tight-fit organizations—those characterized by centralized control and fairly rigid space and furniture standards—enthusiasm for maximizing space efficiency may create working conditions that are counterproductive: too small, insufficient privacy, too few informal meeting areas, and inadequate storage. In what I call elastic organizations—those consciously trying to balance the need to contain costs with the need to provide a supportive work environment—maximizing the effective use of space rather than simply reducing its amount is the goal. The distinction is a significant one and is reflected in the difference between redistributing space and reducing overall space use or between being efficient at the expense of being effective.

In tight-fit organizations the first place in which increases in space efficiency are sought is in smaller space allotments for lower-level support staff: clerks, typists, word-processing operators, data entry personnel. The ultimate expression of pure space efficiency in this model is what American office planners call the *bullpen:* a large, undifferentiated area in which a large number of desks are located side by side. One's work area is quite literally defined by the size of one's desk or work surface and the ancillary space needed to accommodate a single chair (see Figures 11-1 and 11-2).

What Americans call *open plan* offices, in which a large undifferentiated area is divided into individual and small group work areas by the use of panels, is an attempt at a compromise: It has more privacy than the bullpen offers but less than does the fully enclosed office with floor-to-ceiling walls. The original intent of the open plan, was to mirror better the work flow in the physical layout of furniture and to provide more flexibility in response to organizational change. The biggest gain, in fact, has been in space efficiency. Indeed, the International Facility Management Association Research Report #1 (IFMA 1984) shows that for every level in the company pyramid, open plan offices are smaller than their enclosed counterparts.

The efficiency of a smaller-sized footprint in open plan offices is further enhanced by the ability to increase storage by means of hanging shelves and "binder bins" on the panels. However, to maximize the vertical storage potential of panel systems, the panels must be four to six feet high. But to avoid the feeling of working in a large packing crate, panels this high require an office footprint of sixty square feet and preferably more. In today's high-priced property world, this is not efficient enough. The result, seen widely in London, is the use of higher panels only to create boundaries

Figure 11-1.   "Bullpen" arrangements in which small groups are separated from other groups by higher walls or panels are space efficient and can work very well when privacy is not important.

between different work groups and departments, but not individual privacy. With this approach, individual workstations of thirty square feet are possible. Efficiency is increased, but at what cost to effectiveness? How can one concentrate with a colleague talking on the telephone three or four feet away? Where can one spread out reports, printouts, or plans in space not occupied by office equipment: telephone, computer, calculator? (see Figure 11-3).

Figure 11-2.   The American open plan, using systems furniture and interlocking panels with furniture attached to it has increased space efficiency and can be effective if planned in conjunction with other spaces that offer both more privacy and more opportunities for informal meeting.

Figure 11-3.   Using low panels to separate workstations and higher panels to separate work groups and departments increases group identity and reduces the impersonality of a sea of workstations cut from the same mold.

Thus another approach to the unending search for greater space efficiency concentrates not so much on reducing the space alloted to lower-level support staff but on redistributing space throughout the organization.

Planning and Design Responses

Redistribution of Space

The goal when redistributing space is to use the same amount of space much more effectively (see Figure 11-4). The major target of opportunity is the senior executive. In many organizations a small number of senior executives use a proportionally large amount of space (The captain's and officers' sumptuous staterooms compared with the crew's cramped and spartan quarters in Lord Nelson's ship at Greenwich, England, illustrates the point brilliantly). There is rarely any functional reason for any manager to have a 300-plus-square-foot office. Privacy can be obtained in enclosed offices half that size. Offices of 200 square feet or less can accommodate conference tables to seat several people, and for larger meetings conference rooms can be located nearby and shared more cost effectively (see Figures 11-4, 11-5, and 11-6). The only justification for offices larger than 250 feet or so is status communication, and there are less expensive ways of visibly communicating status, ranging from the quality of the furnishings to the view outside.

Although top management rarely need offices as large as they have, professionals and other staff using more information technology and who participate in more informal small-group meetings often need more than they have been allocated. Paring down executive offices and using this "captured" space to enlarge the work areas of profes-

Space Allocated to Individuals

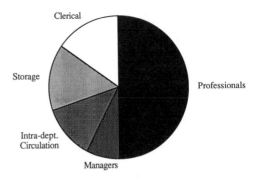

Space for meetings extracted from individual areas
and shared by group

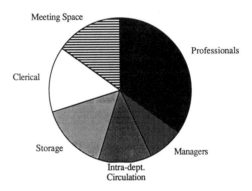

Figure 11-4. A redistribution of existing space, in which individual space allocations shrink while meeting space increases, reflects the importance of supporting face-to-face communication while containing overall space requirements. (Source: Worthington 1988)

sionals or provide more work areas for support staff is thus one facet of a space redistribution program. John de Lucy, Director of Administration for Ernst and Young in London, has been able to increase the number of workplaces per floor from 80 to 140 by making senior management's offices smaller. The space gained by eliminating separate conference tables in these offices was used for new secretarial workstations, and a new teardrop desk design could be used for small meetings in the office. Unfortunately, even more space is usually required, often to the chagrin of senior managers who cannot fathom why the facilities group is projecting greater and greater space requirements at the same time as their own space and headcount is shrinking.

One reason is that headcounts often ignore part-time workers and outside contractors who, though conveniently removed from the full-time salary rolls, still need a place to sit when they come to work. Another reason can be found in the larger number and

TRENDS IN SPACE STANDARDS

GUIDELINES NOT STANDARDS

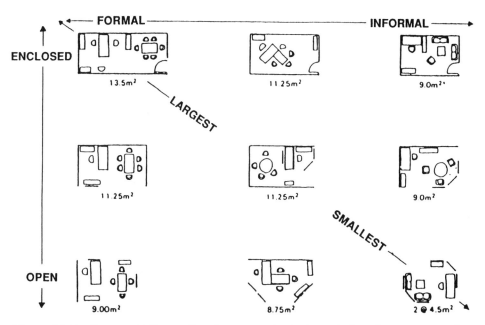

Figure 11-5.   Space guidelines, rather than space standards, make it easier to accommodate different job requirements within a well-defined spatial framework. (Source: Worthington 1988)

greater importance of a variety of "support spaces" ranging from informal break areas and cafeterias to training centers, libraries, conference and project rooms, and fitness facilities.

Cost containment must therefore be calculated in terms of what would have been required if support space had increased and space among office levels had not been redistributed. Using space redistribution to maintain the status quo in overall space requirements becomes a form of space efficiency, given the commitment to provide the kind of environmental support that allows staff—a very expensive resource indeed— to work effectively.

The Nonterritorial Office or Free-Address System

Most forms of traditional office planning are based on the premise not only that employees will come to the office each day but also that they will sit at their desk for virtually the entire time. But this premise is not, nor does it have to be true. In fact, whole classes of employees are expected to be out of the office on most days: field sales representatives, management consultants, account auditors. Even staff who are in the office often are in places other than their desks: library, project room, conference

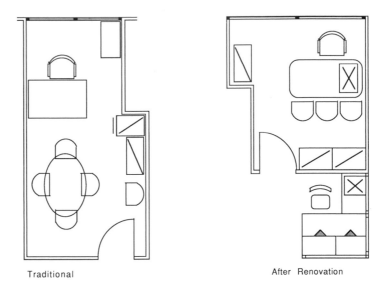

Traditional   After Renovation

Figure 11-6. Under pressure of extremely high space costs, traditional professional offices are being scaled down to create offices for a partner and a secretary in the space formerly occupied by the partner only.

room, break area. Many workers are actually highly mobile. Many others could be. The ultimate in space efficiency therefore is not the small office but the shared office.

This can and increasingly is taking many forms. Whether called the *free-address* or the *nonterritorial* office, this new form of shared office uses information technology but depends on new organizational norms.

In the early 1970s Thomas Allen (1977) reported on a fascinating experiment with an R&D group at IBM. He called it the *nonterritorial office.* Its governing concept was that individual offices and desks "owned" by a single employee would be replaced with a group territory. An area owned by a group of about twenty engineers and their manager was used for the experiment. Within this area the space was laid out so that the manager's enclosed office became a highly confidential quiet area to be used on an "as-needed" basis by those requiring that kind of privacy. Other zones were created by designating some tables as areas for interaction, others where talking was prohibited, and so on. Allen found that space efficiency increased by 30 percent, communication was significantly better—which his research showed was directly related to the quality of engineering design solutions—and the engineers ended up being highly satisfied with the new office (see Figures 11-7, 11-8, and 11-9).

More recently, the Tokyo-based Shimizu Corporation, one of the largest construction firms in the world, initiated a similar experiment, which it called the *free-address* system. Here, too, no one owned a particular office or desk. Shimizu's research had shown that on any given day fewer than 50 percent of the staff were present (see Figure 11-10). To alleviate the extreme density in the typical Japanese office, the company instituted a system in which professional workers were assigned to a work area with two different kinds of workplaces: either desks arranged front to front in the center of the room (the

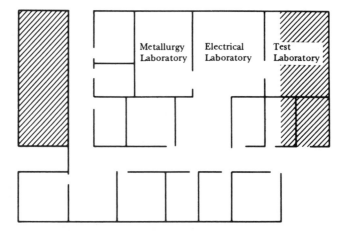

Figure 11-7. The original floor plan for a group of design engineers, with cellular offices "owned" by specific individuals. (Source: Thomas J. Allen copyright © The Massachusetts Institute of Technology 1977 *Managing the Flow of Technology* Cambridge, Mass.: MIT Press. Reprinted by permission of MIT Press.)

traditional arrangement) or small workstations surrounded by panels. There were about 30 percent fewer desks than there would have been if every employee "owned" his or her own workplace.

On coming to work each day, rather than going to an assigned desk, each employee picked up a cordless telephone and a laptop computer and wheeled a rolling pedestal

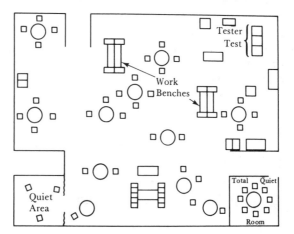

Figure 11-8. The floor plan of a nonterritorial office, in which the traditional office (see Figure 11-7) has been reconfigured into zones for different activities. Individuals use whatever space within the overall office is suitable to the work they are doing at the moment. (Source: Thomas J. Allen copyright © The Massachusetts Institute of Technology 1977 *Managing the Flow of Technology* Cambridge, Mass.: MIT Press. Reprinted by permission of MIT Press.)

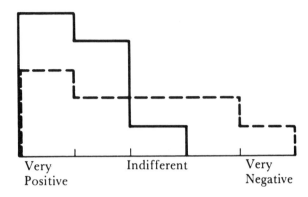

– – – June 1970
——— April 1971

Very Positive   Indifferent   Very Negative

Figure 11-9. A comparison of feelings about working in a nonterritorial office, before and after the experience. (Source: Thomas J. Allen copyright © The Massachusetts Institute of Technology 1977 *Managing the Flow of Technology* Cambridge, Mass.: MIT Press. Reprinted by permission of MIT Press.)

with his or her files to any desk or workstation that was not occupied. The employee could spread work out over two desks, if the one next to him or her was not occupied, or could choose to work in a workstation with more privacy than he or she had ever experienced before. Like Allen, Shimizu found that the employees' initial skepticism gave way to enthusiasm when they discovered they actually had more space to work in (they could spread out onto an adjacent, empty desk), and groups could get together easily for discussions without reserving or moving to meeting rooms. Thus cost was contained, and effectiveness and satisfaction actually increased (see Figures 11-11, 11-12, 11-13, 11-14).

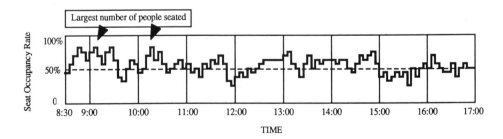

Figure 11-10. An actual occupancy pattern based on observations in a Japanese office for engineers. (Source: Shimizu Corporation 1989)

- Design and use of non-exclusive furniture with drawers which separate from desks.

- Concentrated use of cordless telephones which are not fixed on desks.

- Use of lap-top personal computers which are not fixed on desks.

Figure 11-11.   Furniture and electronic equipment that supports the Japanese free-address (nonterritorial) office system. (Source: Shimizu Corporation 1989)

Similar arrangements are being tried by Hewlett-Packard outside London and by Ernst & Young in London. At Ernst & Young, John de Lucy, the Director of Administration, now calculates space efficiency in terms of both square feet per employee and number of employees per desk! In some parts of the organization the ratio of management consultants to desks is five to one and, for accountants, three to one (see Figure 11-15).

De Lucy is also encouraging some of the staff to work at home and is providing them with laptop computers and eventually fax machines to make them truly effective. Rank Xerox went even further several years ago when it asked a number of its professional staff to leave the company and then set up long-term consulting contracts with them in which little has changed in the way of work but a great deal had changed in where the work was conducted.

The shared office concept improves efficiency, but for many organizations this is not enough. The reason is that efficiency, in terms of amount of space per person, does not resolve the problem of flexibility or the ability to reconfigure workstations and offices to meet changing and unpredictable organizational changes and to accommodate new information technologies. And so other approaches, many dictated by the need to cope with churn (the physical reconfiguration of offices and workstations), are being tried.

CHURN

Churn, or the percentage of total offices and workstations that are reconfigured annually, averages about 30 percent in American companies (IFMA 1984), with rates of 57 to 70 percent relatively common in financial services and other high-change organizations

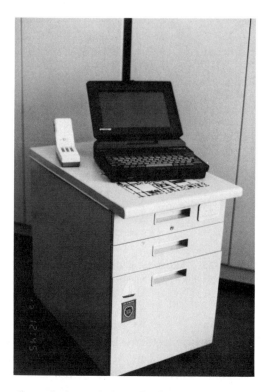

Figure 11-12.   A cordless telephone, desktop plug-in computer, and rolling pedestal are picked up by the Japanese engineer each morning and moved to the desk or workstation where he will work that day. (Photo: Shimizu Corporation 1989)

and departments. Organizational restructuring, changes in management style, acquisitions and divestitures, and development of new product lines—as well as the need to accommodate new computers and their proliferating peripherals—drive frequent organizational change. A number of different planning design concepts have been devised to cope with churn.

Planning and Design Responses

Panel-based Open Planning

The first response to frequent organizational change was to maximize internal planning flexibility by installing panel-based systems furniture that could be taken apart and reconnected in new combinations many times, did not require construction tradespeople, and was presumably less disruptive in regard to dust, noise, and downtime than was conventional drywall construction. Ironically, many organizations found that the panel systems actually stimulated physical reconfiguration because it was relatively easy (and had been justified on this basis!).

Reconfiguration costs money and is disruptive. Moreover, to reach its full potential,

Figure 11-13.   Typical offices of an engineering department in a Japanese company. (Photo: Shimizu Corporation 1989)

panel-based systems furniture also requires more flexible means of distributing power and regulating air flow and temperature. Raised flooring does this, for example, but it is dependent on buildings with sufficient floor-to-ceiling heights to accommodate the raised floor, and it costs more initially than does more conventional wire management and air distribution systems.

Figure 11-14.   Offices of an engineering department in a Japanese company after implementing the free-address concept. (Photo: Shimizu Corporation 1989)

Figure 11-15. The free-address concept for field engineers in a British firm focuses on a large common table with computers and rolling pedestals nearby.

Fixed Service Spines

Companies like Corning Glass in Corning, New York, Aetna Life and Casualty Company, Herman Miller, and IBM UK have deliberately begun to restrict flexibility by adding fixed service elements and rigid planning grids to their planning. The intent is to minimize the overall reconfiguration of workstations while actually making it easier to reconfigure some panels.

The key is a fixed service spine that distributes power and air along a formal grid. Services are never relocated, but it is easy to plug in equipment or direct air along the spine. The fixed planning modules help prevent the decay over time of circulation routes that could affect emergency egress and reduce the cost and time of change, as only unwired panels are moved; decrease the overall amount of physical change; and increase freedom and ease of change around the fixed elements (see Figures 11-16 and 11-17).

Same-sized Offices

In Europe, particularly Scandinavia, same-sized offices are common. The reason has more to do with social ideology than with cost, but the concept also has a strong utility value. Same-sized offices mean that no reconfiguration is needed to accommodate employees of different ranks. Again, people and not panels are moved. Reorganizations proceed more quickly and with no disruption. Union Carbide employed the concept in the United States, and it has worked very successfully (Froggatt 1985). Offices are large enough to house one person with visitors or two persons who do not require

Figure 11-16. Herman Miller's "fat walls" concept provides a fixed space planning grid that defines space architecturally while deliberately reducing possible reconfigurations of the overall layout. Same-sized office footprints that can accommodate different furniture components to support different job functions and work-styles also help minimize the disruption of reconfiguring the overall layout.

much privacy. The same-sized 13.5 × 13.5 foot office serves as a conference room or small lounge, and because of the modularity of the grid, several offices can easily be combined to create larger conference space or other specialized rooms (e.g., computer, dark room, resource center). Union Carbide is a good example of the principle of redistribution of space cited earlier (see Figure 11-18).

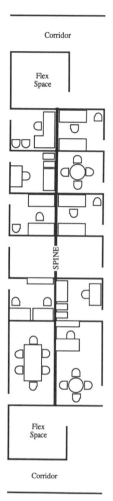

Figure 11-17. A fixed service spine within which all power distribution runs reduces the physical churn of whole layouts, maintains clear circulation, and increases the flexibility of the workstation configuration along and at the ends of the spine.

Narrow Space Bands

Same-sized offices are, for many organizations, too radical a planning concept. More typical are the identification of two to three "bands" of office size, each of which accommodates employees spanning many different job levels (reflected in pay, title, and responsibilities). Thus there may be a single clerical-sized office, and a single-sized professional and middle manager–level office, which together are likely to represent over 75 percent of the total number of office, and then a third band of more senior manager's offices for directors, vice-presidents, and the like. Because most of the reconfiguration involves staff below the senior management level, this system has many of the same advantages as does the same-sized office concept (see Figures 11-19 and 11-20).

Kit of Parts

To widen choice while controlling furniture inventory chaos and incompatibility among different furniture systems, more organizations are allowing employees to select from

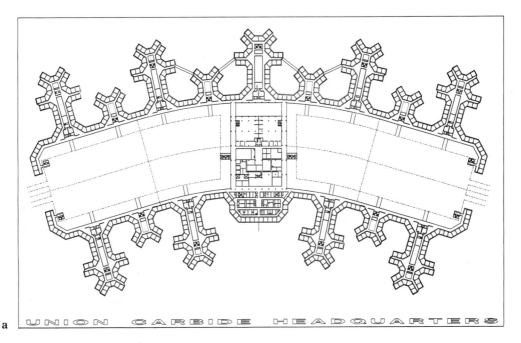

UNION CARBIDE HEADQUARTERS

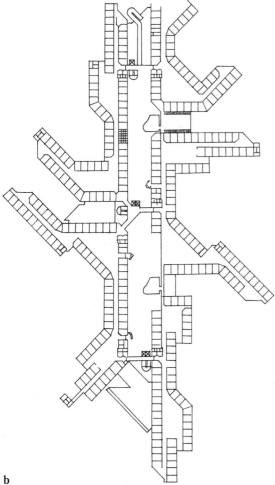

Figure 11-18. Same-sized offices in articulated forms or organized around an atrium reduce physical churn by moving people rather than partitions, and they give employees the most opportunities for access to natural light and interesting views. (Source: a, Union Carbide and Sunbelt Investments 1989; b, SAS Airlines 1989)

b

STANDARD FOOTPRINTS

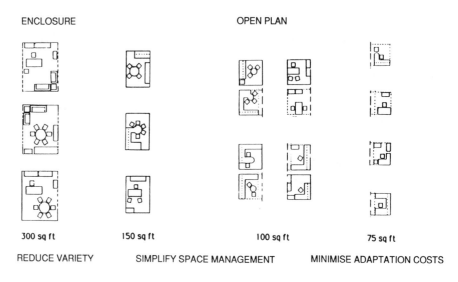

SAVINGS TO BE GAINED THROUGH RATIONALISATION
FIXED LAYOUT INFRASTRUCTURE

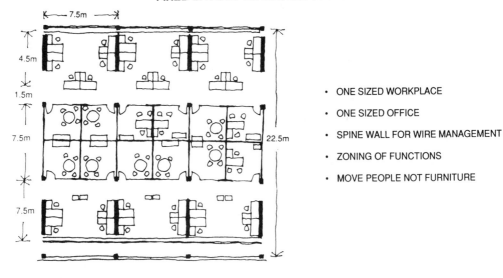

Figure 11-19 and 11-20. Same-sized office footprints and fixed service spines increase flexibility and minimize adaptation costs. (Source: Worthington 1988)

a predetermined kit of parts those furniture components that best suit their own work habits and style. Choice may range from a round conference table rather than a traditional desk to the number and type of shelves and binder bins. The idea is to select a single system within which parts can be mixed and matched without losing their functional and aesthetic compatibility and without the need to maintain extensive inventories of incompatible components. Such an approach to space planning and facility design implies space guidelines based on functional use rather than on what are often rigid and arbitrary highly detailed space and furniture standards rooted in the desire to use office size and furniture to communicate internal status differences.

Building Grid or Window Mullions

Space management is highly dependent on building form, particularly in regard to the service grid and window mullions. Grids must have a functional use when subdivided. Seven-foot grids, for example, mean that the smallest office will be fourteen feet wide, too large for many offices, just as seven feet is too small for any office or usable space (besides storage of materials or equipment). A five-foot grid, which can accommodate offices ten or fifteen feet wide (or larger), makes more sense (see Chapter 13). The planning goal is to be able to subdivide space easily into many different offices sizes and functional uses (see Figure 11-21).

COMMUNICATION AND PRIVACY

The need to share technical information and coordinate tasks is taken for granted in most organizations. But until recently, little attention has been paid to a third type of communication: informal, serendipitous face-to-face communication intended to spark new ideas. For organizations concerned with generating new ideas, services, and products—and these have expanded far beyond the bounds of R & D units within manufacturing organizations to include companies as diverse as insurance and university biotechnology laboratories—the importance of informal communication has become paramount. To shorten product development cycles, promote innovation, improve product quality, and reduce unwanted duplication and overlap, a wide range of expertise and experience is needed, and Professor Thomas Allen's research in R & D organizations (1977) shows that informal communication, especially with people outside one's own discipline, department, or project team is critical to the exchange of ideas.

Planning and Design Response

There are a number of ways in which the design and layout of space and groups can support informal communication (see Chapter 10, the CDC case study, for a more detailed analysis).

Functional Inconvenience

Most adjacency planning assumes that people who have strong organizational reporting or functional relationships should be located close to one another. The intent is to maximize efficiency by reducing the amount of time wasted in unnecessary travel. But

Figure 11-21. Raised-access floors and modular planning allow this Swedish speculative office to accommodate different-sized conference rooms, and common areas, as the occupying tenant desires.

Spatial Bond / Organizational Bond

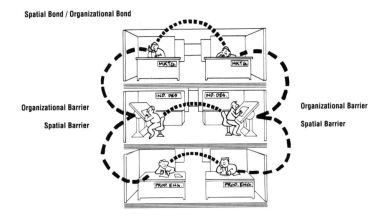

Organizational Barrier

Spatial Barrier

Organizational Barrier

Spatial Barrier

Figure 11-22.   Typical adjacency planning reinforces organizational bonds and barriers with spatial bonds and barriers. (Source: Steelcase, Inc. 1989)

Organizational Barrier / Spatial Bond

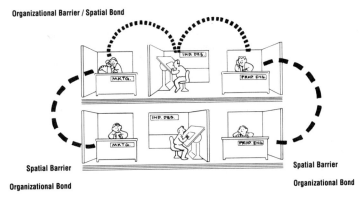

Spatial Barrier

Organizational Bond

Spatial Barrier

Organizational Bond

Figure 11-23.   The concept of functional inconvenience uses adjacency planning to overcome organizational barriers and increase informal communication across departments and disciplines. (Source: Steelcase, Inc. 1989)

being efficient is not the same as being effective. Allen's (1977) research suggests that if the goal is the generation of new ideas, then serendipitous contact is essential; that is, one wants to maximize the potential for people whose organizational relationships make it unlikely they will meet to bump into one another informally. Figures 11-22 and 11-23 show how physical proximity, or adjacencies, can be used to complement and compensate for organizational structure and increase informal communication.

Multiple Work Areas

Organizations want to increase informal communication, but they also recognize the legitimate need for privacy to allow concentration as well as to protect confidentiality. The answer is space planning viewed as part of a total system.

The ability to use information technology to obtain information and communicate with others without respect to distance, and to store information that can be quickly retrieved, promotes employees' spatial mobility and enables the use of multiple work areas within a main office, in branch offices, in different buildings within a large complex, and at home. Information goes with the worker, and the worker goes to the location where, at a given time, it makes most sense to work because it may be quieter, there may be others there with whom he or she wants to interact, transportation may be more convenient, scheduling easier, and so on. Multiple offices may mean smaller offices, but with more specialized purposes and possibly shared by several employees.

The underlying premise is that no single office, no matter how well designed, is likely to support equally well all the tasks and activities and forms of interaction in which many workers today are involved. Thus some of the loosely coupled settings may be very small and under individual control. Others may be larger areas under the control of a project team. Still others may be accessible to whole departments or the whole organization. The individually controlled areas may be more permanent, providing stability, whereas the group areas are assigned on a project basis and provide the opportunity for dealing with new projects, new teams, and other aspects of organizational change. The mobility inherent in this systems view serves informal communication by increasing the probability that employees from different projects and disciplines and departments will run into one another unintentionally as they move about the building.

Shared Meeting and Social Spaces

If workers are mobile and have multiple work areas, each of which is relatively small in size and not intended for small-group meetings, there will remain a need for rooms for scheduled as well as spontaneous meetings and face-to-face interaction. Conference rooms of varying sizes distributed throughout the building, even in increased numbers, are only a partial solution. What are needed are small lounge and break areas. At the Steelcase Corporation's new Corporate Development Center, "Corner Commons" have been situated in the corners of the building for this purpose. At Aetna Life and Casualty, small commons rooms distributed around floors are called *oases*. Placing an activity generator such as a coffeepot in these commons work areas, as well as locating them near frequently used services such as mail and copy that enhance the likelihood of serendipitous meetings.

Circulation

A key to "functional inconvenience" is the nature of circulation and the activities and events encountered while one moves around the building. Central escalators and open central staircases that make travel visible increase eye contact and the likelihood of people initiating contact. Wide corridors and landings on stairs and near lounges create comfortable places to get out of traffic without making the kind of commitment that going to someone's office or a conference room implies.

Break and Lounge Areas

Break and lounge areas need to be located centrally, and along major circulation paths where people will pass them as they move around the building. Such areas can also act as a magnet that pulls people through and to areas where they might not otherwise go. It is important that the furniture in these areas support legitimate activities. Seeing an employee sitting in an easy chair with a cup of coffee in hand bothers many managers. Sitting at a table in an office chair, however, is closer to "normal" business routines and so is less likely to raise management eyebrows. Placing a whiteboard near the area gives the area even more legitimacy. Indeed, for these kinds of areas to work, the activity they support must be viewed by management as "time-in," that is, real work, not time out or loafing.

Group and Project Spaces

Project teams are integral to the rugby model, and they cannot rely on scheduled review sessions in conference rooms, which tend to become too formal and too static. Nor can they rely on serendipitous contacts, which tend to occur too infrequently. Dedicated project rooms provide a focal point for team members who otherwise may not "run into" one another during the workday. Such rooms reduce setup and breakdown time and can help create a sense of cohesion among project groups by giving them and their project a spatial identity (see Figure 11-24).

ATTRACTING AND RETAINING STAFF

Highly qualified workers, particularly in R & D-intensive industries, are in short supply and becoming more so. Therefore, the physical environment has become, for many employees, one of the factors they use in selecting an employer and staying on the job.

Expanding, often round-the-clock time-use patterns of buildings have created the need for employees to have access to food, transportation, recreation, and the opportunity to socialize and relax at all times of the day and night. Facilities to support these activities should be pleasant and easily accessible, and their provision is especially important in greenfield sites located away from commercial development. These facilities include a range of amenities that in the not-too-distant past were more associated with a town center than an office building or complex. Examples are fitness centers and facilities, break areas, dining services, shops and other services, day care centers, and medical services.

IMAGE AND IDENTITY

Image and identity are concerns of the individual and work group and the corporation as a whole, yet for the most part planning and design have considered only the corporate image. But this is changing as organizations realize that expressions of personal and group identity are more tonic than poison and that they can be managed positively without struggling (usually unsuccessfully) to stifle them.

Figure 11-24.   Scheduled conference rooms are not a substitute for dedicated project rooms. (Bottom photo: Joseph Pobereskin Photography 1989).

Planning and Design Responses

Bounded Personalization

Few organizations are willing to forsake completely a planned corporate image, but many also realize that employees do not like to feel like interchangeable parts in a well-oiled machine. The Union Carbide Corporation has balanced these competing needs in some innovative ways.

Employees were invited to bring in favorite photos and posters, which were then professionally mounted at company expense. In addition, a corporate art program was established that offered different categories of art, from Asian and modern to English hunting scenes. Employees were given the opportunity to select artwork for their offices from these categories to reflect their own tastes, rather than those of an art director. Both of these programs preserved the company's desire to maintain a professional image, but they did so by giving employees a choice and something of value (i.e., professionally framed personal photos).

Union Carbide went beyond decoration, however, and offered its employees an opportunity to select a complete furniture package from thirty different combinations (fifteen different styles in two different colors). Once again, the company protected its concerns for its corporate image while acknowledging different work-styles and preferences in a framework of choices that varied greatly but all were acceptable to both the architects and top management. According to a series of formal studies we have done (Froggart 1985; Becker 1988c), these offices continue to be among the most highly rated in studies of American office workers.

Front Stage and Back Stage

Related to corporate versus individual identity is the distinction between front stage and back stage areas. Front stage areas are public areas, the living room or parlor of the office world, where the company preens and keeps its hair up and its shoes polished to impress visitors. Back stage ares are the den, the kitchen, the place where the family lives its daily life, feet up, hair down, comfortable, familiar, productive. It is the place for friends, neighbors, and relatives.

Many organizations treat all space as front stage, public areas, even when the only people who enter them are employees. It is like always having breakfast in a suit and tie or keeping the bedroom or the den as tidy as the living room. Differentiating front and back stage areas, with the corporate image—and visitors—restricted to high-visibility public areas such as lobbies, cafeterias, and meeting rooms allow project rooms and office areas to take on the character of lived-in space for working.

INDIVIDUAL AND GROUP CONTROL

Employees want to express their personal and professional identity. They also want their immediate environment to help them work productively and to be comfortable. A balance between individual and organizational needs and between work-styles and preferences among employees is one of those thorny issues that never disappears for long. New systems such as Johnson Controls' "personal environments" offer individual controls for heating, ventilation, and lighting within an open plan work environment and individual fan coil units that can be regulated by the occupant within a four-to-eight degree temperature range are not uncommon in enclosed offices. The company thus uses technology to support individual control of the ambient environment. Union Carbide's furniture packages or a variety of other "choice" policies (described next) are other ways of meeting the employees' rising expectations without sacrificing the concern for corporate image or cost-effective building systems.

SPACE MANAGEMENT: INNOVATIVE POLICIES AND PROCEDURES

The preceding section looked at some of the design and planning approaches to dealing with recurrent organizational issues, from churn to attracting and retaining staff. In addition, a wide range of administrative policies and procedures interact with and are linked to specific approaches to planning and design. Primarily aimed at containing costs, they recognize the more dynamic nature of business today and the need to share both responsibility and authority more broadly.

Chargeback Systems

Chargeback systems are accounting systems in which individual departments and, in some cases, even individuals are charged for the specific amount of space they occupy and the costs of operating and maintaining it. In some companies the chargeback is extended to the cost of moving furniture, equipment, and panels, with the cost being charged to the department or group that initiates the move. Costs are based on market values and actual operating expenses. Sometimes they are partially subsidized, usually when the program is phased in.

As part of a general movement toward greater administrative decentralization and the establishment of relatively autonomous profit centers, one goal is to make department or area managers aware of the costs of facilities so that they will make more prudent space and change requests.

Another objective is to build into the accounting system a more realistic picture of costs by charging facilities expenses at closer to their fair market value. This also reduces the likelihood that takeover specialists will target a company whose book value is far below market value because of tremendously undervalued real estate assets that can be sold off, piecemeal, at enormous profit.

To minimize chaos, these chargeback systems can be implemented in stages, with the corporate subsidies gradually diminishing. The systems also must be coupled with minimum space and furniture standards so that no single department, in an effort to lower its overhead costs and improve its profitability, creates slum working conditions. Protecting the opposite end of the spectrum needs to be considered as well, both for the demoralizing effect that great differences in accommodation may have on employees whose departments cannot afford luxurious furnishings and because incompatible components and planning approaches can severely limit flexibility and interchangeability and thereby raise costs for the organization as a whole. Some firms, like CitiBank in its new Long Island City tower—which treats each department like a separate tenant, each with its own space and furniture standards—are willing to push the chargeback system to its full potential at the departmental level.

Inventory Control and Bar Coding

Organizations often have a poor grasp of how much furniture, and in what condition, is being used in various locations within a building or in different buildings and different sites. As a consequence, furniture is sometimes ordered for new projects or renovations when existing furniture could be used. CAD and CAFM systems can reduce the amount of unnecessary furniture purchased by helping the facilities group maintain accurate inventory records.

Group Allocation of Space

Most American space and furniture standards are based on the individual workstation or office. In Europe it is more common for space to be assigned to a group or department, based on an allocation of gross square feet per person. Each department or group then works with the facilities group to plan its own layout, based on its idiosyncratic work-style and preferences. There does not seem to be a need for every group to have the same layout or the same way of allocating space. Freestanding furniture and a common furniture standard (i.e., the same furniture is used throughout the organization) enhances flexibility in response to organizational change.

Last-Minute Detailed Space Planning

Many companies try to draw up detailed floor plans months in advance of the actual move. Inevitably, by the time of the move, the group has grown or shrunk, a new group has been assigned to the space, or the work patterns have shifted. So the whole detailed planning effort begins once again, representing an enormous waste of time, money, and energy.

An alternative is simply to assign groups to an area (based on an average number of square feet per person) and to order furniture components to meet a generic workstation, with an inventory of components available from which employees can choose those that fit their standard-sized workstation footprint. These components can be estimated by doing a detailed design brief to understand work patterns and work-styles (see Chapter 8). The layout is not detailed or implemented until only a few weeks before the move.

Simple Guidelines

To help maintain an acceptable work environment and provide some consistency in overall planning efforts while optimizing individual and group control over layouts, some organizations allow departments to plan their own layout within a few space-planning rules, as noted earlier.

In a few companies CAD systems are used to help employees plan their layout by having a CAD operator transform roughly drawn plans from user groups into CAD drawings in which initial layouts can be matched to the power and lighting grid, circulation needs, and so on. The user groups then review the drawings before they are implemented.

Inventing new layouts or new FM policies and procedures is not difficult, but inventing ones that are acceptable to both users and management, that reflect how the organization wants to work and think of itself, is far more difficult. Getting space management right means understanding organizational culture, and that is what Chapter 12 explores.

MANAGING CHOICE AND CONTROL

Many of these design and planning ideas seek solutions that improve the quality of the workplace for the individual employee while preserving the organization's commitment to maintaining its corporate image and controlling costs. The fundamental issue is control and how it can be shared among all the stakeholders in the workplace: management, occupants, and experts like facility managers, engineers, interior designers, and architects. From containing costs to increasing productivity, from organizational restructuring to new management styles, senior management continues to look for ways of maintaining a competitive edge. Sharing control in facility management now means widening the role of employee participation in planning and design.

Most organizations know that their largest organizational cost is salaries and that their single largest asset is the people earning them. How these people work underlies virtually everything any organization does to sharpen its competitive edge. People drive innovation, and facilities affect people. From office layout and block planning to the design of building systems, facilities influence employees' ability to concentrate and communicate effectively, to use necessary resources, and to maintain their comfort, satisfaction, and health.

National surveys of office workers (Brill, Margulis, and Konar 1984; Steelcase/Harris 1987) consistently show, for example, that American office workers want greater involvement in decisions affecting their work environment than most of them now have and that higher levels of user involvement are associated with the employees' subsequently greater satisfaction with the workplace and greater commitment to the planning and design decisions. European research on participatory decision making (DIO 1983) found that involving employees does not necessarily take more time than top-down planning approaches do and that it is most effective when it occurs in the early problem-definition stages of the process rather than in the later implementation stages.

Given the billions of dollars spent annually on office planning and design, raising employees' satisfaction with their workplace through more opportunities for their involvement in the planning process would seem to be an FM program valued by many organizations. Why isn't it? Differences in the definition of the role of the "good manager" and concerns that employee participation is tantamount to planned chaos underlie, I believe, much of the resistance to widespread employee involvement.

Tension among the individual's, the group's, and top management's needs to control will always exist. The challenge is to find policies, programs, and designs that balance them. A starting point is understanding that including rank-and-file employees in decisions about their workplace does not necessarily result in chaos or undermine expert or management authority.

Fear of Chaos

"Utter disorder and confusion" is how the dictionary defines *chaos*. My sense is that many managers also equate variety and visible diversity with chaos. Yet variety is not inherently chaotic; in fact, as biologists and ecologists have shown, differentiation can contribute to stability and strength.

For many managers, broad user involvement creates images of endless and fruitless discussions with every employee, arguing about not only his or her own interminable wish list but also virtually no consensus on the items' priorities. But in fact, American research indicates that employees agree about many aspects of office design, including preferred colors and finishes (presumably the most personal of all preferences). Michael Brill's and his collegues' (1984) study of American office workers, for example, found wide consensus on colors and finishes that employees like and do not like in the workplace. The stark white and black of the modern movement, tepid beige and gray, or the bright intense colors often favored by architects and designers are the least liked. Brill's data show that people overwhelmingly prefer colors and materials associated with traditional homes, executive offices, and prestige: pastels, warm and cool colors, natural materials such as wood and fabric for walls and panels, and wood for work surfaces and storage units. Research is equally consistent in showing that employees want to work with direct access to natural light and that they want ergonomic seating and good lighting that minimizes glare (Eastman Kodak 1983; Moore 1986)

Although many user involvement programs seem futile, the problem is generally with the particular process used, not with the principle of involving employees. Few of us would drive a car without brakes and then conclude that all automobiles are inherently dangerous, but something akin to this seems to occur with poorly designed user involvement experiences.

Undermining Management's Authority

Any program that appears to undermine experts' and managements' authority by shifting control down the line to staff is likely to be resisted by managers. By virtue of their position, managers have the right and responsibility to make certain decisions, based when appropriate on input from knowledgeable experts. This is without question a legitimate and necessary management role. The main issue, of course, is what kind of control?

Managers are likely to discourage user involvement if their concept of the "good" manager or expert is one who dictates not only what needs to be done, and when, but also how and where and with what tools it should be done (a tactical orientation). This kind of manager is likely to view user involvement as undermining management's authority. If, however, managers see their role as developing policies, programs, guidelines, and frameworks guided by expert knowledge (a strategic orientation) within which individuals and groups are allowed to make choices, then user involvement becomes a way of freeing management to concentrate on broader policy issues. Let us look at some of these frameworks or guidelines.

Types of User Involvement

Before embarking on major renovation or new construction projects, most organizations solicit information in some form from their employees about their workplace needs and requirements. This kind of involvement, in which employees are permitted to participate in the design process, is useful in identifying basic features to include in a new design, but it does not offer them a sense of control over their immediate work environment, nor does it result, by itself, in the kind of variety that reflects actual differences in how people choose to work most effectively. Such variety can come only with some form of individual or group choice, such as the following:

1. *The Free Market*
   The free market approach allows individual occupants to design their own work area without restriction but within a given office footprint. In a corporation, this much freedom is allowed only at the highest executive levels, and even then relatively rarely.
2. *The Cost Ceiling*
   In organizations with a high percentage of professional staff such as lawyers, accountants, or advertising writers, a modified version of unregulated choice allows the organization to set a cost ceiling, often keyed to organizational rank, on how much the staff can spend on furniture and furnishings. But within this budget, there are no restrictions on the style or arrangement of the furniture in the office.
3. *The Cafeteria*
   The cafeteria option, in which individuals or groups are allowed to select furniture components or whole office interiors from a set of options determined centrally by corporate designers or facility managers can be highly successful (see the earlier discussion of Union Carbide's corporate headquarters in Danbury, Connecticut).
4. *The Puzzle*
   In the puzzle option at the level of the individual work area, employees are given a set of workstation components selected by the facility manager or interior designer (e.g., table, pedestals, cabinets, work surfaces) that they can arrange within a predetermined work area footprint in any way they like.
5. *Guidelines*
   In Europe an interesting variant of the puzzle approach is its application to the group or task team level. A department or work group is assigned a location in the building, a set amount of space, and a particular furniture system or set of components. The group then determines how to lay out its own work area, using guidelines determined by a central facility manager. These guidelines are typically few and straightforward: High panels cannot be placed near windows where they would block daylight; all workstations must meet the building codes for circulation and fire safety; and equipment must be located so that it can be easily connected to power sources. Within these guidelines, groups are free to arrange their assigned components as they want. There is no attempt to maintain a consistent corporate image in the office layouts. Rather, the corporate image is maintained by means of common furniture elements and building design features, particularly in public spaces.
6. *The Mechanic*
   When integrated furniture systems are used, in the mechanic option, the choice available to the individual is effectively limited to ergonomic seat adjustments, positioning of task lights, and the location of telephones, calculators, computers and other equipment on work surfaces.
7. *The Mirror*
   The mirror option takes the form of personalization, or the display of photos, posters, and memorabilia that reflect personal and professional identity, an important concern

for many people. This is the most common form of choice available to employees at every level.

Functional Diversity: Freedom Within a Framework

Each of the preceding choice options maintains a significant degree of corporate control, usually including the size of the office footprint, the nature and style of basic furniture components, and the location of individuals and groups within the building. Yet nearly all share a commitment to functional diversity, the opportunity for employees to select and/or arrange preselected furniture elements in ways that support their own work-style and work effectiveness. Thus, while these choice programs acknowledge that people work differently and need different environmental supports to be effective, they still address the corporation's concerns for efficiency and flexibility (components can be interchanged), cost control (savings from large purchases can be realized), and overall image (components come from a single line or compatible styles of furniture).

Input programs, including input from experts and employees, help identify appropriate components or features of the office environment, whereas choice programs permit individual freedom within decision frameworks determined by facility management. Together, they provide an integrated facility management strategy that can work for the individual and the group as well as for the organization.

Well-structured programs avoid chaos and actually strengthen management's authority by concentrating on more strategic resource allocation issues. They increase the likelihood that space, furniture, and equipment will be used close to their full potential, and they promote greater employee commitment to and satisfaction with facility decisions. These newer approaches to space planing and management reflect the approach of an elastic organization. They significantly reduce the cost of space while providing what may actually be better working conditions. They are a hidden FM resource.

These approaches to increasing space efficiency are fascinating, but they leave many questions unanswered. What supervision and management styles are needed to make some of these arrangements work? What kinds of workers and work are suitable for these kinds of arrangements, and can both be expanded to larger segments of the work force? What kinds of technology, management and staff training, and financial and other incentives are needed to support these approaches? The cost of space is not dropping, and neither are workers' expectations. Facility managers should learn how leading-edge firms are coping with these challenges, and they must understand their cost and other organizational implications. Collecting examples of innovative approaches to maximizing space efficiency is a first step. The next step is to investigate systematically the cost and organizational implications of these approaches to managing space effectively. This means that organizations, and especially their facility management groups, will have to become much more committed to research than they are at the moment.

Skeptics Speak

As a corporation, we have worked very hard to develop and communicate a clear corporate image. It seems to me that encouraging what you call "functional diversity" undermines a clear, strong corporate image, thereby confusing the customer, visitor, and employee alike.

Remember, we are not talking about everybody doing his or her own thing, without regard to how these decisions will affect neighbors or the organization as a whole. I am advocating choice within frameworks, ideally frameworks that are constructed by representatives of all the parties concerned, so that the "middle ground" I noted can be identified and implemented.

Many managers do believe that clients and customers will interpret visible diversity as a lack of business rigor and weak management. It is equally possible, of course, that visible diversity can be used to communicate the corporation's commitment to treating employees as individuals and respecting their diversity (often proclaimed in official documents but rather less often demonstrated in the physical surroundings).

Much less often considered is the equally undesired possibility that customers might be bored by and indifferent to the bland uniformity of many corporate public spaces or interpret it as an organization's weak commitment to innovation, to creating a humane and pleasant work environment, and to recognizing and accommodating individual differences in work-style that might increase effectiveness, produce better products, and improve service.

Although I do not know of any studies that have investigated customers' impressions and expectations based on the design of corporate facilities and offices, there have been studies of the influence of faculty design, layout, and "messiness" on students' impressions of a professor, which have found, for example, that very messy offices, in which books, papers, and reports are scattered everywhere create the impression that the occupant does not really have time to meet with the advisor and that he or she is disorganized and uncaring (Morrow and McElroy, 1981). The opposite extreme, the clean desk policy, was not, however, very appealing either. Occupants of these kinds of offices were seen as rather dull and boring. The most positive impressions were from offices with neat stacks of books and reports, a clear sense of order but also of activity. They seemed lived-in. In an earlier book I wrote about advertising agencies that corporate clients liked to visit just because they were so different from their own tightly controlled, bland facilities. The kind of vitality and energy observed in offices that are more personal and that have a human imprint, reflecting real people doing real work, can be appealing, refreshing, and invigorating, without being disheveled or communicating a disorganized mind.

It is also worth remembering that most people work in back stage areas, where client contact is minimal or nonexistent. Extending the corporate image beyond the entrance lobby, cafeteria, and other highly visible public spaces into back stage office areas would seem to be difficult to justify, as it is hard to confuse people with environmental diversity that they are unlikely to ever witness.

Space Management and Organizational Culture

Space management, which includes the planning, design, allocation, use, and management of space and furniture, can be thought of as a form of technology in which principles and processes are organized to achieve a certain objective. Any time we discuss any form of technology we need to distinguish between the possible and the probable, that is, between what can be achieved technologically and what is likely to be acceptable and, therefore, done in practice.

One of my favorite examples of the failure to make this distinction involved an aborigine tribe and the introduction, by well-meaning missionaries, of steel axes into their stone axe culture (Sharp 1952). The missionaries gave the tribe the steel axes with the expectation that their technological superiority and the time saved because the axes were ready-made would substantially improve the tribe's productivity. The axes also would be sharper and last longer. There was only one problem. The culture of this tribe valued—above all else—sleep. And so, although the new axes did save time, it was used to sleep more, not to produce more. At the same time, the new axes, which were distributed to everyone, including women, disturbed the tribe's fragile social system by undermining and confusing well-established role definitions among men and women without replacing them with other equally acceptable new ones.

The failure to consider new technologies in their social and organizational context is neither rare nor restricted to nonindustrialized societies. Sociotechnical theory was used first by members of the Tavistock Institute in the 1950s as part of their study of the introduction of new long-wall strip coal-mining techniques. Their work illustrated how the social organization of groups could undermine and counteract new technological advances unless these were designed and introduced in a way that supported fundamental group values and personal and professional identities (e.g., Trist and Bamforth 1951). Subsequent studies in Indian textile mills, on ships, and in other work settings have provided additional evidence showing how the social and organizational context into which technology is placed—as well as in which it is developed—can have an enormous influence on the degree to which it actually improves productivity (Pasmore and Sherwood 1978).

The purpose of space management is to help the organization prosper in a competitive business environment. Technology is not an end in itself, and it is unlikely, by itself, to support organizational effectiveness unless it is designed and implemented with the social and organizational ramifications in mind. Such issues constitute a universe of constraints that in practice limit the take-up rate and usefulness of any new technology, whether office automation, chargeback systems, a fixed service spine, or same-sized offices.

ORGANIZATIONAL ECOLOGY

This way of thinking about the connections between space planning and design and organizational effectiveness has been called the study of *organizational ecology* (Becker 1981; Steele 1986). Its domain is how the planning, design, and management of the physical settings of offices affects and is affected by organizational patterns and practices. Within this context a "smart" building is one in which there is a good fit between the technologies' capabilities and the organization's work patterns and culture. Whatever technologies are put in place should support and even enhance the kinds of work practices the organization considers acceptable. "Acceptable" needs some definition, which leads to a major theme of this chapter: the need for technical innovation to be matched by innovations in work practice and culture.

The proliferation of high-powered personal computers linked by telephone lines with one another and with central mainframe computers without respect to geographical distance (i.e., telecommuting) makes it technically possible, for example, for people to work at home. But what actually governs how many people work at home is "acceptability," not technical feasibility. Acceptability takes many forms: the levels of social contact that employees consider acceptable, the amount of face-to-face contact and supervision that managers consider acceptable, the amount of money allocated to personal computers and their servicing, the potential for security breaches that organizations consider acceptable, the amount of time and money that the organization is willing to commit to employees' training, and so on. The failure of office automation to produce the paperless office illustrates beautifully the constraining influence of people's attitudes and values on the use of technological innovation. We want hard copy. The failure of centralized word-processing centers built on a factory model of information processing (which transformed secretaries from administrative assistants to machine operators) is still another example of the ways in which existing cultures affect technology use.

Existing values and practices do not eliminate the adoption of new technologies; they simply shape how they are used. Typically, the new technology is adapted to existing work patterns. The result is that those aspects of the technology's full potential that might stimulate new ways of working and managing are avoided or neglected. In facility management, for example, computers have been used to promote rigid space and furniture standards. The computer's ability to monitor and track enormous amounts of information—including where different pieces of furniture and components are located, who is using them, and for what purposes—has not been used to explore opportunities for expanding individual choice and diversity in workstations' design or layout. Organizations wishing to explore the full potential of new technologies, rather than simply integrating them into existing work patterns, must be prepared to reassess and modify their own work cultures.

CORPORATE CULTURE

Organizational or corporate culture refers (Schein 1985) to the often implicit, but still widely understood, shared expectations about what is acceptable in an organization, in other words, "the pattern of assumptions underlying what people do and value." These assumptions define the "shared patterns of thought, belief, feelings, and values that result from shared experience and common learning." Strong corporate cultures help guide action and define goals and suggest means for achieving them. In addition to influencing how organizational members think about themselves and their operating environment, the corporate culture embodies the organization's assumptions about how space is structured and about staff and management relations. These latter assumptions, in particular, directly impinge on space planning and design, that is, acceptable ways of structuring the physical environment to achieve organizational objectives.

Assumptions About How Space Is Structured

Several of the design innovations outlined in Chapter 11 imply particular assumptions about how space is structured, that is, about how to symbolize status and power, how to support peer relationships, how to allocate "turf" and privacy, and what are considered the "right" distances for formal and informal meetings and interaction.

Smaller, multiple offices and a redistribution of space within the organization (more for those lower in the hierarchy and less for those higher up) contradict conventional assumptions about how to symbolize status and power. Convention, in most large American organizations, is very clear: Those at the top get more space, more privacy, better views, more and better furnishings, and more opportunities for personalization and choice (Konar and Sundstrom 1985). The (untested) assumption and justification (when it is considered necessary to give one at all) is that such policies act as an incentive for those expecting to rise in the organization and that visitors use such spatial symbolism to gauge the influence and power of the organizational members with whom they interact.

Reducing the size of senior managers' offices or placing them on the inner core of the building rather than next to the windows thus requires shifting either the communication of status to other aspects of the environment (e.g., emphasizing the quality of furnishings) or the symbolic role of the environment to emphasize the direct support of functional job and organizational requirements (e.g., computer support, need for more spatial flexibility to accommodate organizational reconfigurations and churn). This latter orientation, of course, is as symbolic as the former. The difference is in the specific content, not in the importance or inevitability of the environment acting as a communication medium.

Redefining the organization's assumptions about how to symbolize status and power is probably the most difficult aspect of corporate culture to change. It is like pulling on a loose thread: It stubbornly refuses to break loose, but once it does the whole garment may unravel. When a corporate culture does change, it is usually a top-down phenomenon. At Union Carbide, for example, where all staff, regardless of job level, occupy the same-sized offices, furnished from the same set of choices, this decision (which turned completely on end the existing finely wrought space-by-rank policies) was originally made by the chairman of the board. Its justification was the savings in time, disruptions, and money that could be gained by moving people rather than partitions during reorganizations and the widespread feeling that fine-grained status distinctions embedded in rigid space and furniture standards had become dysfunctional.

Assumptions About Peer Relationships and Interaction Patterns

Implicit in several of the design approaches in Chapter 11 is the assumption that innovation, and often simply effectiveness, requires sharing information and expertise without respect to either departmental or job-level boundaries. Highly networked communication patterns are vital to manufacturing, professional, and other organizations that depend for their survival on new ideas. Such sharing cannot occur easily in highly structured organizational hierarchies in which communication, especially informal and spontaneous communication, is primarily among peers or wholly within departmental and project team boundaries.

Spaces intended for interaction scattered coffee bars, work areas, lounges, and seating near mail rooms and along major circulation routes imply that what may look like idle chatting is not only acceptable but intended and desirable! This contradicts the typical view of much of American management that people who are working should look like they are working; that is, they should be sitting at their desk writing, reading, talking on the telephone, or be in a scheduled meeting.

Work, in most American corporations, is place bound. We do not expect people to work in the cafeteria or the hallways, or to take a seat in the empty auditorium to read a book. The computer, with its potential for allowing people to work almost anywhere (at home or in other remote and nonvisible settings), can transform the central workplace into a setting for socializing with workers. But this challenges conventional assumptions about what counts as "work," what is "time in," and what is loafing, gabbing, or just shooting the breeze, or "time out," unproductive labor. Even more threatening are workplaces that are intended to stimulate thinking and creativity but in which no obvious work activity of any kind may be visible to someone passing by; for example, sitting outside on a terrace with one's feet up staring off into space. Many managers have difficulty appreciating such activities as "real" work (except, perhaps, when they find themselves sipping a drink at a business lunch!).

Designing innovative workplaces is easy, but persuading management to authorize them and employees to use them can be something else. The actual use of such workspaces requires a significant change in management's view of work. In particular, it requires shifting from an emphasis on the visible appearance of working to an emphasis on actual productivity. The question becomes what work, at what level of quality, and in what amounts was done within what time frame and with what resources? Ironically, it is the ivy tower, academia, which comes closest to this model.

No professor watches his or her students do their work. In fact, I do not want to know where, when, or with whom my students do their work, or what they are drinking and ingesting while they do it. I give an assignment, describe my expectations, indicate when the project is due, and what readings would be useful to them. I also lecture on the topic to give students background ideas and material. I do not care how long it takes the student (within the allotted time), or whether the work was finished two hours, two days, or two weeks before it was turned in. I am interested in what the students produce, not how many hours they spent in the library. Thus the most typical productivity indicator in many companies—simply being present—is replaced by direct indicators of performance: the work itself.

Assumptions About Turf and Privacy

Along with more space, privacy is one of the most important indicators of status in American organizations. Despite the enormous amount of open office design created by using panels to divide space, most senior managers occupy offices with floor-to-ceiling walls. The justification is typically the need to conduct confidential meetings with staff and visitors and to impress visitors with one's good standing and high rank in the organization.

Some of these confidential and ceremonial meetings could be held in a well-appointed conference room or in a private office reserved for such purposes on an "as needed" basis. The ambiguity of such spatial ownership can be deliberate and positive for visitors, who are likely to use the visual cues of the physical setting to interpret and make sense of the position of their host and, therefore, their own. In meeting with persons below the executive rank, for whom lavish appointments are uncommon, such spatial ambiguity enhances the visitors' own status.

The point is not that top management does not need privacy, but that many employees in middle management and technical and professional positions also need it to work effectively. Using privacy as a scarce resource to communicate status thus lowers its value as a functional component of the everyday work environment for employees representing a cross section of job functions and levels.

Individually assigned and controlled space is characteristic of American offices not only because it provides visual (and sometimes auditory) privacy, but also because of strong assumptions in American society about the right of everyone to his or her own place and the importance of individual identity. The lessons start at an early age. Many parents ask their five-year-old children what they want for dinner, and it is not uncommon for parents to knock before entering their children's rooms.

Shared space implies group rather than individual identity. The individual entrepreneur model—active at least symbolically in American life—places a stronger emphasis on individual achievement than on group achievement. Sharing also requires more social skills, greater coordination, communication, trust, and—perhaps most difficult—conformity to group expectations and norms. These attributes are not highly developed in most American employees or organizations.

Shared space also increases the likelihood of conflict, partially from competition for scarce resources (e.g., space, privacy, equipment) and partially from the need to monitor and possibly modify one's own behavior (e.g., speech, posture, gestures). If the shared space is combined with temporal freedom, as in the free-address or non-territorial office described in Chapter 11, it will require the ability to work well independently and without constant supervision and a commitment to being available at certain times and places to meet with colleagues. Management's role shifts from detailed instructions on how to carry out an assignment to providing general guidelines within which individuals and small groups can organize their work. Neither of these assumptions about workers (independence or the capability of self-organization) are ingrained in American business life and management practice. The design of offices to permit visual supervision of workers, though less prevalent today than in earlier years, is by no means uncommon.

Thus shared offices and spatial mobility, and the greater invisibility and independence of the employee (in relation to management) they foster, create pressures for significant changes in organizational culture. Organizations would have to commit resources to training programs designed to encourage cooperation and to help managers redefine their model of the "good manager" from one that is control-oriented to one that emphasizes the development of policies and guidelines that promote sharing ideas and information; from one in which the manager is like a steamroller, grinding everything beneath its weight, to one in which the manager is more like a snowplow, clearing the bureaucratic highways so that employees can do their work with a minimum of unnecessary interference. Such training programs must be reinforced with new incentive systems that reward individuals and groups with demonstrated abilities in these areas.

Summary of Organizational Implications

One of the values of new information technology beyond its technical capabilities is its ability to stimulate thinking about how work is done now and how it might be changed. It is thus a force for innovation, whether or not the technology is actually used in a new way. Many work innovations do not need office automation. Spatial mobility, shared offices, offices used on an "as needed" reserved basis only, smaller offices for top management, and multiple offices do not depend on information technology. The technology does not make them possible. It only makes them easier.

For these innovations in space planning and design to be adopted successfully, the organization's culture must value independence and cooperation, actual performance and not only the appearance of working hard, and it must create new forms of symbolic communication. The use of office size and privacy to convey status and to reward achievement, for example, could be diminished and replaced with aspects of office design that have only symbolic meaning (e.g., certificates, furniture and finishes, accessories).

The limits to design innovation are thus largely social–psychological and organizational, not technical. Design innovations such as automated security and energy-saving systems or visually stunning atria and more elaborate cafeterias and resource centers rarely encounter much resistance because they do not challenge accepted organizational practices and expectations. They are perfect symbols of technological and design sophistication for firms unwilling to accept genuine organizational innovation.

LINKING FACILITY AND ORGANIZATIONAL INNOVATION

From the printing press to automobiles and indoor plumbing and from representative government to flatter decision structures and quality circles, organizational and technological innovation has had a long history of initial resistance. Yet good inventions and new ways of doing things seem eventually to grab hold, to break through the crust of tradition, driven by the sheer force, perseverance, and the unrelenting persuasion of their advocates. Inventions have, in addition to their advocates, an even stronger ally: the obvious failure of existing tools and techniques to serve their purposes as well as the new invention does. Horses and buggies were great until they were compared with automobiles. The Morse code was a tremendous leap forward until the telephone was invented. Handset type was fine until the computer could be used to set it electronically. Perhaps the same can now be said about the traditional approach to planning and designing offices.

Rarely do mature, profitable organizations use a major building project to stimulate changes in organizational practices, management style, and the daily work patterns of its employees. But the Steelcase Corporation's Corporate Development Center (CDC) illustrates how one company linked facility innovation directly to organizational innovation and—ultimately—to competitive advantage.

A CASE STUDY: THE STEELCASE CORPORATE DEVELOPMENT CENTER (CDC)

The Steelcase Corporation, with its headquarters in Grand Rapids, Michigan, is the world's largest manufacturer of contract office furniture. About six miles away from its corporate headquarters, in the center of a field on the outskirts of Grand Rapids, is Steelcase's new Corporate Development Center (CDC). Like a vehicle from outer space, it literally glows at night, soft white bands of light narrowing to deep pink stripes outlining the tip of an ancient shape, the pyramid. Deceptively small at close range, the pyramid is visible from miles around, unexpectedly appearing, like an apparition,

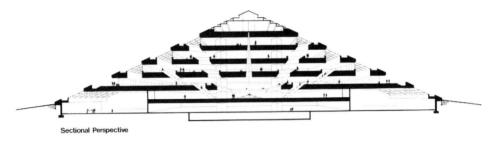

Sectional Perspective

Figure 12-1.   A sectional perspective of the Steelcase Corporate Development Center (CDC). (Source: The WBDC Group, 1989)

over the trees lining a farmer's field. A bold step forward, the CDC challenges conventional space planning and design approaches as well as the existing organizational culture (see Figures 12-1, 12-2, and 12-3).

In May of 1986, construction began on the seven-level, 575 thousand square foot pyramid. Built on a 125 acre site, 809 employees would eventually occupy it, including all personnel in the product development process. Move-in was accomplished in only three years with total costs being $117 million—furniture included.

At first, the CDC's pyramid shape seems a monument to organizational hierarchy, the perfect embodiment of an obsolete management style. This impression would be valid if the tip of the pyramid were reserved for executives and all direction and decision making fed from the top down; if senior management viewed the building as an ode to their egos; and if the lower one went in the building, the lower the rank of the occupants would be. But nothing could be further from the truth.

The building's design is intended, instead, to meet two major objectives: (1) to contribute to the development of innovative products that will enable Steelcase to maintain its preeminent position in the furniture industry, and (2) to speed the product development cycle so that new products can be brought to market faster, thereby better exploiting shifts in the marketplace. These goals derive from the simple fact that although Steelcase

Partial Section : Office-Terrace-Cafeteria

Figure 12-2.   A partial section of the Steelcase Development Center (CDC) office and terrace areas. (Source: The WBDC Group, 1989)

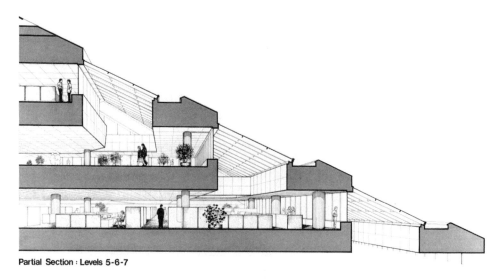

Partial Section : Levels 5-6-7

Figure 12-3.   A partial section of the Steelcase Corporate Development Center (CDC), levels 5 through 7. (Source: The WBDC Group, 1989)

is a leader in its industry, the competition is growing stronger and more international. At the same time, the furniture market is slowing down from its wild boom years of the late 1970s and early 1980s. To survive under these changing circumstances, Steelcase realized that it must strengthen its already strong position. As a company dedicated to improving the quality of the work environment for others, it decided to use its need for a new development facility as the starting point for a broad-based reexamination of the product development process and how a new facility might support it.

THE TOTAL WORKPLACE CONCEPT

Good buildings require good clients. One aspect of being a good client is having a clear vision of short-range goals and objectives and also a larger view of what the organization stands for and should do to prosper over the long haul. At Steelcase these values included the recognition of individuals' basic worth; the need for the building to be as dynamic as the organization occupying it; and the value of effectiveness, which sometimes must be bought at the expense of simple efficiency.

These ideas came together in the concept of the total workplace, which has three meanings. One is the idea of integrating decisions often considered in isolation by individual departments: human resources, information technology, design and construction, and buildings operations and management. The second meaning of the total workplace concept is that the workplace is more than one's own personal office or workstation. It is the entire workplace (site, amenities, commons areas, project rooms, support areas), a series of loosely coupled settings. The third is the idea that the processes used for planning, designing, and managing the workplace are as much a part of the building's quality as are its physical characteristics.

Quality, from planning to construction, was an indispensable force, not an expendable

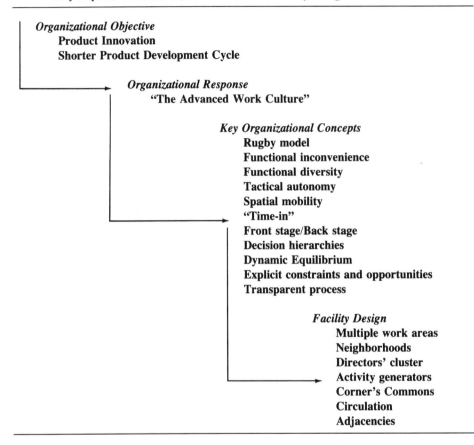

Figure 12-4.   Elements of advanced work culture and facility design. (Source: Becker 1989)

luxury. And quality, in a building intended to promote innovation, required rethinking the product development process itself and how the facility could contribute to it.

THE RELAY VERSUS THE RUGBY MODEL

The assumptions underlying the CDC project was that innovative product solutions require enormous amounts of information about technology, design, the production process, and the market to be widely shared at all stages of the development process. Informal communication across project teams and across disciplines and departments to stimulate creativity was the bedrock of what we came to call the *advanced work culture* (see Figure 12-4).

This view of the product development process contrasts with the traditional serial product development process, in which different subunits in the organization are responsible for each stage in the process. Figure 12-5 differentiates between the serial or "relay race"

Relay Race Model

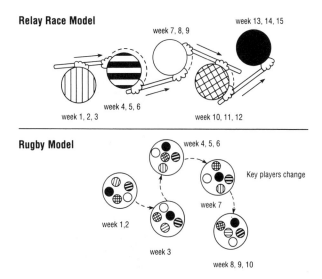

Rugby Model

Figure 12-5. A comparison of the relay race and rugby model of the product development process. (Source: Steelcase, Inc. 1989)

model of communication in the design process, in which information generated by one group or discipline is sequentially handed off to another group (like the first runner handing a baton to the second), and a "rugby team" model of the product development process. In the rugby team model, different disciplines and departments interact in a dynamic, constantly fluctuating fashion.[1] Leadership shifts as the nature of the project evolves. All "players" are involved form the beginning, but with their role and level of involvement changing over time. Its distinguishing features are its emphasis on teamwork that cuts across discipline and departmental boundaries, on free-flowing and serendipitous face-to-face communication, on clear goals reached by taking advantage of unexpected ideas and opportunities, and on information and ideas moving among all players from the very beginning of the process and not in some preordained sequence.

Comparison of Rugby and Relay Race Models

Relay Race Model	Rugby Team Model
Individual	Team
Sequential	Iterative
Static	Dynamic
Pre-planned	Serendipitous
Autocratic	Democratic

1. It recently came to my attention that Hirotaki Takeuchi and Ikujiro Nonaka (1986) wrote an article for the *Harvard Business Review* that described new product development processes as a rugby rather than relay model. At the time of the CDC project (1985) we were unaware of the article.

The great value of the rugby model is that it minimizes the difficulty of managing the transition points between stages, for it is during the transitions that projects are most vulnerable. At this point the nature of the work changes, organizational responsibility changes, and even the personnel assigned to the task change. Changing all these aspects at the same time presents a discontinuity that is difficult to overcome. Decisions made in earlier stages may appear irrational (and sometimes are) in the context of the subsequent stage. Without some continuity of personnel, there is no "memory" for the project, no recollection of why things were done in a particular way. With no one from any of the "downstream" parts of the organization involved in the early decisions, these decisions may result in situations that are totally incompatible with the requirements of later stages.

An integrated process can actually shorten the development time for new products. By smoothing out the organizational discontinuities and providing greater involvement of units other than that with primary responsibility for a given stage, the rugby model reduces the likelihood that a set of drawings, for example, delivered to manufacturing engineering by the product engineering group would result in a product impossible or too costly to produce. Thus less time is spent redesigning, and the overall product development cycle is speeded up.

TYPES OF COMMUNICATION

Good communication is essential to the rugby model of the product development process, but there are different types of communication, and each needs to be considered in its own right (see Figures 12-6, 12-7, and 12-8). Thomas Allen (1977) described these types as (1) communication to coordinate the work, (2) communication to keep individuals informed of new developments in their field of specialization, and (3) communication to stimulate creativity.

By grouping people according to the project or product on which they are working, project organization enhances the coordination among them. And by grouping people according to their discipline or speciality, functional organization enables them to keep up-to-date on developments in their speciality. The need for knowledge-enhancing communication is a function of the rate at which the knowledge is changing. More dynamic technologies require more communication among colleagues in order to keep abreast of new developments.

Communication that stimulates creativity is less predictable and more informal than the other two. It is less influenced by formal organizational structure and more by the physical arrangement of the office space. Inspirational communication is prompted largely by chance encounters at the water cooler, in a corridor, on the stairs, in a break area.

ORGANIZATIONAL PRINCIPLES

The rugby model's emphasis on informal communication makes it important to stimulate face-to-face and serendipitous communication among groups such as product engineering, industrial design, and marketing. But communication by itself will not help attract and retain the highest-quality work force; it will not motivate creative professionals; and it will not encourage employees to contribute their best ideas. What made

Figures 12-6, 12-7 and 12-8. The workplace needs to improve three different types of communication. (Source: Steelcase, Inc. 1989)

the CDC project unusual was the commitment to creating a building that reflected the following interdependent behavioral and organizational concepts, which in combination were likely to improve the creative process as a whole:

Functional Inconvenience

Most adjacency decisions use spatial proximity to reinforce organizational structure. On the principle of the less effort the better, people are located nearest those with whom their job requires that they frequently interact. Allen's (1977) research suggests that such arrangements are efficient but not necessarily effective. The reason is that performance in R & D settings has consistently been shown to be related to the number of informal contacts that one has with people outside one's own department, discipline, and project team. If the goal is to boost creativity, then stimulating face-to-face communication among persons whose jobs do not require interaction (a weak organizational bond) is appropriate. In general, those whose jobs (strong organizational bond) require them to interact will do so, within reason.

We called this deliberate design of inefficient adjacencies *functional inconvenience* to capture the idea that what appears to be inconvenient or inefficient may, in fact, promote effectiveness. For example, encouraging people to walk within the building to go to project rooms, a library, a laboratory, or to see their senior manager may reduce efficiency (in its narrow sense), but increases the probability of informal communication: people unexpectedly bumping into one another as they move around the building. It is this kind of contact that has been demonstrated to contribute positively to innovative engineering design solutions (see Figures 12-9 and 12-10).

Functional Diversity

Disciplines such as engineering, marketing, and design tend to attract very different types of people. Each group's work-styles, attitudes, and values are often poorly understood, let alone accepted by the other groups, and once attitudinal barriers like these are imposed it is difficult to get the groups to communicate and cooperate. The only way to break down such barriers is to bring people into closer contact so that they will realize that, although another group may think and behave differently from them, there is diversity within both groups and that such diversity is needed to generate good ideas and new products. The goal is not, therefore, to "homogenize" the organization, but to help different groups accept and respect these different ways of thinking and working.

Functional diversity also recognizes that within disciplines there can be differences in personal work-style, that is, in how, where, and when people work best. From this perspective, environmental equity lies in giving employees access to those physical resources (work surfaces, privacy, views, storage, display space) they need to work effectively, not in giving everyone the same thing.

Functional diversity, which focuses on the arrangement and use of the entire workplace (including but not limited to the office or workstation) to reflect one's work-style is related to, but different from, personalization, which typically centers on using pho-

Figures 12-9 and 12-10.   Being efficient is not always the same as being effective. (Source: Steelcase, Inc. 1989)

tographs, posters, and small personal objects to communicate one's personal values and interests.

Strategic Leadership and Operational Autonomy

Managers are often more comfortable engaging in the kinds of activities they did before their promotion to manager. Consequently, they often concern themselves with directing the more routine aspects of their subordinates' jobs and thereby neglect the

Figure 12-11. Decision processes, including those for facility design, should distinguish between those intended to strengthen strategic direction and those intended to support tactical control. (Source: Steelcase, Inc. 1989)

longer-term strategic aspects of their own jobs. Strategic leadership refers to the need to distinguish between management's role in setting broad goals and objectives, completion dates, and so on (what should be done) and the subordinate's desire and ability to figure out the best way to accomplish these goals (how something should be done). We called doing the work in one's own way exercising operational autonomy (see Figure 12-11).

Spatial Mobility

Because an individual's work varies over time (day, week, year), the optimal setting for accomplishing that work should vary as well. Unless we live in a studio apartment, we do not cook, eat, sleep, and entertain in the same room in our homes. Then why should we discuss a project, type a report, or read a technical article in the same workspace? We should be able to go to the location where, for a specific activity, it makes the most sense to work (see Figure 12-12). The reason is that no single office, no matter how well designed, is likely to support equally well all of the tasks and activities and interactions in which workers are involved. Spatial mobility also increases the likelihood that people will bump into one another as they move around and through the building during their everyday activities. The design focus shifts from the design of the perfect cockpit with everything one needs to do his or her work within arm's reach (efficiency) to the design of the total workplace, a system of integrated and loosely coupled settings, each of which has a different character and serves different purposes. Employees are encouraged to exploit different areas (e.g., personal workstations, shared commons areas, dedicated project rooms, terraces, an atrium, the cafeteria, a library) as they see fit.

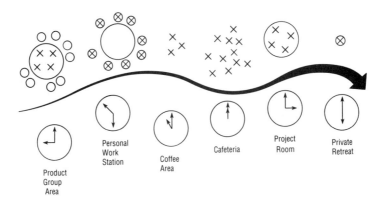

Figure 12-12. A mobile worker free to move among a variety of settings designed to support different work activities increases informal communication and recognizes that no single office is likely to be perfectly designed for every aspect of work.

Time In

Informal communication often takes place in settings like a coffee break area that are relaxed in nature. To managers steeped in the view of "work" as something nonsocial and strictly task oriented, these kinds of social activities are often interpreted as people wasting their time. Yet socializing, arguing, discussing, or just thinking and contemplating are, in fact, all aspects of "real" work. The "time-in" concept is used to capture the idea that looking unproductive (feet up on a desk, staring out into space) can be at the heart of creativity, not a sign of being lazy (see Figure 12-13).

Front Stage and Back Stage

Design intended to reflect a planned, uniform, corporate image is useful in communicating an organization's public face to customers and employees. Such design tends to be relatively formal, stylistic, and static. Communicating corporate image on the front stage, public areas like lobbies, cafeterias, and conference rooms frequently occupied by nonemployees, makes sense. But these spaces should be distinguished from more informal, back stage areas where employees spend most of their day working, for it is in these areas that concepts like functional diversity and tactical autonomy take shape in the physical environment. Treating the entire workplace as a front stage, public area deprives employees of the opportunity to create strong group, project, and individual identities that are motivating and visually reflect the organization's commitment to tolerating diversity. The intent is to have most of the CDC be back stage, so that people can work in ways which are effective, no matter whether they "look right" to outsiders or not.

Planned and implemented carefully, these concepts overlap and intertwine with one another to create a web of reinforcing behaviors that are strong without being brittle. They are the foundation stones of what I have called *elastic organizations*, which, like a rubber band, are resilient. They can take many different forms, easily responding to

Thinking Counts as "Real Work"

Figure 12-13. To be used effectively, innovative designs require top management support and an organizational culture that encourages new ways of working and using space. (Source: Steelcase, Inc. 1989)

changes in work patterns or new technologies without becoming brittle and snapping when submitted to the forces of change. In elastic organizations, design is considered holistically, with as much consideration given to the design process as to the physical design itself.

THE CDC PLANNING PROCESS

From the beginning of the CDC project, one goal of the project team was to capture in its own processes and ways of working the important aspects of the rugby model. This was reflected in the following planning process principles:

Decision Hierarchies

The outcomes of decisions affect different levels of the organization, from site planning and building form to the arrangement of furniture components and the height of the computer keyboard. The concept of a decision hierarchy is that different classes of decisions should be made at different levels of the organizational hierarchy, but that everyone should have some form of decision authority (reflecting a commitment to the concept of tactical autonomy).

In the CDC planning process, certain decisions were made by top management largely without any formal consultation with employees. These included everything from the building's location, the basic building form and materials, and landscaping to the value of functional inconvenience, a commitment to a variety of commons areas, and the decision to use systems furniture in an open plan configuration throughout most of the building. The design and character of commons areas, the policies governing their use, and other interior planning decisions were also made by management, but with considerable input and review by rank-and-file employees. Their involvement took many forms: brief, informal interviews; structured feedback to the design team regarding preliminary workstation and commons areas designs; completion of survey forms; and use of a full-scale mock-up of a section of the building to test employees' reactions to new, specially designed, glare-free glass.

Dynamic Equilibrium

Neither a building nor the processes for designing it are ever complete. Both change continuously in response to altered economic conditions, new technologies, evolving organizational structure, and shifts in the nature of the work force. Over the long term, the design process evolves into facility management. From this perspective, the need to change the facility, even soon after its initial occupancy, should be viewed as inevitable and desirable and not as a failure of the initial planning and design process.

Transparent Process

To be acceptable and to generate employee support, facility decisions should be transparent; that is, the rationale for most facility decisions should be explained to employees so they understand both what is happening and why. Many logical or necessary decisions appear arbitrary and unfair to those who do not understand the reasons behind them. If management cannot justify its decisions to employees in a way that seems sensible, then management probably needs to rethink its decisions.

Explicit Constraints and Opportunities

Realistic expectations flow from an understanding of project constraints and opportunities. There is little reason to ask people for their ideas, work requirements, or response to a proposed design if decisions concerning these areas have already been made. In such cases employee participation becomes an exercise in frustration, resentment, and, ultimately, apathy. In the CDC process employees volunteered information about their work-style and task requirements, and they were consulted about the arrangement of furniture components within the workstation and commons areas. But they were not, for example, asked for advice about workstation size or the overall building form.

THE TOTAL WORKPLACE CONCEPT: SPACE PLANNING AND DESIGN

In the new Steelcase CDC building the organizational concepts just described were translated and expressed in the following ways (see Figure 12-14):

Figure 12-14.   The Steelcase Corporate Development Center (CDC) has many different "real" work areas: informal break areas, individual workstations surrounding common areas, a "town square," and private retreats used on a first-come, first-served basis for total concentration for short periods of time. (Photos: Joseph Pobereskin Photography, 1989).

1. *Multiple work areas: Private/project/shared space.* The concept of employee mobility was encouraged by providing many different work areas for employees to work in, each with a different character and purpose: individual workstation and shared commons areas for a small group of workstations (the cave and commons concept); dedicated project rooms, conference rooms; break areas; cafeteria; outside terraces; laboratories; the atrium ("Town Square"); and a resource center ringed by small, fully enclosed offices used on a temporary basis for work requiring high levels of concentration (see Figure 12-15). The intent of the multiple settings is to recognize

Figure 12-14.   (*Continued*)

that neither open plan offices nor fully enclosed offices by themselves support the full range of activities that are required for creative and productive efforts. Privacy in the CDC is viewed as a matter of degree rather than an all-or-none decision.

2. *Neighborhoods with mixed disciplines.* The conventional wisdom of adjacency analyses, in which everyone in the same department is located together, was largely abandoned in favor of "neighborhoods" in which different disciplines (product engineering, marketing, and design) shared an area (see Figures 12-16 and 12-17). This spatial organization was based on bringing together in a single area all the disciplines working on the same overall product area; for example, seating or case goods. The intent was not only to foster informal communication across disciplines

Figure 12-14.   (*Continued*)

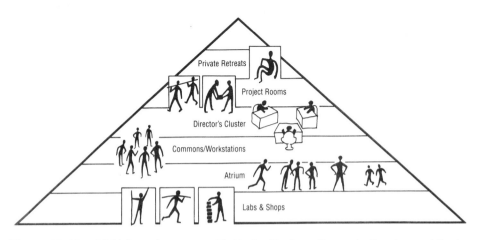

Figure 12-15.   Multiple work areas provided in the Steelcase Corporate Development Center (CDC). (Source: Steelcase, Inc. 1989)

Industrial
Design

Product
Engineering

Product
Marketing

Beverage
Center

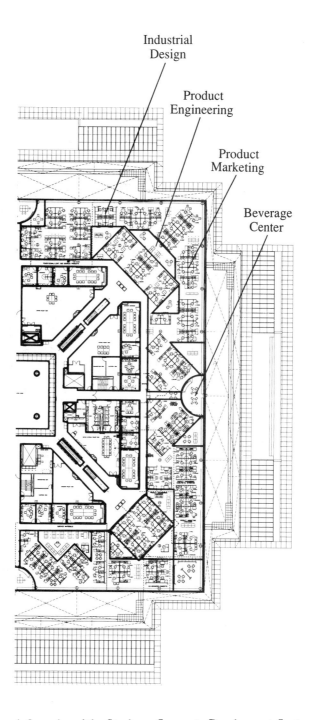

Figure 12-16.   A floor plan of the Steelcase Corporate Development Center (CDC) showing the functional zoning of different areas on the third level. (Source: Steelcase, Inc. 1989)

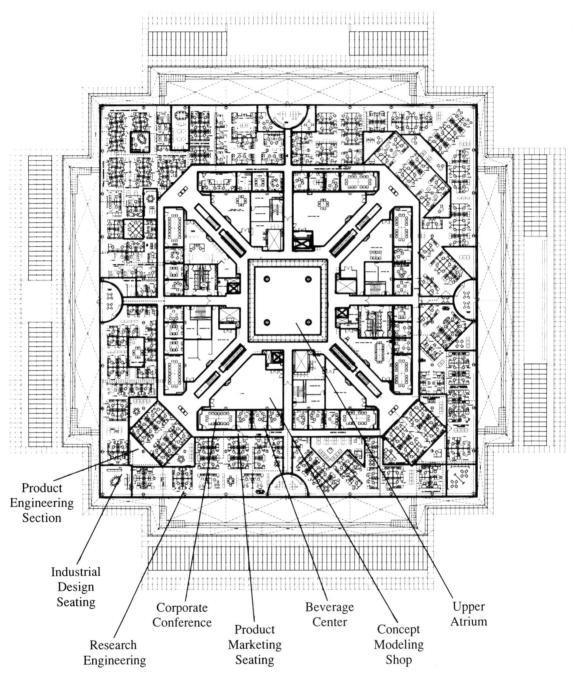

Product
Engineering
Section

Industrial
Design
Seating

Corporate
Conference

Research
Engineering

Product
Marketing
Seating

Beverage
Center

Concept
Modeling
Shop

Upper
Atrium

Figure 12-17.   A floor plan of the Steelcase Corporate Development Center (CDC) showing the mixed (discipline) neighborhood concept. (Source: Steelcase, Inc. 1989)

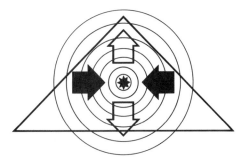

Figure 12-18. Executives in the Steelcase Corporate Development Center (CDC) are clustered in the center of the building, both horizontally and vertically, to maximize their accessibility to others. (Source: Steelcase, Inc. 1989)

but also to create working relationships based on trust and greater tolerance for diversity in work and personal styles. Within the neighborhood, small clusters of engineers or designers are located together so that the encouragement of cross-disciplinary contact is not bought at the expense of professionals' need to share information and talk about new developments in their own specialized areas.

3. *Directors' cluster.* Rather than locating all senior management together at the top of the pyramid in an isolated executive enclave or locating them with their staff in departmental areas separated from one another, a directors' cluster was placed in the middle of the building, easily accessible to others (see Figure 12-18). Its central location increases the likelihood that staff on the way to the Resource Center (on the sixth floor) or to project rooms will run into, or at least have some visual connection to, their senior management. Just as important was the desire to stimulate spontaneous communication among the directors and vice-presidents representing different disciplines in the manufacturing process, something that is difficult to do when senior managers are distributed throughout an entire building.

4. *Activity generators: Town square/cafeteria/break areas.* The building, as a whole, is designed to maximize visibility: between floors, to the outside, and into private offices. One facet of the design to maximize visibility is specialized support spaces such as the atrium, cafeteria, and beverage areas. These are viewed as "activity generators" intended to support chance face-to-face contact. Coffee, whiteboards, barlike seating (deliberately not sofas and lounge chairs) are intended to act like magnets that pull people into these areas because they provide necessary and desired resources (i.e., coffee, mail, current information).

5. *Corner commons.* Placed in corners of the third floor, the corner commons are intended to serve whoever occupies that corner of the floor. With furniture that can be easily manipulated by employees to create more or less enclosure, a miniconference room, display and presentation space, or simply a place to relax, the corner commons are unique in their commitment to encourage the end users to create work areas that are right for them at any particular moment. Like the dedicated project rooms on the fourth and fifth floors, they reflect the commitment to increasing

Figure 12-19.   In the "cave and commons" concept, individual workstations are immediately accessible to small shared areas useful for such things as meetings, spreading out work, and special equipment. (Source: Steelcase, Inc. 1989)

tactical autonomy by giving informal groups and project teams more control over the areas in which they work.

6. *Escalators/stairs.* The anonymity of elevators and stairs hidden behind walls were replaced with escalators, which increase the opportunity for establishing visual contact and communication with other people and other work areas.

7. *Adjacencies.* Project rooms, conference rooms, laboratories, break areas, and the resource center were distributed throughout the building rather than being located to minimize travel distance (e.g., placing a project room immediately adjacent to a laboratory or a particular department or product development group). The intent was to promote functional inconvenience.

8. *Security zones.* Through a sophisticated automated security system, the CDC building is zoned into a front stage, public area where visitors and guests can enter and meet with CDC representatives. Guided tours are on a strict, predetermined route to minimize intrusion into back stage work areas. Restricting visitors to a few front stage areas is intended to reduce the pressure to maintain the building as a showroom and to increase the opportunities for functional diversity and greater informality.

THE ACCEPTABILITY FACTOR AND THE ENCULTURATION PROCESS

To take advantage of these design innovations, employees from the president to the secretaries need to understand the concepts behind the building and feel secure in acting on the building's potential. Design innovations such as multiple work settings, private retreats, and functional inconvenience challenge traditional management styles and assumptions. Employees need to feel confident that if their supervisor sees them having coffee in a lounge area this will be perceived as working, not loitering; that if they remove their tie they will not be viewed as sloppy or indifferent; and that if they are not instantly available because they are in a private study area this will be understood and accepted.

Acceptability requires a good fit between physical design and organizational culture. When design innovation challenges the organizational culture, as it does in the CDC, the social system must be examined and, in some cases, redesigned. The importance of the social system analysis (we called it the *enculturation process*) was understood by the project team from the beginning of the project. Without examining culture changes, facility management policies, organizational practices and structures, and reward systems, we felt it likely that the full potential of the building would never be realized. Such a process requires rethinking (and in some cases changing) the ways in which status and prestige are communicated. It needs to identify social norms that may block new ways of working if unchanged and to propose new social norms that can support the advanced work culture. Policies that determine who uses certain work areas and the extent to and ways in which individuals and groups can modify their work areas themselves must be considered in light of the company's strategic plans and the overall objectives of the building project. At the CDC the enculturation process has taken many forms. Some of these have been formal, but many more were embedded in other aspects of the overall planning and design process, as follows:

- The planning process itself, which included almost every potential occupant of the CDC in small focus group sessions to discover their environmental requirements and to solicit their reactions to preliminary design proposals
- A monthly newsletter, "CDC Update," which discussed the project, its concepts, goals and objectives, and the people planning and designing it
- Informal "wandering interviews" in which members of the project team explained something about the project while asking for informal feedback about its design
- A series of formal "professional forum" symposia in which both senior management and project team members and outside consultants talked about the concepts and ideas behind the CDC's development and design
- For all the staff providing services to the building, from facility management, telecommunications, and computers to food service and administrative services (paper, supplies, etc.), a series of training workshops on what a service orientation would mean in the CDC, its implications for how the services staff did their jobs and worked together, and the changes it might require in their relationship to the groups they served and to corporate administrative and facility management services

No single method, certainly not limited to a single point in time, will suffice to change any organization's culture. This is a bit like hoping that with an extra heave a strong man can yank an eighteen-wheel truck out of the mud. Not likely. It is too early to know how the building will actually be used, but the anecdotal evidence is promising. The key to success, I believe, will be threefold: top management's actually demonstrating appropriate use of the building; that is, senior management being seen in break areas, on terraces, in private study areas, in the Information Center, talking on platforms near escalators, and so on; top management's reinforcing staff for engaging in these kinds of activities; and the staff themselves being willing to try out new behavior patterns, to test the commitment of management to the ideas for which management has paid.

THE INTELLIGENT BUILDING: MORE THAN HARDWARE

The CDC incorporates a number of sophisticated automated building systems and energy-saving design features, but by current world standards it is not at the cutting edge of building technology. The technology in place does, however, serve Steelcase's own existing and projected needs: for energy conservation, wire management, organizational restructuring, power and cooling capacity, security, electronic networking, and computing. In contrast with the current fashion of labeling an "intelligent building" one loaded with sophisticated, automated building systems and information technology, the Steelcase CDC has the potential to redefine "intelligent building" in a much broader way.

CDC Technology Overview

Technology

- Cellular floor deck
- IBM "Profs" electronic mail
- Programmable, proximity card reading security system
- Heat recovery energy saving system with underground ponds
- 300 HVAC programmable zones within the building
- UPS
- Newly designed completely glare-free uplighting
- New Steelcase "Context" furniture system
- Specially-designed glare free windows treated with ceramic "frit"

Many "intelligent" buildings today, in the United States and around the world, including Japan, have been constructed mainly as marketing devices for new information technology. In some cases—in the United States several years ago, for example—sophisticated electronic systems were regarded as a means of marginally differentiating what were essentially identical speculative office buildings. The impetus was from developers, technology manufacturers, and consultants; not clients. Technology was viewed, simplistically (and usually erroneously), as doing everything from reducing headcount and increasing efficiency to promoting group cohesion.

From the perspective of what Fritz Steele (1986) and I (1981) have called *organizational ecology*, an "intelligent" building is, first, client driven. It is one with the capacity to use technology and building design effectively to support corporate objectives. Second, it requires an organizational culture and set of work practices that can support the innovative use of the technology. Third, it should be able to evolve in response to unpredictable changes in the marketplace, the work force, and technology.

By this definition, the Steelcase CDC Building can be an intelligent building. It will take time and the evaluation of actual use patterns to determine whether it is, in fact, an intelligent building: one in which design innovation is matched with organizational innovation in a way that allows for the continual evolution of both. Whatever the final verdict, the extent to which research and theory were used to guide facility planning and design in the CDC is unique. For those who sometimes despair over integrating research into practice, it provides a useful beacon of hope. For practitioners it offers a tangible, kick-the-tires model of planning and design processes that they can examine, point to, and learn from.

GENERALIZING BEYOND THE CDC

In thinking about what aspects of the CDC project might be applied to other organizations and to different cultures, one needs to distinguish between the basic organizational concepts and how they were realized through specific architectural, space planning, and design solutions. One also should consider some of the more unusual aspects of Steelcase as an organization.

Most of the basic organizational principles are broadly applicable. The rugby team model, with its emphasis on all three types of communication and functional inconvenience, should be relevant to any organization dedicated to developing new products and services, whether these be computers, automobiles, furniture, insurance policies, architectural design, or financial programs.

Concepts such as tactical autonomy and functional diversity are meaningful in most organizations but will be more acceptable to some organizations than others. Power cultures (control is invested primarily in senior management) and role cultures (employees have clearly and relatively narrowly defined expectations about what behaviors are appropriate to persons in different roles) will find these concepts—which distribute control more widely and make diversity more visible—difficult to accept. Task cultures (the focus is on getting a job done, using whatever resources and expertise are necessary, wherever these may reside) and relationship cultures (in which the expectation is that all persons will help one another in whatever way they can to get their job done, whether or not it is related to their own) will be less threatened by these concepts. Japan, which simultaneously combines strong hierarchical relationships with strong support and task cultures would, I think, find many of the concepts of the advanced work culture easy to understand, if not familiar.

The aspect of the CDC project that is harder to generalize is the particular ways in which the organizational concepts were realized through physical design. This is certainly the case in cities like Tokyo, London, and even New York City with their astronomical space costs. Although to some extent the generous provision of commons areas in the CDC was justified by providing slightly smaller personal work areas, the fact is that all of the space in the CDC is generous, even by American standards. It is positively luxurious (basically unheard of) by Japanese standards.

Steelcase, as a leader in the furniture industry and a firm committed to positioning itself as "The Office Environment Company," can justify such generous space use in part as a form of marketing. The low cost of space in Grand Rapids also means less pressure for space efficiency than in cities like Tokyo and London. Yet to dismiss the CDC (and the processes used in its planning and design) as particular to Steelcase and Grand Rapids misses the point. And that point is that the justification for the building's design was that Steelcase's top management had good reason to believe (based on available research and expertise) that the new facility would help Steelcase achieve its business objectives. Thus the commons areas and other design elements are not, like most "break areas," just a pleasant amenity for employees, a frill or luxury that can easily be sliced from the construction budget or replaced with more workstations at a later time. Similarly, the extensive involvement of employees in the design process served the larger purpose of modeling in the building project the ways of working being proposed for the product development process and contributing to a better design. Viewed as the cost of doing business well, such design processes and features take on a different meaning.

They must also be viewed as part of a total system. Whatever the size of the building budget, the question is how these funds are allocated. Steelcase chose to spend much of its available budget on spaces that will directly affect and contribute to its employees' effectiveness. In comparison with many executive enclaves, with their enormous offices and sumptuous furniture and finishes, the CDC senior management areas are modest. Many of the design concepts could be realized with less expensive materials, and depending on the cost of space and the type of work, the individual offices, cafeteria, or commons areas might be smaller. The issue is not space per se; it is how available space is distributed and whether it is serving the organization as a whole or only a small minority of its employees.

Skeptics Speak

The Steelcase CDC is fascinating, but Steelcase is a privately held, extremely profitable company with huge financial resources. How many of its ideas are applicable to the typical publicly owned company?

You must distinguish between the way in which Steelcase translated the organizational concepts into design and the concepts themselves. Without doubt, the concepts can be generalized. They have, in fact, been applied in different forms to many different organizations both in this country and in Europe. What sets the CDC apart is the comprehensive nature of the plan, integrating technology, design, and organizational change into a single project.

The principle of increasing the probability of eye contact while moving around the building can be realized with escalators, an expensive solution (though in some place, like the Centraal Beheer insurance company in the Netherlands, the escalators run up in the morning and down at night, thus reducing the number needed). It can also be realized by using broad, open staircases. Commons areas take up space, but they should be viewed as part of a total system of spaces (loosely coupled settings) in which the total amount of space may remain relatively constant but the distribution of it (slightly smaller professional work areas, smaller managers' offices) changes significantly. Budget was not a major constraint for Steelcase, but more important than money is, first, a strong management commitment to the concepts; second, a creative design and project team with an understanding of the guiding concepts and the imagination to seek creative solutions to them (the pyramid in no way exhausts, for example, the universe of solutions to the problems that the CDC addressed); and third, the organization's willingness to see a building project in broad rather than narrow outline, as related to its ability to achieve its business objectives. Thus, the willingness to commit resources from human resources and other areas is part of a broad-based organizational change effort.

The fact that Steelcase is privately owned and does not have to answer to shareholders is one consideration in thinking about the generalizability of the CDC ideas. What about the fact that Steelcase is also in the "environment" business? Its management is more attuned to the physical environment as an important factor in the organization's success, and it can also use to a much greater extent such a building project in its own marketing and public relations efforts.

Very true, and it does make a big difference. Senior management's awareness and acceptance of the value of a well-designed workplace is critical, but it does occur also in companies with no connection to the "environment" business. Scandinavian Airline Systems' corporate headquarters building on the outskirts of Stockholm is easily as good an example of a building used to advance corporate business objectives as the CDC, and firms like the NMB bank in Amsterdam and McDonalds in this country have created buildings that are carefully and artfully designed to support the organization. The Union Carbide headquarters in Danbury, Connecticut, remains a fascinating example of a facility that combines at a high level behavioral principles, information technology, and outstanding design.

The key is senior management's understanding the potential value of a good facility. This requires bringing such examples to their attention and taking managers to the actual sites and having them meet their counterparts in these organizations who can explain why they spent the money and time to do what they did (and how they feel it benefits their organization). It means sending articles and books (or the relevant parts of them) to them and organizing seminars in which practitioners, consultants, and academicians discuss their research and explain the concepts behind the planning and design of interesting buildings. There are many ways of educating top management. But what is certain is that if you wait for managers to issue you an invitation to organize such a project, you are likely to wait a very long time, indeed. The initiative must come from you.

What about the time frame for a culture change? How long will it take?

You will need a long time, real perseverance, and strong champions at the top to support the change effort. A building project can act as the catalyst of a change effort, but it cannot carry it off by itself. Open planning concepts in the schools did not create an open education process; it created mini-facility managers in the form of teachers who moved around freestanding bookshelves and furniture to recreate barriers and boundaries around their classroom to protect their familiar and comfortable teaching routines. The great benefit of using a major building project to stimulate organizational change is that it is highly visible, tangible evidence of management's commitment. But to work, it takes equal effort to help people learn new roles, to define old behaviors in new ways, and to expand their repertoire of skills and abilities. It can be done.

PART 4

Assessing Performance

CHAPTER 13

Assessing Building Performance

Franklin Becker and William Sims

It is ironic, but even today we often have more information about the relative merits of different cars or copiers costing a few thousand dollars than we have about buildings costing hundreds or even thousands of times as much. Yet buildings are really only "products" writ large, purchased or leased by firms for specific purposes. They are tools of the trade, meant to help get a job done.

Like a Porsche, excelling at speed and style but wholly inadequate for hauling children or file cabinets, some buildings are better as some things than others are. But how do we know which is "right" for different types of organizations? The answer is that we usually guess. Not blindly or stupidly, but erratically and narrowly. Sometimes we guess right. Often we do not. Given the cost of buildings initially and over their life cycle, their asset value, and their influence on the organization's ability to achieve its business objectives, getting it right "sometimes" is no longer a luxury that most organizations can afford.

HISTORY OF BUILDING PERFORMANCE MEASUREMENT

Buildings have always been evaluated. What is changing is the emergence in recent years of more formal and systematic building appraisal methods. The interest in systematically measuring the performance of buildings had its genesis in a number of things that happened during the 1960s. One of these was the movement to develop rational or systematic methods for designing buildings. These methods required models that could predict the outcome of proposed design actions and an evaluation procedure that could compare the overall pros and cons of different designs. Unfortunately, the available knowledge base did not match the complexity of the problem, nor did the necessary computing power exist to combine all of the disparate models into one master system.

The social concerns of the 1960s also contributed to the emergence of more deliberate approaches to assessing building performance. Architects, in particular, became interested in how well buildings were meeting their occupants' needs. Here, too, it quickly became apparent that we had no real knowledge base for these human–environment relations. So architects turned to social scientists for help, and from this union evolved post-occupancy evaluation (see Chapter 14).

Though useful, a major drawback to POE was its singular focus on occupant satisfaction. The importance of the failure to judge buildings on a broader basis became obvious with the onset of the energy crisis of the 1970s. Cumulatively, billions of dollars were being spent on energy in buildings, and yet little work had been done to monitor (or predict) how well different types of buildings, using different building materials and systems, actually performed from either an engineering or a human perspective. Out of this debacle evolved today's rather sophisticated energy management systems, with their capacity to monitor and regulate energy use continuously in order to contain costs while maintaining acceptable levels of comfort. The problem was that energy concerns, like POE, focused on only one subset of issues on which buildings needed to be assessed.

To concerns with occupant satisfaction and energy conservation there were added during the 1970s several other factors stimulating the development of more sophisticated building appraisal methods. One was the tremendous inflation in building and capital costs resulting from the major economic restructuring brought on by the energy crisis. Second were advances in applied economics. During this period, models for predicting the cost effectiveness of different building configurations were devised. Third was the development of cheap and powerful computing which spawned the rapid development of computer-aided design and computer-aided facility management systems. Last was the emergence of the professional facility manager.

All service groups organizations are being held more accountable than ever before for demonstrating that their activities are helping the organization achieve its business objectives. Many organizations are also moving toward more decentralized decision making, letting those most directly affected by decisions influence them, subject to some basic overall policy guidelines and principles of accountability. Both of these trends require some means of measuring and accounting for the results of actions. Facilities represent a substantial percentage of most organizations' assets and also a substantial proportion of their operating costs. Thus it is hardly surprising that building performance appraisal is becoming a formal and regular part of the facility management process.

Yet in most organizations, building appraisal remains relatively primitive: fragmented, semi-automated, partially systematic, and only weakly connected to the organizational demands that presumably necessitated the building appraisal in the first place. Organizations that are relatively good at managing the rest of their assets and costs often do not even have good records of their facilities. Some have sophisticated and precise data on energy costs but no database on the relation between energy performance and occupancy satisfaction and comfort, or on the relation between building characteristics and the requirements of different segments and subgroups within the organizations. Even though buildings are occupied over time and all organizations are preoccupied with organizational change, very few systems directly relate building assessment to what the organization will be like in the future.

The realization that facilities affect the productivity of the organization and its employees makes imperative the development of such databases and an understanding of such relationships. In a certain sense, facilities represent a new and untapped frontier for improving organizations' performance. Benefits range from the organization's ability to implement its business plans faster because its facilities can accommodate new information technologies quickly and with minimal disruption to being able to support new management styles and work patterns because the facility has building characteristics that enable space to be organized and designed in many different ways. But to exploit this potential there must be better ways to determine how well different sorts of buildings meet the needs of different types of organizations. There also must be a clearer understanding of the kinds of decisions that a building appraisal process can influence.

USES AND BENEFITS OF BUILDING APPRAISAL

Although all decisions are ultimately made on the basis of judgments (some founded in expertise, some in politics), a good building appraisal system should help make more informed judgments about the following questions:

- Which buildings being considered are acceptable?
- Which buildings being considered are the most cost effective?
- Am I paying for things I do not need?
- Am I paying for things I am not getting?
- What modifications should I ask for?
- Which organizational subgroups should occupy a particular building (or part of it)?
- What should the purchase price or rental rate be?
- Which leases should be renewed or be allowed to expire?
- Which buildings should we sell or retain but lease?
- What should the term of the lease be?
- Which buildings most need renovation?
- What renovations are most cost effective?
- If we want to lease or sell, what market should we target?

Simply asking these questions makes clear that building appraisal does not pertain just to existing buildings nor to just cost, occupant satisfaction, flexibility, or change. It is as valuable when organizations are shrinking as when they are expanding, when they are renovating as when building new, and when divesting or merging. It can be used to evaluate buildings in the planning stages as well as those already built. It can be used as a preliminary form of architectural programming—to guide the search for design solutions—as well as a method for assessing buildings in use.

For long-range strategic planning, building appraisal provides information about what kinds of buildings will be needed in the future to accommodate the organization's expected evolution. Knowledge of which buildings are performing poorly and well is an important component of such a long-term replacement strategy. Phasing-out operations or other downsizing operations require a similar knowledge.

Many shorter-range decisions also require building performance data. Selecting among buildings being offered for lease or purchase requires both performance and cost data. Decisions about whether or not to renovate an existing building and in turn exactly what should be renovated to obtain the most cost-effective building requires systematic performance data. Similarly, the process of designing and building a new building requires the ability to identify the organization's performance requirements and to be able to use that information to guide and monitor the search for the best design and to evaluate and select among the alternatives being offered.

Decisions about managing the occupancy of the building stock require comparable and reliable data. Which buildings or leases should be retained or disposed of? Which buildings or which areas within the current stock of buildings have the best location for a particular unit? Which building will best meet the needs of that unit over the next several years so that the disruption and cost incurred by frequent relocations or renovations can be minimized? Operational and maintenance decisions can also benefit from building performance data. Which types of buildings or which elements within buildings require the least maintenance, are the most energy efficient, and incur the fewest breakdowns and repairs? Which are the easiest to clean? What cleaning or maintenance strategies work best for particular buildings? All are questions that benefit from having a reliable database on building performance.

When the FM organization lacks reliable and comparable data on building performance and costs, its ability to make its most basic decisions is impaired, as is its ability to make a convincing case for its recommendations. The ability to demonstrate the FM unit's organizational effectiveness is hampered without such information and a procedure for generating, maintaining, and manipulating it to answer questions. Reporting to management and customer units is easier and more convincing when the consequences of decisions can be demonstrated. Feedback, planning, control, allocation, and reporting functions all benefit from having performance indicators that are grounded in the building's effectiveness in meeting the organization's needs. The FM unit should be able to show, for example, that new planning processes, procedures, or space guidelines have lowered the cost or the number of renovations and have better enabled the building to accommodate organizational change, a new management style, or dramatic shifts in group size.

With all these benefits, why do not more organizations regularly use building performance appraisal to manage their facilities? The main reason is that, until very recently, the measurement technology or methodology did not exist. Furthermore, there was no cadre of trained FM professionals who understood the need for and the use of building performance appraisal techniques to help manage buildings. As a consequence, formal, systematic appraisals of the performance of buildings are relatively rare and are fairly new.

CHARACTERISTICS OF A MODEL BUILDING APPRAISAL SYSTEM

What are some of the characteristics of a performance system? First, it should consist of measures that have meaning for the organization and the decision makers in that organization who must use them, for example, the management to which the FM unit reports and the people occupying the space. Good examples are initial and operating costs, ease of renovation, number and types of different units that could occupy a particular space without renovation, and the ease of relocation of employees and equipment.

Second, the measures on which the system depends should be easily accessible. They should not require expensive, difficult, and disruptive data collection procedures. They need to be reliable, valid, and easy to analyze. Different people using the same system should get the same answer. Elaborate training should not be required to use the measures or to understand the data and reports obtained from them.

Third, for general facility management purposes the measures should not focus solely on one narrow aspect of building performance such as cost or energy efficiency. Rather, they should represent a broad range of the types of performance that a building must provide for an organization, such as cost, maintenance, employee satisfaction, ease of relocations, and security.

Fourth, the system should be able to compare the performance of different buildings for different organizations at different times.

Fifth, it should be possible to link the system to the organization's other databases. For example, if the finance department calculates the rent chargebacks for space and the facilities unit monitors compliance with company space standards, both should calculate how much space the various units use. When one unit changes the information, it should automatically change it throughout the system. Although different units use the same information, they often measure or calculate it in different ways. With an integrated system this information would need to be collected only once and would be instantly available to all who use it.

For analytical purposes it should also be possible to relate data from, for example, the human resources department on rates of respiratory illness to occupancy of different buildings or parts of them, or to examine whether organizations in buildings that give staff good window access have lower employee turnover rates, or that buildings with certain characteristics are much more adaptable to changes in information technology than others are. A computer-aided facility management system (CAFM) with a database that includes building performance data can enable a company to reduce the time needed to collect and use information.

Sixth, the system should be linked to a financial database that can be used to estimate both the cost of different building modifications and how these will influence performance, as well as showing how building modifications will affect the building's market value and operating costs.

Once such a system is used, the FM organization can begin to establish benchmarks and performance profiles that will enable them to compare performance over time and with other units. Having a consistent and easily used information base improves the speed with which the FM unit can respond to inquiries, including "what if?" questions. As decision makers become familiar with the system, the speed and quality of the communication between the FM unit and management will improve. Reporting will become easier and more effective, as will the perception of the professionalism and value of the FM unit.

DIMENSIONS OF BUILDING PERFORMANCE APPRAISAL

Simply measuring a building's physical attributes, such as its size or its power capacity, is a gauge of "performance," but not a very good one. The implicit and untested assumption underlying such approaches is that if one knows something about capacity, one also will know how well it serves the organization's demands. But unless the organization's demands themselves are measured and compared with that capacity, the performance assessment will be a bit like trying to clap with one hand. How one moves from describing the physical characteristics of a facility to relating such attributes to the organization's objectives is one of the differences among performance assessment techniques.

A building's performance can be judged on an almost infinite variety of dimensions. Table 13-1 suggests some of the types of organizational demands or objectives against which a building can be assessed.

Which of these factors should be used to determine building performance? Equally important is the evidence generated. How reliable is it? How verifiable? For any approach, the following questions should be asked:

- Is the process objective or subjective? Are the measures operationally defined, or do they require expert judgments? In systems that rely extensively on expert judgment, the only way to reduce the variation in measurements is to use the same evaluator. Is the system designed so that, after completing a training program in-house, staff can make the evaluations?
- Are the systems standardized, or do they use measures that are constructed for each new situation?
- Can the system be used to evaluate both existing and proposed buildings?
- Can the system be used to judge the adequacy of a building for future and current needs?
- How comprehensive are the performance attributes? Does the system focus on just a few dimensions of performance, such as energy consumption or individual employees' satisfaction with their workstations?
- Is the system designed so that the measures can be used to track the performance of buildings over time in relation to actions designed to improve performance?
- Can the system be used to identify and account for the relative importance of different issues or performance dimensions (e.g., is flexibility more important than image?)?

Table 13-1. Indicators of Building Performance

Financial	*Space Use Efficiency*
• Asset value of real estate portfolio	• Rentable or usable/gross
• Income from leases and disposals	• Space/employee
• Expenses of real estate occupancy	• Space/unit of income
• Construction costs	• Renovations required
• Energy costs	• Turnaround time
• Maintenance costs	• Change orders
	• Response time
Performance/productivity	• Disruption
• Quality of work	
• Quantity of work	*Organizational Issues*
• Absenteeism	• Changes in work force size
• Innovation	• Need to relocate employees
	• Ability to attract and retain staff
Information Technology	• Security
• Networking IT	• Communication of status
• Changing location of cables	• Informal communication
• Protecting equipment	• Image to outside
• Electrical power capacity	
• Telecommunications	

A LOOK AT SOME BUILDING PERFORMANCE APPRAISAL SYSTEMS

In regard to who conducts the assessment, existing building appraisal systems fall into one of two categories: user-based systems or expert-based systems. The first uses the building's occupants' responses to evaluate the adequacy of a building, primarily their satisfaction with different aspects of the building's design. The second set of procedures relies on experts' assessments, which typically span a much wider range of concerns, many central to the facility management role: ability to accommodate information technology; organizational growth, decline, and churn; changes in workers' expectations, work-style, and time-use patterns; and space and energy efficiency.

User-based Systems (POE)

POE (post-occupancy evaluation) is a formal evaluation of a building by its occupants after it is completed. The focus is on user satisfaction, measured with social science–based tools of interviews, surveys, focus groups, systematic observation, and behavioral mapping. What is measured ranges from aspects of the physical environment (e.g., parking, lighting, temperature, seating) to the occupants' judgments about how such physical characteristics affect their work behaviors and attitudes (e.g., morale, informal communication, teamwork, productivity). POE is limited to existing buildings, but the information generated can be used as part of the briefing process for a new building, as well as to improve the conditions through renovation of the building for which the data were initially collected. The POE's greatest strength is for improving prototype buildings that are built over and over again as variations on a theme. There are three main types of POE: (1) Custom (individually tailored), (2) standardized (uniformly applied), and (3) mixed (standard components mixed and modified).

Custom POEs

Custom POEs are constructed by individual researchers and are tailored to the specific circumstances of the building and its occupants. For the most part they provide information to the architects and the clients on how well the completed building is meeting the needs of its occupants, especially in relation to their personal work environment. The adequacy of the building systems in terms of maintenance and repair or operating costs, the effect of the building form on organizational and group functioning, its ability to accommodate new information technologies with minimal disruption, and other organizational objectives tend to be overlooked.

Custom POEs rarely become part of a systematic database, and the methods themselves are often relatively informal, relying on casual observations and selected interviews with management or staff. Usually relatively small in scale and short in duration, the custom POE does not permit comparisons with other buildings, with other sectors of the industry, or with earlier time periods. they also tend to be one-shot affairs; that is, they are done at one point in the life of the building, and their use is confined to identifying and occasionally correcting oversights and defects in the building. Seldom are follow-up studies done to see whether the changes made actually corrected the defects in the building (or produced other unanticipated changes, positive or negative).

Standardized POEs

In recent years a number of researchers and FM practitioners have begun to see the value of having standardized tools and measures that were valid and reliable and, most importantly, would allow for comparisons with other buildings, organizations, and time periods (Preiser 1989; Preiser, Rabinowitz, and White 1988). The voluntary standards organization ASTM is now constructing a standardized battery of valid and reliable tools that will be publicly available to any one doing a POE (see Figure 13-1).

This system would have a standard core of measures supplemented by additional measures. They would have the advantage of allowing for comparison with either an in-house database or ultimately with a national database maintained by organizations such as IFMA, BOMA or ASTM.

The standardized POE shares a number of the drawbacks of the custom POE, but some of its limitations, particularly its original focus on the response of the individual employee to his or her workstation and immediate environment, are beginning to be addressed. Preiser, Rabinowitz, and White (1988) recommend including other factors such as code compliance, structural integrity, security, and energy efficiency. By definition, this means broadening the range of participants in the building assessment far beyond the immediate building occupants. There is no reason that facility managers, architects, telecommunication specialists, and other "stakeholders" in the building should not be directly involved.

Section 3. Common workplace requirement

USER SURVEY (I-1-U)

Please rate common workplace on each of the characteristics below. First indicate your satisfaction with each one, and fill the number corresponding to your answer in the left side box. Then rate how important each one of the characteristics is to you, and fill your answer in the right side box. If you have some specific reason or explanation about you rating, please put your comments on the last column of each question

1 Dissatisfied	1 Not Important
2 Somewhat Dissatisfied	2 Hardly Important
3 Neutral	3 Neutral
4 Somewhat Satisfied	4 Somewhat Important
5 Satisfied	5 Very important

Physical settings

Satisfaction		Importance	Comments
☐	1. Overall workspace size	☐	________
☐	2. Shape of workspace	☐	________
☐	3. Density of people	☐	________
☐	4. Location of workplace on the floor	☐	________
☐	5. Quality of lighting	☐	________
☐	6. Quality of air conditioning	☐	________
☐	7. Color of floor covering	☐	________
☐	8. Color of overall furniture	☐	________
☐	9. Noise level at workplace	☐	________
☐	10. Overall image (color, atmosphere)	☐	________
☐	11. Overall environment (comfort)	☐	________

Communication on the floor

Satisfaction		Importance	Comments
☐	12. Number of meeting space	☐	________
☐	13. Size of meeting space	☐	________
☐	14. Privacy of meeting space	☐	________
☐	15. Location of meeting space	☐	________
☐	16. Furniture of meeting space	☐	________
☐	17. Visibility to co-workers	☐	________

Figure 13-1. Example of a postoccupancy evaluation (POE) survey.

Please rate <u>your personal workplace</u> on each of the characteristics below. <u>First</u> indicate your <u>satisfaction</u> with each one, and fill the number corresponding to your answer in the <u>left</u> side box. Then rate how <u>important</u> each one of the characteristics is to you, and fill your answer in the <u>right</u> side box. If you have some specific reason or explanation about your rating, please put your comments on the last column of each question

1 Dissatisfied	1 Not Important
2 Somewhat Dissatisfied	2 Hardly Important
3 Neutral	3 Neutral
4 Somewhat Satisfied	4 Somewhat Important
5 Satisfied	5 Very important

Satisfaction   Importance   Comments

☐ 1. Location of your workplace   ☐ _____

☐ 2. Arrangement of furniture   ☐ _____

☐ 3. Amount of work surface   ☐ _____

☐ 4. Function of furniture   ☐ _____

☐ 5. Amount of storage for work materials   ☐ _____

☐ 6. Function of storage   ☐ _____

☐ 7. Display area for graphic materials   ☐ _____

☐ 8. Style of furniture   ☐ _____

☐ 9. Color of furniture   ☐ _____

☐ 10. Comfort of chair   ☐ _____

☐ 11. Degree of privacy   ☐ _____

☐ 12. Suitability to your work   ☐ _____

☐ 13. Opportunity to personalize workplace   ☐ _____

☐ 14. Image of workplace   ☐ _____

☐ 15. Overall satisfaction with workplace   ☐ _____

16. What do you like <u>most</u> about your current <u>personal workplace</u>?

_____

17. What do you like <u>least</u> about your current <u>personal workplace</u>?

_____

Figure 13-1. (*Continued*) Example of a postoccupancy evaluation (POE) survey.

Coding, analyzing, integrating, and interpreting these kinds of data can be a daunting task. No POEs are yet designed to provide data in the form of easily conceptualized and communicated profiles or performance summaries. In a sense, they have not yet fully made the transition from social science tool to a fully developed building appraisal methodology. The most serious defect of the POE, however, is its assessment of the performance of only existing buildings occupied by the concerned organization and as the organization currently exists. It is not possible to use the technique to determine the suitability of a building for an organization as its needs evolve and change over time.

Expert-based Systems

Another approach to assessing building performance is to rely on experts to judge the building's performance. The expert assessment can take a variety of forms, but it usually has a much broader focus and considers a wider range of attributes than does the POE. Such assessments typically concentrate on the adequacy of the building for the organization's effective functioning, and they are most often used to help the organization select a new building.

Expert assessments can range from a simple walk-through appraisal by an expert to formal feasibility studies. Their main characteristic is that they rely on the judgment of an expert who makes the appraisal based on experience that cannot easily be passed on to others. Also, although one expert's opinion may be reliable and valid, it cannot easily be compared with the appraisal of another building by another expert. Furthermore, many of these appraisals do not follow a formal or standardized method. Like the custom POE, they are individually designed for each situation.

Checklist Appraisal Systems

The most common expert appraisal method simply uses a checklist of important considerations to rate performance. Many FM texts (cf. Gould 1983; Worthington and Konya 1988) contain checklists to use in evaluating buildings and selecting a site (see Figure 13-2). In some cases they describe what constitutes good and bad characteristics on each of the dimensions; for example, low floor-to-ceiling height restricts cable management options. Using these dimensions, the expert rates (e.g., on a scale of 1 to 10) how well different buildings perform on each one. Yet, unless the basis for assigning a rating is clear, the ratings will be subjective with no objective reason for awarding one site a 5 and the next a 7.

These systems help ensure that important factors are not ignored in the assessment and that there is some way to compare different sites using the same criteria. Different buildings or sites can be compared on these numerical ratings by using a simple matrix in which each building is judged on one scale and the performance dimensions on the other. However, these comparisons are possible only when the judgments are made by the same evaluator or when there are explicit criteria for the ratings (which is relatively rare). It is also not possible to compare these appraisals with a set of norms using a large national database.

Factor	Material	Condition Good	Condition Fair	Condition Poor	Findings
Structural					
Design loadings					
Columns					
Bearing walls					
Floor/roof					
Horizontal framing					
Foundations					
Other					
Water					
Supply					
Metering					
Piping and insulation					
Pumps					
Tanks					
Heating					
Treatment					
Other					
Plumbing Fixtures					
Toilets					
Drinking fountains					
Kitchens					
Janitor's closets					
Other					
Sanitary					
House drain					
Piping, vents					
Traps					
Floor drains					
Roof drainage					
Ejectors and sumps					
Disposal system					
Other					
HVAC					
Boilers and assoc. equip.					
Piping and insulation					
Pumps and compressors					
Ductwork, dampers, insulation					
Fans, filters, louvers					
Cooling system					
Room units					
Roof-mounted equipment and supports					

Figure 13-2. Example of a building appraisal checklist. (Source: Gould, B.R. 1983. *Planning The New Corporate Headquarters*. New York: John Wiley & Sons. Copyright © 1983, John Wiley & Sons. Reprinted by permission of John Wiley & Sons, Inc.)

Table 13–2. Building Characteristics Reviewed in
the Architectural Feasibility Study

Efficiency
- Gross square feet
- Net square feet
- Usable square feet
- Rentable square feet
- Expansion possibilities (site and building)

Space Planning
- Ceiling grid
- Window grid
- Column spacing
- Building depth and shape
- Size and placement of core

Building Services
- Floor-to-ceiling height
- HVAC zoning and design
- Power capacity (including expansion)
- Power distribution system
- Number and location of elevators

Architectural Feasibility

A variant on the checklist method is the architectural feasibility study (see Table 13-2). Designed primarily to determine whether a client organization should remain in the building it now occupies, renovate it to improve its fit with organizational requirements, or move to a different building (on site or at a new location), architectural feasibility studies rely on a combination of expert judgment, a quantitative analysis of the building and site, and a comparison of these data with some form of benchmark data, either industry generated or derived by the architectural firm from its own experience. These data are related to organizational requirements, in the form of headcount projections, changes in the nature and extent of information technology, and, to a lesser extent, possible changes in management structure, style, and overall work patterns and organizational culture.

This approach, more so that any of the others, actually performs a direct cost–benefit analysis; that is, it compares how well the needs of the organization (now and in the future) can be met by remaining in the existing building, renovating the existing building, buying a different building, or constructing a new building. Each of these options is weighed in light of their estimated cost.

The physical analysis has three main components:

1. *Efficiency.* The proportion of gross, net, and usable square feet is taken from "as built" plans (rarely accurate!) or by direct measurements of the building. The definition of each of these terms can be an arcane one, with tremendous cost impli-

cations. The amount of available usable space directly affects leasing costs, and it also determines how much of what one is paying for can actually be used to accommodate workstations, support areas, and other "usable" areas of the building (but not the core with elevators, electrical service closets, toilets, etc.). Many architectural firms recommend minimum levels for these ratios based on experience with many different clients. DEGW, a large architectural and space-planning firm based in London, recommends, for example, a ratio of usable/net square footage of about 80 percent and of usable/gross of about 68 percent (Worthington and Konya 1988).

2. *Space planning.* In planning space, several different kinds of construction factors are reviewed, the most common of which are related to the planning grid, especially the placement of window mullions and ceiling grid, and the spacing and placement of columns throughout the building. Another factor is the size and location of the core housing elevators, vertical power distribution, and toilets. Still another is building depth, with shallow buildings viewed as providing less flexibility in planning open offices or combinations of open and cellular offices.

Again, based on experience laying out offices in different kinds of space, many architectural firms have rules of thumb about the most flexible planning grids. In the United States a five-foot grid is considered ideal. In Europe the comparable measure is a grid 1.5 meters. In both cases the issue is the ease with which the space can be subdivided into offices of useful size, not too large or too small. The placement of the cores and columns affects the amount of available free space, which directly affects the ease with which different-sized departments or work groups can be accommodated on a floor. An additional factor is the opportunity for expansion on the site afforded both by the design and the construction of the existing building and by the size and building constraints of the site.

3. *Building services.* Building services refer to the building's capacity to accommodate such things as existing and projected information technology requirements, goods and people movement (including the ease with which furniture and other equipment can be moved in and through the building during the day without a huge disruption of work), and safety and security issues. The most common building factors assessed are the floor-to-ceiling height (which affects wire management, lighting, and HVAC) and the capacity, zoning, and control characteristics of the HVAC system (which affects heat load and the building's partitioning).

Using standard cost estimating procedures and data, the cost of modifying the building to improve its fit with organizational requirements can easily be estimated. The ability of the existing space configurations (limited by building depth, size, and placement of cores and ceiling and window grids, etc.) can be tested by trying to fit hypothetical layouts onto them, which can be compared with the layouts possible in a modified or different building with different characteristics.

The method is as good as the judgments of those performing the assessment and as reliable as the internal database against which comparisons are made. One drawback of this approach is that different experts assessing the same building are likely to reach different conclusions (unless they all use essentially the same working assumptions to guide their assessment). More important, the organizational factors that can be assessed and systematically factored into the appraisal are limited to headcount projections and the adoption rate of information technology. There is no way of including in a systematic appraisal format of this type such organizational factors as management styles, communication of status, and type of communication desired.

Matrix Method

The matrix method has much in common with the checklist appraisal approaches, as it can be used to compare the suitability of a number of buildings for a particular type of occupant (DEGW 1985). In the example shown in Figure 13-3, the performance of several buildings is compared on twelve criteria. The criteria here, unlike those of the checklist approach, are the result of extensive research and professional practice with particular building and organizational types. The basic criteria remain the same from one study to the next, but each appraisal can be tailored to the circumstances of the study by adding additional criteria. Expert ratings (which may or may not be associated with particular building features) are summarized in an overall rating, seen in the column to the far right of Figure 13-3. Each of the factors is rated in a matrix form as excellent, good, fair, or poor.

The ratings are displayed graphically so that they are easily understood on either a general or a detailed level. Each of the ratings in this table is the result of a more detailed matrix evaluation that is summarized into a single evaluation on that one dimension. For example, the accessibility rating is actually the result of four separate assessments of factors, such as the ability to be dropped off by car, the number of entrances, the visual clarity of the elevators, and the ease of access to the building. Individual ratings on these four factors are then combined into a single overall assessment of the building's accessibility.

Similarly, the usable area efficiency rating examines factors such as the gross floor area, the area in core and circulation, the core area efficiency rating, and the net leasable area. The ratings for each are summarized into a measure called usable area efficiency. Measures such as net leasable area can be defined so that any assessor could carry out the rating. Other factors, however, are not so easily operationalized but require expert staff to make highly refined judgments. The technique also uses graphic analyses such as drawing typical floor plans on the same scale. These can then be used to compare things like the serviceability of floors. Bar graphs of quantitative data such as floor area or the percentage of net leasable area that is highly serviced are used to display and compare the information.

This technique provides valid, reliable, and comparative data on the performance of existing buildings. It can also be applied to proposed buildings, with the analyses made using the building design documents. The technique has no way of identifying an organization's needs (either current or future) or of matching them with the building's performance. The system presumes that the user of the ratings already has information on organizational needs and will judge the match between building performance and organizational needs. But this is obviously quite difficult to do given the number of variables that must be considered.

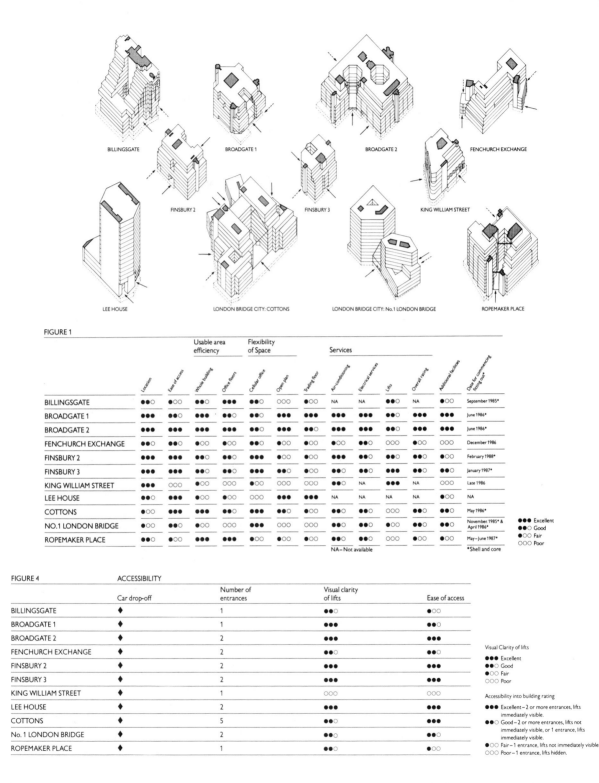

FIGURE 1

| | Location | Ease of access | Usable area efficiency | | Flexibility of Space | | | Services | | | Overall rating | Additional facilities | Date for commencing fitting out* |
			Whole building	Office floors	Cellular office	Open plan	Trading floor	Air-conditioning	Electrical services	Lifts			
BILLINGSGATE	●●○	●○○	●●○	●●●	●●○	○○○	●○○	NA	NA	●●○	NA	●○○	September 1985*
BROADGATE 1	●●●	●●○	●●●	●●○	●●○	●●●	●●●	●●●	●●●	●●○	●●●	●●●	June 1986*
BROADGATE 2	●●●	●●○	●●●	●●●	●●○	●●●	●●○	●●●	●●●	●●○	●●●	●●●	June 1986*
FENCHURCH EXCHANGE	●●○	●●○	●○○	●○○	●●○	●○○	●○○	●○○	●●○	○○○	●○○	○○○	December 1986
FINSBURY 2	●●●	●●●	●●○	●●●	●●●	●○○	●○○	●●●	●●○	●●○	●●○	●○○	February 1988*
FINSBURY 3	●●●	●●●	●●○	●●○	●●●	●●○	●○○	●●○	●●○	●●●	●●○	●●○	January 1987*
KING WILLIAM STREET	●●●	○○○	●○○	○○○	●○○	○○○	○○○	●●○	NA	●●●	NA	○○○	Late 1986
LEE HOUSE	●●○	●●●	●○○	●○○	○○○	●●●	●●●	NA	NA	NA	NA	●○○	NA
COTTONS	●○○	●●●	●●●	●●○	●●●	●●○	●○○	●●○	●●○	○○○	●●○	●●○	May 1986*
NO.1 LONDON BRIDGE	●○○	●●○	●○○	○○○	●●●	○○○	○○○	●●○	●●○	●○○	●●○	●●○	November 1985* & April 1986*
ROPEMAKER PLACE	●●○	●○○	●●●	●●●	●○○	●○○	●○○	●●○	●●○	○○○	●○○	●○○	May–June 1987*

NA – Not available *Shell and core

●●● Excellent
●●○ Good
●○○ Fair
○○○ Poor

FIGURE 4 ACCESSIBILITY

	Car drop-off	Number of entrances	Visual clarity of lifts	Ease of access
BILLINGSGATE	◆	1	●●○	●○○
BROADGATE 1	◆	1	●●●	●●○
BROADGATE 2	◆	2	●●●	●●●
FENCHURCH EXCHANGE	◆	2	●●○	●●○
FINSBURY 2	◆	2	●●●	●●●
FINSBURY 3	◆	2	●●●	●●●
KING WILLIAM STREET	◆	1	○○○	○○○
LEE HOUSE	◆	2	●●●	●●●
COTTONS	◆	5	●●○	●●●
No. 1 LONDON BRIDGE	◆	2	●●○	●●○
ROPEMAKER PLACE	◆	1	●●○	●○○

Visual Clarity of lifts

●●● Excellent
●●○ Good
●○○ Fair
○○○ Poor

Accessibility into building rating

●●● Excellent – 2 or more entrances, lifts immediately visible.
●●○ Good – 2 or more entrances, lifts not immediately visible, or 1 entrance, lifts immediately visible.
●○○ Fair – 1 entrance, lifts not immediately visible.
○○○ Poor – 1 entrance, lifts hidden.

Figure 13-3. Example of matrix-format building appraisal procedure. (Source: DEGW 1985)

Further complicating this assessment is the absence of a formal way of ranking or accounting for differences in the relative importance of the criteria. The system also can be carried out only by the trained experts who developed the system, and thus it is not possible to link this information with a large national database that would enable comparisons with other buildings. It is also not possible for the in-house FM unit to use it as a regular diagnostic tool to manage the organization's facilities.

Finally, the system is labor intensive, as it requires collecting large amounts of data and graphically representing those data in the form of floor plans drawn on a common scale. At the same time it compares the buildings' performance so that, when combined with other information such as cost and organizational needs, can help determine which of several alternative buildings is likely to be the most suitable for a given type of organization. The nested analysis (in which a general factor "accessibility" is derived from the ratings of some of the factors) enables a decision maker to examine in more depth the judgments that went into a particular rating. Most of those assessments are professional judgments based on the experience and insight of specific experts and therefore are not very accessible to others.

Turnkey Expert Systems

The matrix method has many advantages: It uses the judgment of experts that is the result of years of experience in assessing the performance of buildings. But because of its reliance on expert judgment, it is not a system that can be regularly used by in-house FM organizations to plan and manage the facilities of an organization. It also does not allow for the creation of a large multiuser database that could be used to make comparative assessments.

To overcome some of these limitations and yet retain the advantages of expert judgment, the authors, working on their own and with Gerald Davis and DEGW in London, have developed a more comprehensive building appraisal system that improves the fit over time between organizations and the buildings they occupy.

The first project, completed by DEGW and its collaborators in London in 1983, broke new ground by linking specific building characteristics—like a building's depth, its slab-to-slab heights, and the size and location of the cable raceways—to its ability to accommodate new information technologies, both office automation and automated building services. It represented a form of the matrix approach just described.

ORBIT-2 (Davis et al. 1985) took place in North America, and its goal was different. It set out to create a systematic, comprehensive building appraisal methodology that either consultants or organizations themselves could use to rate the suitability of different buildings for specific organizations or their subunits.

To be a useful methodology ORBIT-2 had to be dynamic, capable of responding to changes in technology and design and also to the needs of particular organizations using it in-house or as a consultancy tool. To this end we wanted the rating process to be:

• *Comprehensive.* It integrates information on the organization, information technology, and the building, including its building systems, furniture, and fit.

- *Transparent.* The way in which the rating scores are calculated can be easily traced and understood.
- *Simple.* The process is simple to use, requiring a minimum of training.
- *Selective.* There are dozens of potentially relevant criteria against which buildings can be assessed. Our goal was to identify a number of issues spanning technological and organizational concerns that, if got right, would make it likely that the building would help the organization achieve its business objectives.
- *Dynamic.* Organizations change over time, and so buildings suitable for today may be inappropriate in five years. We thus built in a time dimension in which organizational requirements are recorded both now and in the future (a date is determined by the organization).

The ORBIT-2 project began with a "delphi" type of study which asked a panel of experts in areas such as information technology, organizational change, real estate and development practices, and buildings and building systems to identify the important trends or changes in each of their areas of expertise that were likely to affect buildings or building needs over the next few years. Each of the experts was then asked to revise their prognostications based on the predictions of the others. From these trends papers the ORBIT-2 team derived a list of seventeen issues that most organizations occupying office buildings were likely to face during the next few years. These issues included fluctuations in staff size, relocation of employees or computers as a result of organizational change, and the introduction of new information technology.

Because all organizations differ and change over time, an essential part of the ORBIT-2 method was an instrument that could be used to gauge the relative importance to an organization of each of these issues, both now and at some time in the future. The procedure for identifying the importance of these issues and how they change is a feature differentiating this method from the others we discussed.

ORBIT-2 did succeed, but rather clumsily. Long questionnaires were used to determine organizational facility requirements. Design strategies, which in the ORBIT-2 methodology describe patterns of building components organized to solve problems like power distribution or internal office relocations, were sometimes vague. And the score was complicated, attempting to show where the particular building being appraised stood in relation to a hypothetical "ideal" building.

The third generation of ORBIT work, called ORBIT 2.1, developed by William Sims and Franklin Becker, transformed the original ORBIT-2 building appraisal procedure from an interesting idea into a simple, workable methodology.

THE ORBIT 2.1 RATING PROCESS©

ORBIT 2.1 differs in four ways from ORBIT-2 (Becker 1988a). First, separate and long Organizational and Information Technology Surveys were combined into a single, much shorter instrument. As part of this, the original seventeen key issues were reduced to fourteen as shown below.

Third, the method of calculating the performance scores was simplified and also made more sensitive. Separate scores are now calculated for overperformance and for underperformance, to correct a defect in the previous system, in which overperformance on one issue could cancel out underperformance on another. Building underperformance is likely, for example, to affect organizational performance by making it costly, difficult, and disruptive to reorganize work groups because of the building's shape or its way of distributing power and cooling. Overperformance means the organization is wasting its scarce resources by paying for building characteristics, such as excess power capacity or flexibility, that it does not need. The ideal is a perfect match between organizational requirements and building characteristics. In practice, one decides on the degree of overperformance or underperformance that can be tolerated (see Figures 13-4 and Table 13-3).

Fourteen Key Issues

1. *Change of total staff size.* Is the total number of people to be accommodated in the organization stable or changing?
2. *Attract or retain workforce.* How important is it for the organization's success to ensure that highly qualified staff who are hard to replace feel satisfied enough not only to come but to stay?
3. *Communication of hierarchy, status and power.* How important is it for people to visually recognize differences in rank, status, power within the organizations?
4. *Relocation of staff.* How frequently are people being physically relocated from one workplace location to another inside the office?
5. *Maximizing informal interaction.* How important are informal and spontaneous interaction and face-to-face communication among staff?
6. *Human factors.* How important to the organization is the quality of lighting, air conditioning, temperature, acoustics, and human comfort of its furniture?
7. *High status image to the outside.* How important is the image of the organization which is presented to visitors from the outside?
8. *Security to outside.* How important is protection of information and other valuable objects from outsiders?
9. *Security to inside.* How important is the protection of information from insiders?
10. *Connecting equipment and changing location of cables.* How important is it to the organization to be able to easily connect different pieces of equipment to each other and/or to relocate cables to virtually any location within the building?
11. *Adding or relocating environmentally demanding equipment.* How important is it to the organization to be able to add or relocate environmentally-demanding equipment to virtually any location within the building?
12. *Protecting hardware operations.* How important is it for operations not to be interrupted, even for a few seconds; or for data to be protected against loss, delay, change or misrecording, due to problems with computer or related hardware?
13. *Demand for power.* How important is the need for primary and secondary electrical power capacity and feed, including vertical and horizontal on-floor distribution?

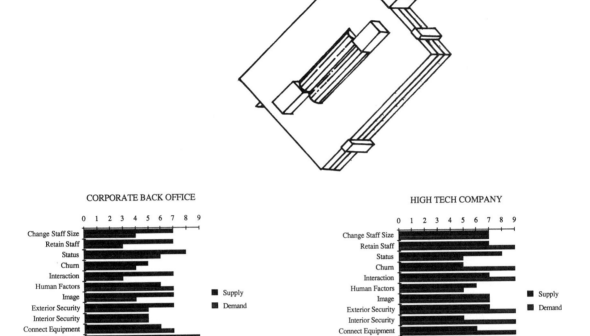

Figure 13-4.   Using the ORBIT 2.1 Building Rating Process to compare the suitability of the same building for different types of organizations. (Source: Becker 1988d)

14. *Telecommunications.* How dependent is the organization on telecommunications inside and to or from outside the building.

The next step was to revise the Building Survey to make it more accurate and sensitive. This included both more detailed and accurate design strategies and a more differentiated system for modifying the ratings of design strategies for each of the fourteen key issues so that they would accurately reflect the characteristics of the buildings being assessed.

Finally, a Design Strategy Rating Modification Guide was added to help modify the rating of design strategies. It also offers a brief rationale for why certain design elements are considered good or bad for resolving an issue.

The combination of these changes has transformed the ORBIT-2 Rating Process from an interesting, somewhat theoretical piece of work to a simple, practical tool for

Table 13-3. ORBIT 2.1's Summary Performance Score Table

	+	−
ORGANIZATIONAL ISSUES		
Change of Total Staff Size	0	
Attract and Retain Staff		−4
Communicate Status	3	
Internal Relocation (Churn)		−4
Interaction	1	
Human Factors	0	
Image to Outside	1	
Security to Outside		−3
Security to Inside		−5
Organizational Subtotals	+5	−16
INFORMATION TECHNOLOGY ISSUES		
Connecting Equipment	0	
Environ Demand Equip	0	
Protecting Hardware	5	
Demand for Power		−1
Telecommunications	4	
Information Technology Subtotals	+9	−1
Overperformance: +14		
Underperformance: −17		

Source: Becker 1988d.

systematic, comprehensive building appraisal. It addresses the kinds of questions noted at the beginning of this chapter related to purchase, leasing, renovation, programming, and occupancy of particular buildings.

How Are Buildings Rated in the ORBIT 2.1 Process?
The ORBIT 2.1 Organizational Survey: The Demand Side

A survey instrument called the Organizational and Information Technology Survey is used to rate the relative importance of each of the fourteen issues on a nine-point scale (see Figure 13-5). Senior people in the organization who are knowledgeable about the organization's current operations and culture as well as its future plans and potential complete the survey, from which a demand profile is created that displays the organization's building-related needs in a simple set of bar charts. These demand profiles can differ for different types of organizations, and they can show considerable change as the organization changes in response to market pressures or the introduction of new technologies.

The ORBIT 2.1 Building Survey: The Supply Side

The next step is rating how well a building is able to resolve or deal with each of the fourteen demand issues. The ORBIT-2.1 Building Survey identifies basic design

ORBIT-2.1
ORGANIZATION AND IT SURVEY

14 KEY ISSUES

<u>Present Year</u>
1985

<u>Future Year</u>
1990-1995

• 1. **Change of total staff size**

not important= less than 5% change in one year; **very important**= more than 50% increase or decrease in one year

not important------------very important
1   2   3   4   5   6   7   8   9

not important------------very important
1   2   3   4   5   6   7   8   9

• 2. **Attract Or Retain Highly Qualified Workforce**

not important= *many qualified applicants for each opening; **very** **important**=very difficult to find qualified applicants*

not important-------very important
1   2   3   4   5   6   7   8   9

not important------------very important
1   2   3   4   5   6   7   8   9

• 3. **Communication of hierarchy, status, and power**

not important= no visible indicators of rank, status, or power; e.g., size and or location of workstation; amount or quality of furnishings; **very important**= nearly all aspects of physical setting used to communicate status

not important------------very important
1   2   3   4   5   6   7   8   9

not important------------very important
1   2   3   4   5   6   7   8   9

Figure 13-5.   Example of the ORBIT 2.1 Organizational and IT Survey. (Source: Becker–Sims Associates 1988)

ORBIT-2.1

BUILDING SURVEY ©

ORBIT Rating	Actual Rating	

(1) CHANGE OF TOTAL STAFF SIZE

Design Strategies

9   ___   • Leased building in desirable suburban office park with options to lease more or sublet space; if owned, options to expand on site; building designed for expansion and subdivision; several actual or potential entrances; medium to deep space with large floors; several cores for vertical transportation; no atrium.
* Mostly open plan; free-standing furniture; movable partitions or panels; small zoned HVAC.

9   ___   • Leased space in high rise, multi-tenant, downtown office building; option to lease additional space; option to sublet; medium depth and floor size ; central transportation core; elevator with ability to lock out floors.
* Systems furniture; largely open plan; small zoned HVAC.

7   ___   • Owned building in greenfield site with expansion potential; potential to lease portion of building to other occupants; low rise; single entrance; medium depth and floor size; single transportation core.
*Systems furniture; movable partitions or panels; medium zoned HVAC.

5   ___   • Owned building in business park; adaptive re-use of former manufacturing space; no option for expansion; low rise; single entrance; large floors; single transportation core.
* Flexible furniture and largely open plan but some fixed partitions; medium zoned HVAC.

3   ___   • Leased space in industrial rehabilitation project in fringe area of city; cannot lease more space; low rise; single entrance; deep space; single vertical transportation core.
* Mainly open plan, systems furniture; large zoned HVAC

1   ___   • Owned building on suburban site; cannot expand; low rise; shallow depth; small to medium floors; single transportation core; atrium.
* Largely compartmented offices; free-standing furniture; large zone HVAC

Figure 13-6a. A building appraisal process should consider different aspects of building design and construction. (Source: Davis et al. 1985)

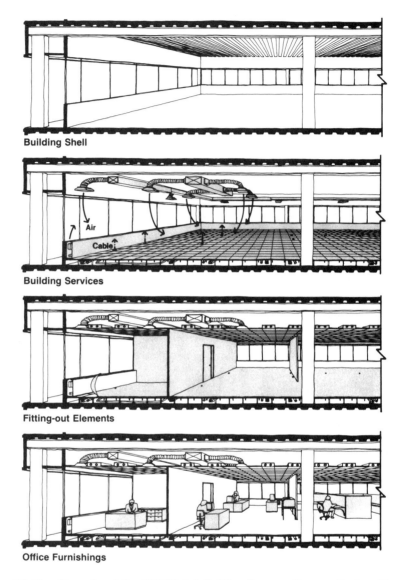

Building Shell

Building Services

Air

Cable

Fitting-out Elements

Office Furnishings

Figure 13-6b. Example of the ORBIT 2.1 Building Survey. (Source: Becker–Sims Associates 1988)

strategies that are used by office building designers (see Figure 13.6a). These design strategies use particular combinations or assemblies of different building elements, including the building shell, the building services, fitting-out elements, and office furnishings (see Figure 13.6b). Each of these strategies was rated by the ORBIT 2.1 team on a nine-point scale for its ability to resolve each of the fourteen issues.

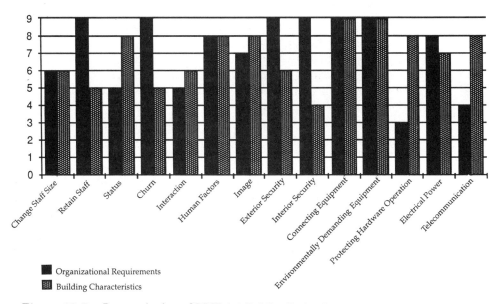

Figure 13-7. Bar graphs from ORBIT 2.1 Building Rating Process comparing organizational requirements and building characteristics. (Source: Becker 1988d)

The Building Survey lists each of the pre-rated design strategies that help resolve a particular issue. By using them it is possible for someone with a minimal amount of training to evaluate a building's performance. All that is necessary is to identify the design strategy described in the survey form that most closely matches the one used in the building being evaluated for each of the issues. In cases when the pre-rated descriptions do not exactly match the building, there is a procedure for adjusting the rating to account for that divergence.

Once the appropriate strategies for each issues are selected (and modified if necessary) building rating scores for each of the fourteen issues are converted into a supply profile that describes the building's performance. The last step in the process matches the organization's demand profile with the building's supply profile (see Figure 13-7). This simple visual matching of the two profiles makes it easy to understand the fit between the building's performance and the organization's requirements.

Benefits of the ORBIT 2.1 Building Rating Process

The ORBIT-2 system solves a number of the problems of the other systems, including the following:

- It is relatively broad and comprehensive in the performance dimensions that it evaluates.
- These dimensions were chosen as a result of an extensive study of current and emerging issues by leading experts in fields related to office organizations.

- The basic structure is open. Additional issues can be added to the system as they emerge or to suit the particular needs of an organization.
- The system does not require experts to use it each time. But it does use the knowledge and judgment of experts by having them "pre-rate" the design strategies.
- The system permits an in-house database to be created and to be linked to a larger national database if desired.
- It enables both existing and proposed buildings to be evaluated and to be matched with the needs of an organization or a subgroup within an organization, such as an department or division.
- It enables an organization to anticipate the match between a building and its future needs. The system can be used to answer "what if?" questions such as what is the most cost-effective strategy for improving the match between building performance and the organization's need for internal flexibility?
- It enables an organization to target its renovation efforts to those that will improve performance, as opposed to a general renovation that might even reduce performance in some areas.
- It provides the information in a simple graphic form that is easy to communicate to decision makers.

Limitations of the ORBIT 2.1 Building Rating Process

What are the limitations of the ORBIT-2 system?

- It does not directly assess the satisfaction of individual employees with their work environment, as does the POE method. It presumes that the expert judgments of several of the issues, such as the one entitled "Human Factors," will reflect the employees' satisfaction.
- Although the system is comprehensive, it does not deal with all the needs that a building must fulfill for an organization. For example, it does not include cost or energy efficiency issues. The system's open structure does, however, enable the addition of other issues, so that it can become increasingly comprehensive over time.

The system's open structure is well illustrated by the work of Gerald Davis, one of the original contributors to the ORBIT-2 work, with the Accommodations Branch of Public Works Canada (PWC). Using the basic rating process developed for ORBIT 2.1, PWC has established an entirely new set of issues (see Figure 13-8). For each of them there are new design strategies. Initially, a target value of 4, the midpoint on a nine point scale, was set by the government as the level that it expects all its buildings to reach. It set a target value of a two-point discrepancy between the building rating and organizational demand as the point at which a mismatch would automatically trigger a need for a building modification. The intent is to use the building rating process to assess, eventually, every building for which PWC is responsible. PWC will also use the process in all decisions about leases, renovations, and new construction.

REQUIREMENT OF TENANT

	-1	0	1	2	3	4	5	6	7	8	9
OCCUPATIONAL HEALTH AND SAFETY											
• Life Safety											
• Health											
INDIVIDUAL EFFECTIVENESS											
• Indoor air											
• Positive stress											
• Cleanliness											
• Temperature and humidity											
• Acoustics and vibration											
• Visual access to daylight and distance											
ACTIVITIES											
• Task-related privacy											
• Task-related illumination											
• Conditions for meetings and teamwork											
• Local control of the environment											
MISSION AND WORK											
• Supportive building systems											
• Adaptability											
• Internal accessibility											
• Structural capacity and rigidity											
• Subdivision into rooms											
• Physical security											
• Computerization and interconnection											
• Location and access to the facility											
• Storage for occupants											
POLICY											
• Barrier-free											
• Federal image											
• Staff services											

Figure 13-8. Issues of building appraisal process being developed by Public Works Canada. (Source: Davis 1989)

SELECTING A BUILDING APPRAISAL SYSTEM

Given the wide diversity of systems available, what are the questions to ask when selecting a building performance appraisal system?

• The first and most important question is whether it evaluates those aspects of the building that need to be evaluated. If the concern is with the building's overall performance for the organization, then a system focused solely on energy consumption is clearly unsuitable. If the concern is with whether the employees are satisfied with their work environment or with identifying ways to improve that satisfaction, then an expert-based system measuring organizational needs is not appropriate.

- Does the system provide a formal method for comparing needs with performance? A system that measures only performance can result in a building that performs well, but in areas that are not needed.
- Can the system evaluate proposed as well as existing buildings? A system that can assess only existing buildings is not very helpful in choosing among alternative proposed designs. Although such a system could be used to identify oversights and errors for correction after occupancy, this is obviously much more costly than identifying and correcting them while they are still only "lines on paper."
- Can the system calculate the adequacy of the building for the organization's future needs? Does it provide a formal means for the organization to identify its future as well as its current needs? If a company is planning to increase its level of office automation and to change its corporate culture with a formal program over the next few years, can the building appraisal process judge existing buildings in light of future organizational demands, as well as for those created by the current way of working and the existing organizational culture?
- Can the system evaluate the entire building, as well as subareas within the building, or is it limited to one or the other? Similarly, can the system be used for the organization as a whole as well as for individual subunits?
- Does the system use standardized measures that permit comparisons with other buildings, areas within buildings, different time periods, and other organizations and their buildings?
- Does the system distinguish the relative importance of the building's various performance characteristics?
- Is the system relatively simple to use and interpret? Does it require outside experts to collect and analyze the information? Does it generate data in a form that is easily understood by decision makers? Can it summarize the information in a form that will clearly show the basic pattern of the building's performance and enable subsequent detailed and sensitive assessments?
- Have the measures been tested and proved to be both reliable and valid?

All of the systems described have obvious benefits, but in all probability none can answer all of an organization's needs. Why not create your own that does? The answer is time. The time required to create a new system can be enormous, and so it is probably better to use (and modify) an existing system or to cobble several together that have needed features.

IMPLEMENTING BUILDING PERFORMANCE APPRAISAL

What are some lessons that might be applied to starting a performance assessment program? First, whenever possible, use a standard system or one composed of standard measures. Second, start small. Begin by collecting information on a few indicators, and then use these to make decisions and recommendations. This will create confidence in the FM unit's competence and will enable the FM unit and its customers to identify the kinds of measures that they will need to make decisions. Third, start by using a test case in a unit that is an ally. Work out all the bugs there until you have a successful approach, and then move to a broader application. Fourth, use measures that are meaningful and important to management and your customers, and then move to more subtle and remote measures if they are needed. Fifth, try to integrate the data into a relational database so that you can ask (and answer) "what if?" questions. Make sure that at least some of the measures are, or could be, related to critical organizational performance issues such as employee turnover, absenteeism, satisfaction, or cost. Use the information to make decisions and recommendations and to plan and manage the FM unit's operations. Finally, use the information to make reports and recommendations to management and to demonstrate the increased effectiveness of the FM unit.

Skeptics Speak

I can appreciate the idea of making building appraisal more systematic, but it seems to me that the kind of comprehensive process you describe for ORBIT 2.1 is time-consuming and therefore unlikely to be used.

Nothing could be further from the truth. The beauty of systems like ORBIT 2.1 is that they consider a wide range of factors, much wider than usually considered in building appraisals, but from the user's viewpoint the system is easy to use. We recommend one day of training to become familiar with the system. After that, actual building ratings, even of complex buildings, will take between thirty and sixty minutes. All that is required is someone knowledgeable about the building. Completing the organizational survey (fourteen questions!) requires about thirty to forty-five minutes of an individual's time and from one to two hours of a group's time, during which individual ratings are discussed and some consensus reached on them. Once these data are available, the actual rating process of matching the supply and demand profiles takes a matter of minutes. This approach is, in fact, far faster than any other form of building appraisal that we know of.

Building appraisal systems like ORBIT 2.1 are comprehensive, but they are too general, never getting down to the levels of detail necessary to make a good decision.

It depends, I think, on what you mean by "general." You are right that the rating process does not replace a detailed inspection by a mechanical engineer or telecommunications specialist. Yet the design strategies are quite specific, and the ability to modify them to reflect specific conditions in a building makes them even more so. Nonetheless, none of the appraisal approaches discussed are intended to or can replace expert judgment. Rather, they are meant to complement it. They are designed to help experts concentrate on those aspects of the facility that need to be examined most closely. They are also useful in quickly eliminating buildings that perform so badly that they need not be analyzed in detail.

Every building is different, and every organization has dozens of different subunits with different requirements. For this reason every building and every assessment should be done on a case-by-case basis. Otherwise it's like trying to fit square pegs in round holes.

Buildings are different, but within classes or types of buildings they really are different only in details or minor features. Buildings constructed for particular purposes and at certain times often have similar floorplates, core layouts, structural systems, ways of handling power distribution and HVAC, and so on. This is the point behind the "design strategies" idea. With the exception of the POE, which makes no attempt to measure or describe the physical characteristics of a building, the other approaches are based on the assumption that there are common issues that every building should be able to accommodate. These issues form the checklist, or matrix, issues or organizational requirements and are the criteria against which the building is assessed.

With respect to internal organizational variation, you are absolutely right. The way ORBIT 2.1 deals with this is by treating departments, divisions, or any other organizational unit that seems to have different requirements as an independent organization; that is, that group completes its own Organizational and Information Technology Survey. These subunit profiles can then be compared with one another. If they are different, then each can be examined independently against the building survey profiles. If there is substantial agreement, then they can be combined. We have done this in several organizations with no difficulty.

Don't all these checklists or ORBIT-like methods quickly become outdated? Building technology is changing all the time, and so is what organizations consider important.

The specific checklist items or survey items do need to be continually monitored and, when necessary, updated. But buildings last for fifty to seventy years on the average, and, although technology continually changes the building shell, and many basic systems stay the same. For the most part, we believe there are issues that virtually every organization occupying typical office space will find relevant. The Organizational Survey in ORBIT 2.1 asks its users to indicate variations in importance on these issues, so that changing values can be directly incorporated. And organizations may add other issues. The Public Works Canada appraisal process illustrates this very well. We also see the need to revise the ratings of existing design strategies to reflect the fact that an excellent solution in 1990 may be only fair in 2000. And of course new strategies, new ways of responding to existing issues, may also have to be constructed to reflect improvements in building systems, architectural design, and the like.

Remember, building appraisal methods of any kind are not a panacea for every building decision, nor are they meant to be used by poorly trained people without any understanding of the building or facility management process. They are simply a useful diagnostic tool that allows one to consider simultaneously many more factors than any individual can keep track of in his or her own mind.

CHAPTER 14

Assessing FM
Performance

Facility management performance is an amalgam not just of the building's performance as a physical product (space, electrical, and cooling capacity; lighting levels; elevator size and frequency; maintenance and running costs) but also of the kinds of outcomes, from cost to human satisfaction and performance, that the building influences in some way and the organization values. These outcomes are influenced by both the processes for developing, delivering, and operating the building and for allocating and using space, equipment, and furniture to support organizational objectives.

FM quality is thus embedded in a network of interdependent outcomes that range from initial construction costs and long term operating costs to the building's capacity to accommodate new techniques and changing user patterns. In the final analysis, the organization must balance these interdependent and (often competing) outcomes so it can achieve its strategic mission. Cutting costs, for example, has little value if salaries become so low that top-quality staff choose not to join or remain in the organization or equipment obsolescence impedes work efficiency.

Although many individual measures of building performance are collected in organizations today (e.g., energy and other operating costs and savings, square footage construction costs), almost no organization is able to provide at a glance a kind of FM balance sheet that shows the relation of these individual indicators to one another.

None, that I know of, are able to communicate, and therefore analyze and use, the relationships among various cost and service indicators.

THE PERFORMANCE PROFILE CONCEPT

The concept of a performance profile is a way of putting into practice a systems perspective. It stresses the overall pattern of outcomes rather than emphasizing one or two important outcomes that may be relatively easy to measure (e.g., number of employees per square foot) or have instant face validity (e.g., reduced operating costs). It provides a graphic analogue to cost–benefit analysis.

Calculating the cost side of the equation is comparatively simple and straightforward, but unfortunately it may be deceptive and even organizationally counterproductive. It is easy to reduce energy costs, for example. Just turn down the heat or lower the air conditioning. Cheaper furniture and less adaptable buildings lower costs, but at what price to the organization? The profile approach is a form of cost–benefit analysis that takes into account a range of organizational outcomes that are fundamental to calculating overall facility performance. These from initial construction costs and ongoing maintenance charges to staff satisfaction with their workplace and the amount of downtime in key information systems.

These kinds of indicators, through a long chain of events virtually impossible to trace, ultimately affect the organization's success, however that is defined: sales volume, return on investment, profit. As Robert Sommer (1972) pointed out, the causal connections between something like downtime and annual sales volume is so tenuous that it makes much more sense to look at the proximate indicators (e.g., downtime, staff satisfaction, amount of staff training) themselves. These are easier to measure and are not rooted in a series of untestable causal links that will always be open to criticism.

The goal is not to maximize efficiency in any single area, but to maximize overall organizational effectiveness. In facility management terms this means, for example, balancing headcount reduction against the level of service provided, energy efficiency against staff discomfort and fatigue, and record keeping against the time required to collect and analyze the information. Balance is achieved at the point that lowered costs do not spawn unacceptable service levels.

WHAT SHOULD BE MEASURED

As a service function, facility management performance must be tied to better "customer" response, with the primary customer often being the staff. As an administrative and operations function, facility management performance will always be under pressure to reduce costs. It is this relationship that defines cost effectiveness.

What is measured and how much weight is given to any one measure depend on the organization's operating environment and culture. Yet despite enormous differences among organizations, in today's dynamic and unpredictable business climate most organizations must respond to the following pressures, regardless of differences in business sector, organizational culture, and perhaps even company size:

- The demand for highly qualified staff with rising expectations about what constitutes an acceptable working environment that often exceeds their supply.
- High property costs that demand the efficient use of premises.
- The location of expensive information technology must be dictated by organizational need, not by building characteristics.
- Frequent changes in organizational structure and ways of working that demand buildings and furniture that can be reconfigured with a minimum of disruption to employees.
- Rapid response to changes in market conditions and the ability to seize unexpected business opportunities that are critical to business success and demand minimum "downtime" and disruption to employees.

This list, though not exhaustive, reflects many of the pressures facing facility managers today and suggest the kinds of overall facility performance measures that are likely to be relevant to facility management.

SELECTING PERFORMANCE INDICATORS

The following performance indicators are likely to be helpful to most organizations, especially those experiencing rapid change:

- *Costs,* including new construction, equipment (e.g., CAD, CAFM[1]), moving (e.g., a typical workstation or department), operating (e.g., energy, rates, rents), renovation (e.g., cost per square foot for a standard workstation, computer room), and furniture, staffing, and premises
- *Disruption,* including the amount of time lost because telephones, computers, and other equipment were not connected to power, furniture and files were not in place, and staff was distracted by the noise of drills and workmen and the dust and moving of goods and materials
- *Satisfaction,* of staff and management with their physical working conditions and the process used to plan and design their work areas
- *Responsiveness,* in terms of hard measures such as the time (e.g., number of hours, days, weeks) in which facility management responds and fixes, if required, facility-related problems
- *Training,* of staff to understand facilities management and learn specific skills
- *Space efficiency,* the ratio of usable to gross square feet in a building

Who Should Be Involved

The first step is for the FM group to think about which individuals should help identify the FM performance profile. They should include the director of facility management

---

[1]CAFM stands for "computer-aided facility management."

and the person to whom he or she reports (probably a senior vice-president), the department heads occupying the facility, and the department heads of other service organizations with whom FM must work (e.g., telecommunications, purchasing, MIS).

This group should understand the FM performance profile and the idea that it is a collaborative consensus-building activity intended to set challenging but feasible performance targets for FM and to establish reasonable expectations about service levels for building occupants. This group will nominate and select the performance indicators and decide on the target performance levels to be achieved.

Indicators and Organizational Objectives

FM indicators must be related to the organization's strategic objectives. On what do they depend on to be achieved, and how can the facilities affect these objectives? Excellence and competitiveness, two common goals, for example, require being able to attract and retain the best-qualified staff (which depend in part on the staff's satisfaction with facility amenities and with their office or workstation appearance, location, and function), being able to respond quickly to changes in staff size and group composition (which are affected by the facility's flexibility and capacity for responding to organizational change), and being able to exploit new technologies quickly (which is influenced by the time and cost of handling wire management and the amount of downtime to install and relocate equipment).

Good performance indicators are directly related to strategic objectives, and the identification and discussion of their facility implications will in themselves likely prove to be an eye-opening experience for business group managers unfamiliar with or skeptical about the importance of facilities to the organization's ability to achieve its business goals.

Performance Inventory

Having identified those outcomes that are valued by senior management, user group managers, and facility management, the next step is to discover which (if any) of these factors are already being measured somewhere in the organization. Does the human resources department, for example, conduct an annual staff survey that contains (or to which could be added) a few questions about environmental satisfaction? Are exit interviews conducted regularly, and could these data be coded to note any facility-related reasons for leaving? Are there project files that record every physical change effort, its cost, and the time and staff involved? Using existing measures (or modifying them in simple ways to serve their new purpose) is a good way to start a performance profile assessment.

Microsectors

Organizations are composed of many different job functions, with people of vastly different experiences, qualifications, and expectations. The R & D people often bear little resemblance—in expectations and environmental requirements—to the marketing and sales, accounting, or clerical staff. Make sure that the performance indicators identified are, first, appropriate to the different microsectors in the organization. Although there may be some indicators that are relevant to everyone, different groups will probably have some different combinations as well. Thus there is no reason that the acceptable response time for a routine clerical function must be the same as that for an R & D group or for a floor housing brokers and traders. This sometimes seems unjust to people in one sector, but uniformity for equity's sake is a luxury that few organizations can afford (because, if there were a single standard, it would have to meet the most stringent requirements, not the least). More sensible is asking which performance indicators, set at what target level, could be sensibly applied across the board, and which cannot. Management needs to know why this is the case and be prepared to discuss these differences with staff and management.

Balance Between Cost and Service

A third step is to see whether there are a sufficient number of cost and service indicators and a reasonable balance between them. Some organizations, for example, those in which the supply of desired employees exceeds their demand, or those with high proportions of employees doing relatively routine work, may decide to include more cost factors or to weigh them more heavily. Even when cost is a high priority, however, it must be balanced by some "service" measures, of which workplace satisfaction is probably the most common. Depending on the situation, medical complaints, absenteeism, and turnover may also be useful reflections of how well the workplace is serving its occupants.

Easy Measurement

Can the appropriate indicators be easily measured? Have the data already been collected? There is little point in listing indicators that sound good on paper but that, because of the difficulty in actually collecting the data, are unlikely ever (or regularly) to be collected.

Once the assessment team has selected the performance indicators, they must determine how to measure them and what level of performance is to be achieved for each indicator.

MEASURING PERFORMANCE

Most of these performance indicators can be measured relatively easily and objectively using one or more of the following techniques:

- *Direct observation of behavior.* This can be either a casual or a systematic observation of human behavior. Casual observation may be just an informal stroll through a space to get a sense of how people are using it (where do people meet besides conference rooms or their own offices?). Systematic observation requires recording accurately how many people use a common area, for instance, during a day or week (this is done by sitting near the area for blocks of time or by recording the number of people and the types of activities they are engaged in at preset times, perhaps every hour during the day and every day of a week). Systematic observation is time-consuming but accurately shows how a given area is being used.

- *Indirect observation of behavior.* This means looking for traces of behavior. How people have rearranged furniture can indicate that an area is being used, how, and for what type of communication (two chairs pulled up together is different from a conference table arrangement or a small circle of chairs). One can get a sense of whether certain areas are is being used by noting whether writing is left on whiteboards or whether trash like coffee cups or printouts are left in meeting areas.

- *Instrument readings.* These include everything from temperature and humidity controls (and their computerized reports) to devices that monitor the number and location of telephone calls, motion sensors that indicate whether a room is occupied, proximity card readers that print out who has entered a particular location and at what time, and so on.

- *Archival data and logging.* Departments like purchasing and human resources routinely collect valuable cost and personnel data, including information on why people joined or left a firm (in exit interviews), the cost of furniture and equipment, and the cost of consultants or outside contractors. Human resources also are the collection point and record keepers for work-related grievances, absenteeism and turnover, and occupational health problems and patterns. These data, if related to particular buildings or parts of buildings, can build a database of employee environmental satisfaction that can complement formal surveys and informal interviews.

- *Computer logging and inventory.* Another form of archival data is generated whenever employee requests for facility-related services are entered into a computer database, thereby enabling the progress in resolving the complaint to be monitored. These data often include information on the length of time between when a complaint was registered and resolved, the time and cost of service personnel, and the costs of materials, parts, and equipment needed to resolve the problem.

  Bar coding and other computerized inventory space and furniture methods can track and compare equipment costs, the type and quality of equipment and space available to different departments, occupancy rates, circulation factors among buildings or sites, the ratio of support to direct office space, the ratio of net usable to net rentable square feet and both to gross square feet, and so forth.

- *Plan analysis.* Detailed analysis of plans to determine the distance between different functional areas (affecting informal communication, for example) or the kinds of paths between the different areas.

- *Interviews.* These can be formal, following a predetermined series of questions, or informal, simply asking people without set questions about their views on some topic.

- *Surveys.* These can vary in length from a few questions to dozens of pages and from open-ended questions (short answers provided by the respondent) to closed-ended questions (the respondents need only check a box or circle an item indicating their agreement or satisfaction level or whether they do or do not have some equipment or think it is important.)

Generally, the shorter and the more closed-ended questions there are, the better. People are likely to complete the survey, and it is much easier to score closed-ended than open-ended questions. These data can be quickly entered into computerized statistical analysis programs that will analyze the data. These packages can generate information on frequencies and means for questions, broken down into categories by job level, job type, years of experience, sex, or whatever other variables are considered important).

- *Sample selection.* For all forms of observation, interviews, and surveys, one can organize a formal selection of people and places, or simply select these in a more or less random fashion. When the goal is to get a feel for a place or an issue, informal methods are ideal: Fast and cheap, they are useful for gaining insight into a situation. When the information is to be used in formal presentations, particularly when there is a controversy, more formal data collection techniques may make sense. Although they are more time-consuming to develop and implement, they are more representative and accurate—and can lead to tables and charts and graphs that are impressive in formal presentations.

These types of measurement techniques can be used to measure the type of FM performance indicators we discussed. Responsiveness, for example, can be measured by the length of time from the point an inquiry is launched until it is resolved, using records from computer-monitored systems that note when a problem is reported, when it is resolved, and how much it cost in time and materials. Automated monitoring systems can record the length of time that telephones or computers are down.

Customers' or employees' satisfaction with the work environment and with the planning and design process can be measured systematically and quantitatively with a post-occupancy evaluation (POE) survey in which staff rate their satisfaction with different aspects of the building before and after a renovation and with the process used to plan and design it. Databases derived from archival records generated by entering into a computer employees' facility-related inquiries and complaints and an analysis of archival data from human resources provide additional indicators of performance for the customer.

Space efficiency can be measured using a ratio of usable to rentable or gross square feet derived from a computerized space inventory or plan analysis.

Training time can be figured from employees personnel records located in human resources.

Construction and project management costs can be analyzed using computerized data from purchasing and finance in the form of work orders for services, materials, and equipment. The costs of moving so many linear feet of wall or panel, whole workstations, and the like can be derived from similar archival data generated as a normal part of the design and construction process.

The secret, if there is one, is analyzing and interpreting in an imaginative and purposeful way the data that are routinely collected, something that sadly is all too seldom done. It is also thinking about data collection as a facility management diagnostic tool that can help managers allocate scarce resources (time, money, staff) as effectively as possible.

THE *KISS* PRINCIPLE

Ray Kroc, the founder of McDonalds, used the term KISS (Keep It Simple, Stupid), to characterize how he liked to run McDonalds. It is a good principle. Because the purpose of performance assessment is to improve FM practice, enhance the quality of the built environment, and improve individual and organizational effectiveness, it must be made part of facility planning and management practice. It must be simple and quick to conduct, and its results must be meaningful to both practitioner and client. To be useful it does not have to meet academic canons of scientific respectability.

A more formal, long-term database is critical to the development of a credible research tradition similar to that found in engineering and medicine. In large part it is this research tradition that has distinguished the medical and engineering professions from architecture. It is the academics' responsibility, working with practitioners, to undertake the more rigorous scientific research that can complement and test the insights and findings of practice-based diagnostic studies.

By distinguishing between what might be called diagnostic or formative performance assessments—with their greater emphasis on influencing events in the particular situation in which data are collected—and more rigorous academic research—intended to develop a general knowledge base—greater pressure can be brought to bear on those with the time, knowledge, and resources needed to conduct formal research. In this way the efforts of the practitioner and the academic build on and expand each other, rather than either diluting or driving each other out.

Thinking of a POE (postoccupancy evaluation study), for example, as a relatively simple, practitioner-driven management technique, distinct from more formal environment–behavior research or sophisticated evaluation studies, may help it gain credence within the organization, where it is most likely to be used regularly and to influence the quality of the built environment.

COLLECTING AS FEW DATA AS NEEDED

Just as was true in the briefing process, good performance assessment does not require huge amounts of data (or time to collect and analyze them). More data are not necessarily good or useful. The challenge is not to collect all the data that are possible to collect but to identify the least amount of data that can be easily collected and analyzed to help make informed management decisions. The time required to collect and analyze the information must be balanced against its possible contribution to significant management decisions. Top managers, facility managers, and department and division managers must work together to identify, first, what indicators are important to the organization (these may change over time with the organization's circumstances, such as market conditions, labor force patterns, competitiors' actions, and new regulations).

SETTING TARGET LEVELS FOR THE PERFORMANCE PROFILE

Individual indicators, whether the POE or cost or response times, are meaningless unless they can be compared; Three dollars a square foot energy costs only begin to be interpretable when one knows the average cost for a comparable building is half as much.

The precise level of performance to be achieved ideally should be jointly developed and agreed on by facility management group and by facility management's customers, the staff. At IBM UK, for example, target levels for staff satisfaction with their physical surroundings (which vary by site and building) are determined by both department managers and facility managers. Achievement is measured through regular staff surveys. Other organizations may set levels for telephone service (no telephone will be "down" more than one hour, and no computer "at all".) Automated equipment that logs use patterns acts as the measurement device.

The targets that are chosen should reflect the organization's own operating environment and company or national culture. The targets should be both realistic and feasible, that is, attainable. Accordingly, target levels for energy or space efficiency or employee satisfaction may vary considerably from one building or site to another, depending on the facility reality at each.

Setting target performance levels requires that service providers and users work together and consider the following:

- *Feasibility*. Can the target be achieved with the available staff and existing facilities? A collaborative process provides a kind of checks-and-balances system in which the user cannot unilaterally set unachievably high targets, nor can the provider set easily achievable low targets. The idea is not to "look good" or to set up some other group to "look bad." The premise of the performance profile approach is that all employees are "in this together." Organizational success depends on service groups and line departments working together. Neither can succeed without the other.
- *Historical performance*. It is useful to collect data on past performance levels. How long, on the average, were computers down last year? How much did it cost, and how long did it take, to move a specified kind of workstation or so many linear feet of panel? If a POE has been done, what were the satisfaction levels overall and for particular sites or buildings?

  These data are a useful starting point for negotiating realistic targets. Were the user groups satisfied with these performance levels? What improvements would be welcome, and what do the service providers believe is realistic, given their resources?
- *Resource allocation*. Discussions about target levels inevitably will lead to discussions about resources, both that more are needed and also about the way in which existing ones are allocated or distributed. In other words, where do priorities lie?
- *Priorities*. The negotiating team should establish priorities, in part by looking back at the earlier stage of the process, in which strategic goals and objectives were identified. They may also have to ask senior management for clarification or to establish their own priorities (and the rationale for them). If it becomes clear the high-priority goals cannot be met at desired performance levels because of insufficient resources (not enough or competing claims on them), then additional resources can be requested, priorities can be shifted, or expectations (target values) can be lowered.
- *Reporting intervals*. Having decided what indicators to use and what level of performance is to be achieved, the next question is how performance will be reported and

who should see this information. At first, it probably makes sense for the FM performance profile team to meet relatively frequently, perhaps once a month, to see whether the measurements are actually working. If they are not, they can be modified as needed. These meetings can also serve as a time to see whether the customers' perceptions of the level of service being provided match what the indicators show, another test of the indicators' usefulness and validity.

Collecting and analyzing performance information will have little value if it is not communicated to those who can benefit from it. Far too many companies treat all kinds of information as though it were top secret. Performance data should go, first, to those who are being assessed. What is their response? Are there mitigating circumstances that help explain why certain things occurred? Much more of this information, especially that pertaining to the group or department, should be made public. IBM UK posts its frequent performance appraisals of outside cleaning and maintenance contractors in the break area where these groups gather. Part of the reason for doing this is the desire to reward outstanding performance. I see no reasons that occupant groups should not receive periodic reports that show that the facilities group has achieved or exceeded agreed-upon target levels or that they have fallen short of them (with an explanation of why and what they expect to do about it).

This kind of collaborative exercise should lead to a clarification of mismatches between expectations and resources, and should be made known to senior management. Thus their expectations, too, can be brought in line with reality as defined and described by the combined user/provider FM performance profile team.

BENCHMARKING: MANAGEMENT BY VARIANCE

The expected (target) values should be compared with actual performance; how long was the computer actually down? What was the average rating on the POE? This simple analysis underscores the complement to management by objectives (MBO), which is MBV, or management by variance, which shows where actual performance deviated from expected performance and why.

These analyses are needed for performance evaluations at the individual, department, or area level. As part of the benchmarking process, they also can guide management's planning and action. For example, if a regional facility group consistently underperforms when compared with sites with comparable facilities, one can begin to ask whether additional training is needed, or more headquarters support, or additional staff. Thus MBV is intended to trigger management's intervention in order to improve performance over time.

It is likely that industrywide benchmark data, now available through organizations such as the Building Owners Managers Association (BOMA), the International Facility Management Association (IFMA), and the Urban Land Institute (ULI) will expand to cover a wider range of facility performance indicators, thus making external as well as internal comparisons possible.

Figure 14-1 illustrates the idea of management by variance (MBV), in which actual versus target scores are compared in a hypothetical profile. In this chart all the target

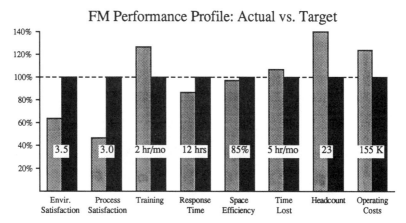

Figure 14-1. A facility management performance profile comparing actual achievements with target levels. (Source: Becker 1988a)

values are treated as 100 percent, thereby offering a standard yardstick for different target measures, from ratings on an employee survey to space efficiency or downtime. This is a way of comparing apples with apples when one started with apples and oranges.

Figure 14-2 shows prototypical FM performance profiles. Their value is in helping an organization think about the level of performance it believes is appropriate.

The ideal FM profile is low cost/high service, and the worst case is high cost/low service. High cost/high service is tolerable during prosperous times, when inefficiency is buried in profit. Low cost/low service should always be avoided. Remember that stringent financial conditions demand innovation, not poor service. The point is that looking at only one side of the profile may result in an entirely false conclusion about overall facility performance; that is, costs may be down (great), but if service is also very low, not much has been achieved. Similarly, a high service measure loses some of its luster when associated with higher than expected costs.

BENEFITS OF THE PERFORMANCE PROFILE

The value of the performance profile approach is that expectations are clear, both the customer's and the administration's, and so is—so far as possible—the extent to which they have beeen achieved. Because organizations are dynamic, the objectives can be negotiated over time.

Second, such a series of performance indicators should help rectify the untenable position in which many facility managers find themselves: If they do a great job, no one notices. If they do a poor job, they are a very easy target. The performance profile makes it easy to communicate quickly and graphically just how well facility management is doing, as well as where it needs to improve.

Third, such indicators represent a facility management database. By pinpointing by building, region, or country (any area or location) where performance is especially good or poor, and in what specific areas, one can begin to judge the resources, skills, and administrative support needed to improve performance. The indicators thus become a

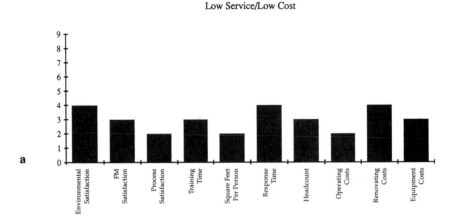

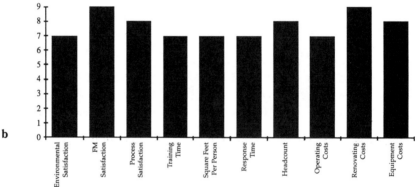

Figure 14-2 (a–d). Prototypical facility management cost–service performance profiles. (Source: Becker 1988a)

management tool, not merely a quarterly or annual ritual related to performance evaluation.

To return to the first point, the FM performance profile links cost to service, measuring value for money. This can be done subjectively, by analyzing the individual indicators in relation to one another. With some work, ratios and indices can be combined. Robertson Ward, for example, developed a measure that he calls the *density function per capita,* which is a ratio defined by staff costs divided by the net square feet of space occupied.[2] Such measures are helpful, but in a world where performance is and always will be tied to professional judgments, just comparing actual with expected performance is a step forward in its own right. It reduces the likelihood that only one

---

[2]Robertson Ward, personal communication, June 1988.

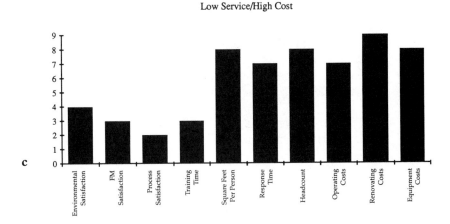

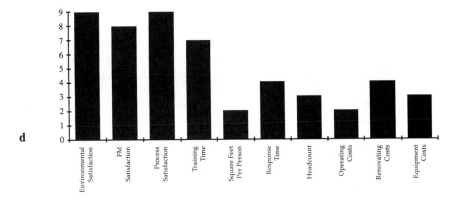

Figure 14-2. *(Continued)*

or two factors, such as cost or headcount, will submerge other components of the "value for money" equation.

FROM THEORY TO PRACTICE

If the performance profile approach were to become an industrywide technique for evaluating overall facility performance, it would require:

1. Agreement on a core set of measures, based on how such information would help the organization meet its business objectives. The analysis of the information should lead to management's making better decisions about how the facility is planned, designed, and managed.
2. The development of common measurement procedures based on how a wide range of organizations actually work. That is, the measures must be feasible, and so the data must be easy to collect and analyze.

3. A commitment to understanding how the overall facility function, not just the physical facility itself, is working. This will take some courage, as it opens the facility manager to criticism of the FM's performance in a way that is more visible and more directly linked to organizational effectiveness issues. But the threat of visible assessment should be balanced by the opportunity to communicate outstanding performance equally effectively.

The long-term benefit is likely to be facilities that can satisfy the competing and diverse needs of management and staff and in doing so help the organization achieve its objectives.

Skeptics Speak

The performance profile concept still is not as "clean" as are traditional financial measures such as ROI (return on investment) or profitability. Top management is interested in bottom-line measures, and that means dollars.

The "bottom line" is really more like a basket; it holds a variety of valued outcomes, not just one called money. Making money is surely the goal of most companies, but to succeed, they must support many enormously diverse outcomes: obtaining and keeping the best employees possible, maintaining an image of quality, satisfying customers, and keeping abreast of new technologies. Each of these outcomes, in turn, depends on other factors (which themselves become valued): attractive and well-planned facilities, challenging work, good pay, positive management style, effective training programs, and time to explore new technical and organizational trends.

These valued outcomes often cannot be precisely related to profit or ROI, just as it is impossible to demonstrate conclusively that a good diet for children by itself produces higher grades, better social adjustment, or outstanding athletic achievement. Rather, it is the overall pattern of valued outcomes, not any single element, that we associate with excellence. Because this is true, Bob Sommer, as I noted earlier, made the valid observation that the only sensible thing to measure is the proximate indicators: communication, training time, employees' perception of work, and reported satisfaction. We believe, based on a variety of research, that these kinds of outcomes increase an organization's effectiveness and ultimately help the company prosper. In service areas like FM, in which making a profit is not the primary objective, these other variables, which can be linked to facilities decisions, become useful to track and monitor.

Your idea of "fit" suggests, I believe, that no companywide standards should exist, that instead targets should be set by site or even building. But this would just lead to everyone's making excuses for his or her performance, arguing that the site or building has special characteristics that make it impossible to improve performance.

I do not think so, and the reason is that targets are negotiated by both providers and users. Users will not accept targets that they believe are unrealistically low. Remember, also, that historical data will be collected as part of the target-setting process, so that performance levels will be related to what has occurred over time. This becomes the starting point, not necessarily the final achievement level. Finally, in large multi-building and site organizations, targets and achievement levels at any site or building can be benchmarked internally to see how they stack up against comparable facilities, either informally or systematically. Each building or site can, for example, be categorized by assigning it a numerical score (from 1 to 10, for example) on a number of factors: type of building (laboratory, office, sales, warehouse), size, age, condition, and construction. This score then enables similar buildings (comparable age, condition, size, type) to be compared according to operating costs, responsiveness, employee satisfaction and the like. These figures can be calculated using FM staffing profiles: number of staff, type and level of education, experience, and so on.

What will be the role of headquarters staff if all the local areas set their own targets? Doesn't it make the headquarters group redundant?

No, and the reason relates to a characteristic of the elastic organization; that is, the idea that headquarters groups act as a resource to local areas by providing technical expertise in the form of guidelines, particularly in setting resource levels and boundary points for performance, and also by offering training programs and developing processes and procedures to help structure local decision making without determining its final outcome. In the elastic organizational model, the headquarters is responsible for setting strategic direction, whereas the local area is responsible for tactical decisions.

You talk about performance profiles and FM performance, but you don't say anything about one of the most important areas in facilities today: environmental quality, or things like air quality, temperature, ventilation and lighting. The performance profile idea doesn't seem useful to me if it doesn't consider these kinds of issues.

I agree. It does, or at least it can. For example, POE typically includes questions about satisfaction with HVAC, lighting, air quality, privacy, noise, and distractions. These data provide an excellent measure of employees' perception of environmental quality. In addition, objective measures can be established by using instrument readings for pollutant, noise, and lighting levels, and target values for these can be determined by using a combination of technical standards and employees' responses to these levels.

The point to remember is that environmental quality is not the same as FM quality (e.g., policies, processes, procedures, costs, staffing) or even facility quality (e.g., flexibility, adaptability, power capacity, safety, asset appreciation, subdivisibility, way finding). Environmental quality is an important factor, but it should not be the sole focus of facility performance.

The Total Workplace

It is ironic that in the United States—which takes great pride in its democratic insitutions and where rugged individualism is a cherished myth—that the place where millions of Americans spend much of their time—their workplace—is so centrally controlled, bureaucratic, and conformist. To be sure, there are many exceptions, particularly among small firms and to some extent in organizations (or subgroups in them like R & D or advertising) that are professionally defined as being "creative." We are not alone, of course, in having impersonal firms. Japanese offices, for example, are not exactly a paragon of individual freedom. One could also argue that tight control, or at least some forms of it, make sense. After all, American and Japanese firms have been immensely successful over the past eighty years. Why?

Dumb luck helps, and so does being in the right place at the right time. The Xerox Corporation, for example, developed commercially available copy machines at a time when there was little competition and a completely untapped market. Its problem was not convincing companies to buy its products. The problem was determining how to organize the waiting line. But companies with brand names that define the product, whether hot sauce (Tabasco), facial tissues (Kleenex), breakfast cereal (Kelloggs), cake mix (Duncan-Hines), cameras (Kodak), or copy machines (Xerox) are exceptions.

The most common characteristic of successful companies, it seems to me, is that they capture and exploit the talent, imagination, knowledge, experience, commitment, and energy of their employees. And they do this with all the resources at their disposal. The issue is not the presence or absence of tight central authority or bureaucracy per se; it is the ability to devise control mechanisms that better enable the organization's resources to be used to their fullest to achieve strategic business objectives.

The "organization's resources" are everything the organization has at its disposal to improve its competitive advantage or to achieve its mission: people, money, equipment, information, facilities. Its "control mechanisms" include formal review policies and procedures; hiring, promoting and firing of staff; profit and loss statements; the structure of departments and divisions; employee training and development programs; and incentive structure (often a combination of money, recongition, access to more challenging work, the "best" projects, and more personal freedom and responsibility). There is also an invisible control mechanism—the organizational culture and its values, norms, and expectations that do such things as define a "good" worker and a "good" manager, set the acceptable level of risk taking, and structure communication processes.

An organization is like a living, dynamic organism, and creating one that is capable of growth, able to learn from experience, and smart enough and willing to take advantage of opportunities when they arise or—better yet—creating them where others see only elephant traps or unassailable peaks is an immensely difficult task. It is, in fact, an impossible challenge unless one sees it not as giving birth to a fully developed adult that pops out of the womb in a pin-striped suit and red suspenders ready to go to work, but as creating the conditions within which latent talent can mature. The ability to create the right conditions for development is what, over the long run, determines the ability of any self-supporting organization to prosper. One facet of getting these conditions right is the nature of the total workplace.

I began this book talking about Venice, a smelly but beautiful and wonderful place. Venice captures in a way few places can the gift of transforming adversity into advantage. Similarly, few organizations open their doors with only bright people, great products, predictable and expanding markets, and dim-witted competition. Using existing resources well requires a clear vision, one concerned as much with process as product and focused on setting healthy conditions for growth rather than trying to determine at every moment in time exactly what the organism should do or think or be.

What are these conditions? Psychological studies of self-esteem in children suggest that the right conditions are not total freedom and complete indulgence. Rather, confidence in oneself and one's abilities comes from parents, teachers, and other authority figures setting clear boundaries and indicating what constitutes acceptable behavior, as well as targets for achievements. These boundaries should not be so constraining that every new situation would require a new policy. Nor should they be designed, like a jail or an operating theater, to keep the outside world at bay. Rather, they should be frameworks for behavior that allow children to make choices, to take risks, to challenge the world around them without threatening their life, or their parents' or their teachers'! Setting boundaries helps children know that adults care about them and also tells them what they need to do to win and to gain adult approval.

The only significant similarity between children and employees is that both need the freedom to develop and exercise their skills, knowledge, and experience. But in too many large organizations one finds talented men and women, enthusiastic and dedicated to the company, but with no effective outlet for their creative energy. In effect, they are not permitted to contribute to the organization's success. The irony is that these same companies often have a field army of human resource specialists whose job it is to motivate, train, and develop staff.

What, you might say, does this have to do with facility planning and management? The answer is that facility management activities and responsibilities influence significantly the form and character of the everyday world of work. FM decisions large and small help shape the sense of a place. Decisions about building size, shape, location, finishes, materials, furniture, lighting, layout, and heating and ventilation have aesthetic and economic implications, to be sure. But much more far-reaching are the consequences of such decisions in terms of how it feels to come to work; how easy or difficult it is to meet with colleagues informally; having the space, privacy, and equipment necessary to work productively; or sufficiently comfortable to be able to concentrate on one's work. And it is not just the physical environment that counts, but also the policies and procedures for how the workplace is used and modified and how employees are helped to adapt to physical changes that FM initiates. Is there an opportunity to express individual or team identity so that one does not feel like a replaceable cog in an institutional wheel? Are the reasons for physical changes explained so that employees will know where they fit into the big picture? Is the emphasis on creating a visual order that symbolizes efficiency or on creating a dynamic workplace that allows different kinds of people with different work-styles to create personal work environments that help them work effectively? And then there is the process through which the workplace and policies and procedures for managing are developed. Are these designed as a form of organizational development, with the process itself intended to motivate, to release creative energies, to foster cooperation and collaboration?

It is the way that these thousands of decisions are orchestrated that defines the nature of the total workplace. The total workplace affects the organization's ability to prosper in a competitive world: to attract and retain the highest-quality staff possible and to create the conditions in which they want to and are able to use their knowledge, imagination, and skills to the organization's (and their own) best possible advantage.

The total workplace cannot be just a brilliant building. Being at the architectural or technological cutting edge is always just that: close to but not at anywhere. It may be the end point for the architect or the engineer, but it should never be for senior management or the facility manager. It is the facility manager's job to see that facilities and equipment, and the policies and procedures for planning, designing, and managing them, use human potential and creativity, not stomp it underfoot or shove it to one side. This requires more than just being proactive. It means formulating a vision of the role of facility management in the organization that is broad, imaginative, and connected to strategic organization goals. And such goals are never just to cut costs, but to maintain and gain competitive advantage, and to fulfill the organization's mission.

The goal is excellence. It does not (how could it?) generate controversy. The issue is how best to achieve it. The answer lies in control and how to manage it. It does (how could it not?) generate enormous controversy. It is at the heart of all management debates and has been since people started "managing" others. Not surprisingly, it is a fundamental issue for facility management.

How facility managers conceive, express, and manage control is the unifying theme of this book. Whether in strategic planning, the briefing process, managing environmental change, planning and designing workspace, even in selecting HVAC or wire management systems, the underlying questions always are who selects the furniture, who lays out the furniture, who shapes the vision, and who controls the temperature or the lights? These are hardly trivial questions, because how they are answered influences every day the ability of millions of office workers to be effective. The questions may arise within the FM domain, but the consequences are organizationwide.

The answer is not anarchy, everybody doing his or her own thing. Nor is it rigid control mechanisms. It is the creation of elastic frameworks that define boundaries without eliminating meaningful choice, that release energy but do not stifle it, that support taking risks without encouraging recklessness, that value diversity but do not fear it, that measure performance and not attendance, and that evolve from an understanding of how people really work and not how we wished they did.

I like to say that "forms follows income," and it is true that money makes some decisions easier. But the secret to creating responsive, first-rate facilities is not the amount of money available. It is the choices about how available funds are allocated and how these reflect how control is managed. And it is having confidence, in one's colleagues, in one's boss, and in the decision-making process itself. When he was chair of the psychology department at the University of California at Davis, my friend and mentor Bob Sommer once explained to me that when he set up a committee to look at constructing animal research facilities, he appointed only people who were actually involved in animal research. He set a budget limit and then let the committee make the decisions. He was willing to accept whatever decisions they made within the budget ceiling. As a manager, he saw his job as defining frameworks and creating structures within which responsible people would make thoughtful decisions. He realized that in a democratic society many of them might not be the ones he himself would make. He thought of himself as the phantom chairman, invisibly providing a guiding hand that allowed many flowers to bloom. He finally stepped down after ten years as department chair, leaving behing a much stronger department than the one he took over and a faculty that asked him to continue as chair.

The kind of total workplace that enhances the organization's ability to compete successfully in a turbulent and unpredictable world is one in which expertise is recognized in many guises and sought in many places. It is one in which those with technical expertise and managerial authority are confident enought not to be threatened by involving others in decision making, in which sharing control is seen as part of one's job and not as a dereliction of duty and in which the search for "excellence" is visible, tangible, and palpable. Facilities that support the organization in all its endeavors do not happen by accident but emerge from good information, imaginations, cooperation, confidence, and senior management's commitment. It is a simple vision, but also a powerful one.

References

Ackoff, R. L. 1979. *The Art of Problem Solving.* New York: Wiley.

Ahituv, N., and B. Ronen. 1985. Centralization and distribution of CAD/CAM systems. *Human Systems Management* 5(4):301–308.

Allen, T. 1977. *Managing the Flow of Technology.* Cambridge, Mass.: MIT Press.

Becker, F. 1981. *Workspace: Creating Environments in Organizations.* New York: Praeger.

Becker, F. 1987. New facilities for architects. *Architects Journal,* November, pp. 82–83.

Becker, F. 1988a. *The Changing Facilities Organization.* Haverhill, England: Project Office Furniture.

Becker, F. 1988b. Form follows process at dynamic Lloyds of London. *Facility Design & Management,* February, pp. 55–58.

Becker, F. 1988c. How to take the crisis out of office relocations. *International Facility Management Journal* Fall, pp. 38–44.

Becker, F. 1988d. ORBIT 2.1. *Facilities* 6(3):5–7.

Becker, F. 1988e. International FM: Taking off the blinders. *Premises Management and Facilities Planning,* October 19–20.

Becker, F. 1989. Design for innovation: The total workplace concept. *Illume* (Japan) 1(2):60–81.

Becker, F., and A. Hoogesteger. 1986. Employee adjustment to an office relocation. *Human Ecology Forum* 15(4):6–9.

Becker-Sims Associates. 1988. *The ORBIT 2.1 Workbook.* Unpublished consulting report. Ithaca, New York: Becker-Sims Associates, Inc.

Becker, F., and J. Spitznagel. 1986. Managing multinational facilities. Final research report to the International Facility Management Association, Houston.

Brill, M., with S. Margulis and E. Konar. 1984. *Using Office Design to Increase Productivity.* Buffalo, N.Y.: Workplace Design and Productivity.

Brooke, M. Z. 1984. Autonomy and centralization in multinational firms. *International Studies of Management and Organization* 14(1):3–22.

Buller, P. F. 1988. Successful partnerships: HR and strategic planning at eight top firms. *Organizational Dynamics* 17(2):27–43.

Butler Cox. 1989. *Information Technology and Buildings.* London: Butler Cox Plc.

Carlzon, J. 1987. *Moments of Truth.* New York: Ballinger.

Davis, G. 1989. Unpublished consulting report prepared by G. Davis and D. Sinclair for Public Works Canada, Ottawa, Canada, Centre for International Facilities.

Davis, G., F. Becker, F. Duffy, and W. Sims. 1985. *ORBIT-2: Organizations, Buildings, and Information Technology.* Norwalk, Conn.: The Harbinger.

DEGW. 1985. *Eleven Contemporary Office Buildings: A Comparative Study.* London: DEGW Architects Space Planners.

DEGW. 1987. *The Space Requirements for Professional Firms in the City of London.* London: DEGW Architects Space Planners.

DEGW. 1988. *Trading in Three Cities: London, New York, Tokyo.* London: DEGW Architects Space Planners.

DIO International Research Team. 1983. A contingency model of participative decision making: An analysis of 56 decisions in three Dutch organizations. *Journal of Occupational Psychology* 56:1–18.

Duffy, F., C. Cave, and J. Worthington. 1976. *Planning Office Space.* London: Architectural Press.

Eastman Kodak Company. 1983. *Ergonomic Design for People at Work. Vol. 1.* Belmont, Calif.: Lifetime Learning Publications.

Steele, F. 1987. Unpublished adaptation of a table originally developed for the Steelcase Corporation as part of consultancy for the Steelcase Corporate Development Center.

Froggatt, C. 1985. The effect of corporate space and furnishings policies on employee workspace and policy satisfaction. M.A. thesis, Cornell University, Ithaca, N.Y.

Gates, S. R., and W. G. Egelhoff. 1986. Centralization in headquarters–subsidiary relationships. *Journal of International Business Studies* 17(2):71–92.

Gould, B. P. 1983. *Planning the New Corporate Headquarters.* New York: Wiley.

Grant, R. M., A. P. Jammine, and T. Howard. 1988. Diversity, diversification, and profitability among British manufacturing companies, 1972–84. *Journal of International Business Studies* 31(4):771–804.

Hill, C. W. L., and J. F. Pickering. 1986. Divisionalization, decentralization and performance of large United Kingdom companies. *Journal of Management Studies.* 23(1):26–50.

Hoos, I. R. 1978. Methodological shortcomings in futures research. In J. Fowles (ed.), *Handbook of Futures Research.* Westport, Conn.: Greenwood Press.

International Facility Management Association. 1984. *IFMA Research Report #1.* Houston: International Facility Management Association.

IFMA Education Committee. 1989. *Facility Management Model Curriculum: Baccalaureate Degree.* Houston: International Facility Management Association.

Konar, E., and E. Sundstrom. 1985. Status demarcation in the office. In J. Wineman (ed.), *Behavioral Issues in Office Design.* New York: Van Nostrand Reinhold.

Lauenstein, M. C. 1986. The failure of strategic planning. *Journal of Business Strategy.* 6(4):75–80.

Louis, M. R. 1980. Surprise and sense making: What newcomers experience in entering unfamiliar organizational settings. *Administrative Science Quarterly.* 25:225–251.

Markoff, J. 1989. Cray's future without Cray. *New York Times,* business section, Sunday, May 21, pp. 1, 8.

Mason, R. O., and I. Mitroff. 1981. *Challenging Strategic Planning Assumptions: Theory, Cases, and Techniques.* New York: Wiley.

Mintzberg, H., and J. A. Waters. 1985. Of strategies, deliberate and emergent. *Strategic Management Journal.* 6:257–272.

Moore, G. (ed.) 1986. *Environmental Stress.* Cambridge, England: Cambridge University Press.

Morrow, P. C., and McElroy, J. C. 1981. Interior office design and visitor response. *Journal of Applied Psychology.* 66, 630–646.

Naisbett, J. 1982. *Megatrends: Ten New Directions Transforming Our Lives.* New York: Warner Books.

Pasmore, W., and J. Sherwood. 1978. *Socio-Technical Systems: A Sourcebook.* La Jolla, Calif.: University Associates.

Perin, C. 1974. *Everything in its Place.* Cambridge, Mass.: MIT Press.

Peters, T. 1988. The destruction of hierarchy. *Industry Week* 237(4):33–35.

Peters, T. J., and R. H. Waterman, 1981. *In Search of Excellence: Lessons from America's Best-run Companies.* New York: Harper & Row.

Preiser, W. F. G. 1989. *Building Evaluation.* New York: Van Nostrand Reinhold.

Preiser, W. F. G., H. Z. Rabinowitz, and E. T. White. 1988. *Post-Occupancy Evaluation.* New York: Van Nostrand Reinhold.

Rapoport, A. 1970. Symbolism and environmental design. *International Journal of Symbology* 1:1–9.

Schein, E. 1985. *Organizational Culture.* San Francisco: Jossey-Bass.

Sharp, L. 1952. Steel axes for stone age Australians. In E. Spicer (ed.), *Human Problems in Technological Change.* New York: Russell Sage Foundation.

Shimizu Corporation. 1989. Personal communication illustrations based on an internal study of the "free-address" space planning system at the Shimizu Institute of Technology, Tokyo, Japan.

Sommer, R. 1972. *Design Awareness.* San Francisco: Rinehart Corporate Press.

Sommer, R. and B. Sommer. 1980. *A Political Guide to Behavioral Research.* New York: Oxford University Press.

Steelcase, Inc., Illustrations originally developed by the Steelcase Corporate Development Center Project Team, and produced by Steelcase. Grand Rapids, Michigan: Steelcase, Inc.

Steelcase/Harris. 1987. *Office Environment Index.* Grand Rapids, Mich.: Steelcase Corporation.

Steel, F. 1986. *Making and Managing High Quality Workplaces.* New York: Teachers College Press.

Takeuchi, H. and Nonaka, I. 1986. The new product development game: Stop running the relay race and take up rugby. *Harvard Business Review.* January–February (1):137–146.

Trist, E., and K. Bamforth. 1951. Some social and psychological consequences of the Longwall methods of coal-getting. *Human Relations* 4:3–38.

Wack, P. 1985a. Scenarios: Shooting the rapids. *Harvard Business Review* 63(6):139–150.

Wack, P. 1985b. Scenarios: Uncharted waters ahead. *Harvard Business Review* 63(5):73–89.

Wandersman, A. 1979. User participation: A study of types of participation, effects, mediators, and individual differences. *Environment and Behavior* 11:465–482.

Weick, K. 1984. Small wins: Redefining the scale of social problems. *American Psychologist* 39:40–49.

Worthington, J. 1988. Presentations given at "Profiting From Change" Seminar, Cambridge, England, June 1988 sponsored by PROJECT OFFICE Furniture: Hoverhill, England.

Worthington, J. and A. Konya. 1988. *Fitting Out the Workplace.* London: Architectural Press.

Yee, R. 1986. The 1986 corporate real estate executive survey. *Corporate Design & Realty,* February, pp. 56–58.

Zechhauser, S., and R. Silverman. 1983. Rediscover your company's real estate. *Harvard Business Review,* January–February, pp. 111–117.

Zeisel, J. 1981. *Inquiry By Design.* Monterey, Calif.: Brooks-Cole.

Further Reading

Baetz, M. L. 1985. *Planning for People in the Electronic Office.* Toronto: Holt, Rinehart and Winston of Canada.

Binder, S. 1989. *Corporate Facility Planning.* New York: McGraw-Hill.

Brauer, R. L. 1986. *Facilities Planning: The User Requirements Method.* New York: American Management Association.

Brinkerhoff, R. O., and D. E. Dressler. 1990. *Productivity Measurement: A Guide for Managers and Evaluators.* New York: Sage Productions.

Goumain, P. (ed.) 1989. *High-Technology Workplaces.* New York: Van Nostrand Reinhold.

Hammer, J. M. 1988. *Facility Management Systems.* New York: Van Nostrand Reinhold.

Helander, M. (ed.). 1988. *Handbook of Human–Computer Interaction.* New York: Elsevier Science.

Kanter, R. M. 1983. *Changemasters: Innovation for Productivity in the American Corporation.* New York: Simon S. Schuster.

Kerzner, H. 1989. *Project Management: A Systems Approach to Planning, Scheduling, and Controlling.* 3rd ed. New York: Van Nostrand Reinhold.

Levi, L. 1981. *Preventing Work Stress.* Reading, Mass.: Addison-Wesley.

Lueder, R. (ed.) 1986. *The Ergonomics Payoff.* New York: Nichols.

Ruck, N. C. (ed.) 1989. *Building Design and Human Performance.* New York: Van Nostrand Reinhold.

Sundstrom, E. 1986. *Work Places: The Psychology of the Physical Environment in Offices and Factories.* Cambridge, England: Cambridge University Press.

Vischer, J. C. 1989. *Environmental Quality in Offices.* New York: Van Nostrand Reinhold.

Index